ADDITIONAL PRAISE FOR
JONATHAN MILLER AND
THE COMPASSIONATE COMMUNITY:

"Jonathan Miller's well-crafted new book shows that simple Biblical Sunday School lessons have surprising applicability to public issues and progressive politics."

—Robert Putnam, Malkin Professor of Public Policy,
Harvard University, author of *Bowling Alone*

"Jonathan Miller draws deeply from the Hebrew Scriptures to challenge contemporary Americans to build a truly compassionate community in the United States. This deeply felt work underscores the truth of the observation of Jesus in the New Testament that the good householder draws forth old things and new. From the ancient wisdom of Israel Jonathan Miller draws forth something fresh, urgent, pertinent, and wise in order to speak to our times. This book is obedient to the challenge of 'Tikkun Olam'—to repair the world—and, as such, deserves a wide readership."

—Lawrence S. Cunningham, John A. O'Brien Professor of Theology,
University of Notre Dame

"Jonathan Miller has gone to the Hebrew Bible to explore the values that are essential for Americans if we are to have a good society. This book should be read by Christians and Jews alike, in that it is truly an interfaith message that we all need to hear."

—Tony Campolo, Founder of the Evangelical Association for the
Promotion of Education, Professor Emeritus, Eastern University,
and author of several books including *Speaking My Mind*

"*The Compassionate Community* is an intriguing mix of biblical insights and policy analysis, reflecting the author's obvious faith, good sense, and experience as a state elected official. It builds from Hebrew scriptural stories to foundational values, and combines that moral analysis with practical knowledge of what does and can work to improve the lives of poor Americans. It's full of smart ideas, and full of hope. It's a great antidote to cynical and partisan 'faith wars' and is a good read as well. And it's a call to commitment and community that all those interested in the public good should read—and follow."

—Mary Jo Bane, Thorton Bradshaw Professor of Public Policy and Management,
Kennedy School of Government, Harvard University

"Jonathan Miller has proved to be a master storyteller in whose words we recognize our deepest struggles as a people and catch a glimpse of who we wish to become In *The Compassionate Community*, he brings the virtues of biblical heroes and heroines to life in his account of people and programs contesting today's politics of self-interest. It's a story of the greater good that Americans yearn to hear, and we are indebted to Jonathan Miller for telling it so well."

—Bob Edgar, General Secretary, National Council of Churches USA

"*The Compassionate Community* examines the unfortunate contrast between the current debate about 'values' and the universal values that are at the core of the Judeo-Christian ethic. Miller's vision of a Compassionate Community is one that should be embraced and implemented by policy makers on both sides of the political divide."

—Donna L. Brazile, Chair of the Democratic National Committee
Voting Rights Institute and former campaign manager
for Gore for President 2000

"Miller offers a compelling roadmap of how to ensure we leave our children a strong, safe, and just America. Through a frank discussion of the importance of policy girded by our moral values, Miller illustrates the kind of policy proposals that will be able to unite Americans and make sure that everyone who works hard and plays by the rules has the opportunity to share in the American Dream."

—U. S. Senator Evan Bayh (D-IN)

THE
COMPASSIONATE
COMMUNITY

TEN VALUES TO UNITE AMERICA

JONATHAN MILLER

palgrave
macmillan

THE COMPASSIONATE COMMUNITY: TEN VALUES TO UNITE AMERICA
Copyright © Jonathan Miller, 2006.

First published 2006 by
PALGRAVE MACMILLAN™
175 Fifth Avenue, New York, N.Y. 10010 and
Houndmills, Basingstoke, Hampshire, England RG21 6XS.
Companies and representatives throughout the world.

PALGRAVE MACMILLAN is the global academic imprint of the Palgrave Macmillan division of St. Martin's Press, LLC and of Palgrave Macmillan Ltd. Macmillan® is a registered trademark in the United States, United Kingdom and other countries. Palgrave is a registered trademark in the European Union and other countries.

ISBN 1-4039-7408-X hardback
978-1-4039-7408-2

Library of Congress Cataloging-in-Publication Data
Miller, Jonathan, 1967–
    The compassionate community: ten values to unite America/by Jonathan Miller.
        p.   cm.
    Includes bibliographical references (p.)
    Contents: Noah and the value of opportunity—Abraham and value of responsibility—Jacob and the value of work—Joseph and the value of family—Moses and the value of freedom—Joshua and the value of faith—Deborah and the value of justice—Jonathan and the value of peace—David and the value of respect—Esther and the value of life.
    ISBN 1-4039-7408-X (alk. paper)
    1. Compassion.   2. Compassion—Religious aspects.   3. Caring.
4. Values—United States.   I. Title.
BJ1475.M55   2006
170'.44—dc22

                                                            2006043205

A catalogue record for this book is available from the British Library.

Design by Letra Libre.

First edition: October 2006
10 9 8 7 6 5 4 3 2 1
Printed in the United States of America

To my Dad,

Who never got the chance to write his book,

But whose voice echoes throughout these pages.

CONTENTS

ACKNOWLEDGMENTS

The "Compassionate Community" was born in the Sunday School class I have taught since 1997 to ninth and tenth graders at Temple Adath Israel in Lexington, Kentucky. I have called the course *Tikkun Olam*, after the Jewish tradition that means literally "to repair the world" and deems everyone responsible to help make the world a better place. Thanks to the flexibility provided me by principals Marsha Rose and Jane Grise and Rabbis Jonathan Adland and Marc Kline, I have been able to continue to change and innovate, and ultimately expand the class to discuss the concepts of faith, values, and politics, all within the umbrella of the Judeo-Christian and American traditions. My task has been made easier by the help of regular guests to my class, including Jim Newberry, John Roach, and Kathy Stein, who taught me their own faith perspectives.

I was inspired to put pen to paper (actually finger to keyboard) by a seminar I attended at the Aspen Institute, sponsored by the Democratic Leadership Council (DLC). Shortly after the 2004 election, the DLC brought together a few dozen young leaders to talk about the future, and I was inspired both by their vision and optimism, as well as their encouragement about my ideas and perspective. A second Aspen Institute event—the inaugural Rodel Fellowship program, which involves 24 young elected officials (12 Democrats and 12 Republicans) from across the country—helped me refine my thoughts and explore new avenues for discussion. I am in debt to each of the participants, as well as to the organizers, particularly Aspen moderator and Wofford College President Ben Dunlap, whose teachings on political philosophy were very influential on my writing, especially his notion that Thomas Jefferson's Declaration of Independence, Abraham Lincoln's *Gettysburg Address*, and Martin Luther King, Jr.'s, *Letter from a Birmingham Jail* represent the three great documents of American liberty.

There are several people whom I have never met who have inspired and educated me through this process. Rabbis Mark Gopin, Mark Levine, and Sid Schwartz's *Jewish Civics: A* tikkun olam/*World Repair Manual* serves as the textbook for my Sunday School class, and has directed me to many of the Talmud's great lessons that are included in this book. I am also indebted to Rabbis Joseph Telushkin and Harold Kushner for their inspiring and instructive texts on Jewish law and tradition. And Rabbi Ken Carr (my college roommate and best man at my wedding) gave me invaluable advice and instruction.

Christian authors such as Rick Warren, Jim Wallis, and my friends Tony Campolo and Roy Herron provided me with a broad introduction to Jesus and his teachings, and directed me to key passages in the New Testament for education and inspiration. The Reverend Christopher Skidmore provided me extensive assistance on New Testament translation and interpretation. And Huston Smith, William Eerdmans, and Karen Armstrong gave me a greater understanding of Eastern religious philosophy and teaching.

I never imagined that the process of publishing a book would be so complex. I am very grateful to my agent, Will Lippincott, whose enthusiasm and expertise helped guide this project to completion, as well as to my friends Michael Bloomfield and David Sirota for introducing me to Will and giving me advice on the publishing process. I am also grateful to Amanda Johnson, my outstanding editor, and all of the staff at Palgrave Macmillan for having the faith to publish this book and help bring it to its finished form.

The actual writing was a labor of love, and I am fortunate to have so many friends who offered their advice and support during the process. These include Josh Bowen, Gene Brockopp, John Y. Brown, III, Chad Brownstein, Julian Carroll, Josh Cherwin, David Dixon, Mickey Edwards, Al From, Ron Granieri, Rebecca Herpick, Greg Jones, Martin Kaplan, Nancy Jo Kemper, Kit Kincaide, Ivan Kronenfeld, Jeffrey Liebman, Crit Luallen, Mindy Lubber, Clark Mandel, Will Marshall, Bob Massie, Brent McKim, Steve Neal, Avinash Sathaye, Ted Schlechter, Steven Schulman, Bill Stone, Sayeed Syeed, Barbara Dafoe Whitehead, and Alan Young.

I am also blessed with a cadre of former and current staffers who, in their free time, helped make this book a possibility. They include Chad Aull, Rachel Belin, Angela Burton, Dan Logsdon, Kenneth Mansfield, Becky McCauley, and Dianne Wilson.

My family has been a never-ending source of support and love. My mom, Penny Miller, an accomplished author herself, gave me great encouragement. My sister, Jennifer Miller, was a valuable fountain of ideas and editing suggestions. And my two daughters, Emily and Abigail, consistently provided perspective and inspiration.

I owe three people above all my thanks for making this book possible: Brooke Parker, my chief of staff, who provided me with invaluable knowledge by guiding me through the doorways of a thousand classrooms and courthouses in Kentucky; David Hale, my consigliere and best friend, for serving as my sounding board on all issues of policy and faith, and as my primary teacher on Christianity, both in word and practice; and most of all, my wife Lisa Miller, for reminding me every day of what is truly important, and whose love and support sustains me and our family.

INTRODUCTION

THE COMPASSIONATE COMMUNITY

Two thousand years ago, there was a great rabbi by the name of Hillel the Elder. Hillel was widely known and respected in all of Israel for his wisdom and knowledge. Even today, his moral and legal decisions serve as a cornerstone of Jewish tradition.

One day the rabbi was approached by a cynical pagan who did not believe in Hillel's God. The pagan issued Hillel a challenge: If the rabbi could teach him the entire Torah—the first five books of the Hebrew Bible—while standing on one foot, the nonbeliever would convert to Judaism. The rabbi accepted the challenge. Hillel declared: "What is hateful to you, do not do unto your neighbor. That is the whole of the Torah; all the rest is commentary. Now go and learn it."[1]

A few years later, Jesus of Nazareth was walking many of the same paths of ancient Israel preaching his Gospel (good news). He was approached by a skeptical group of rabbis who asked a question similar to the one posed to Hillel: "Teacher, which is the greatest commandment in the Law?" Jesus replied that all of God's law could be summed up in two commandments. First, "you shall love the Lord your God with all your heart and with all your soul and with all your mind." And second, "you shall love your neighbor as yourself." Jesus's "Golden Rule" echoed Hillel's teachings: "Treat people the same way you want them to treat you."

These two stories illuminate an eternal, universal truth. There is no value more celebrated in the human experience than compassion for others. As the renowned Christian author C. S. Lewis recognized, nearly every world religion—despite enormous geographic and cultural differences over many centuries—has accepted God's revelation of compassion for others.[2] (See table 1 for an illustration of Lewis's principle.)

These same traditions teach us that there is a group to whom special compassion is owed: society's most vulnerable. This includes the elderly and the young, the widowed and the orphaned, the disabled and the powerless. Jesus opened his "Sermon on the Mount" by extolling the "poor," "those who mourn," the "gentle," and the "persecuted." In the days before his crucifixion, Jesus affirmed that we can tell the righteous from the damned by whether they had fed the hungry, given the thirsty something to drink, clothed the naked, visited the prisoner, and welcomed the stranger. His teachings echoed the Hebrew prophets who proclaimed that a society's moral virtue was defined by its compassion for the disadvantaged and the vulnerable.

Indeed, these traditions teach us that showing compassion for others, particularly the needy, is a manifestation of God's love for us all. The Hebrew Bible instructs that because of God's covenant with the Jewish people, we must be a "light unto the nations" and share that love with the blind, the prisoner, and the homeless. The Hebrew prophets decreed that the highest form of worship is "to do justice, to love goodness and to walk modestly with your God." Accordingly, God's Chosen People are considered by Jewish law to be congenitally compassionate.

Jesus expanded on this notion, teaching that when humans show compassion for others, we are actually returning God's love: "Truly I say to you, to the extent that you did it to one of these brothers of Mine, even the least of them, you did it to Me." As the renowned Catholic activist Dorothy Day concluded: "The mystery of the poor is this: That they are Jesus, and what you do for them, you do for Him."[3]

This ethic of compassion for others is deeply ingrained into American history and culture. The Declaration of Independence—the Founders' mission statement—concludes that with God's protection, "we mutually pledge to each other our Lives, our Fortunes and our sacred Honor." Fifty years later, the esteemed political observer Alexis de Tocqueville identified this shared sense of community—the willingness of Americans to recognize that there is a greater good above ourselves as individuals—as a key factor in the nation's rise toward greatness. And in 1977, Vice President Hubert Humphrey beautifully encapsulated centuries of teachings to define the moral foundation of the American experience by stating that the "moral test of government is how it treats those who are at the dawn of life, the children; those who are in the twilight of life, the aged; and those who are in the shadow of life, the sick, the needy, and the handicapped."[4]

More than 200 years after the nation's founding, and more than 2,000 years after Hillel and Jesus, Americans continue to struggle with our moral responsibilities to our neighbors. In fact, the debate over moral values lies at the epicenter of today's political discourse. The widely read 2004 National Election Pool exit poll revealed that a plurality of voters chose "moral values" as the most important issue that influenced their vote. Eighty percent of these Americans voted to reelect Republican President George W. Bush, providing him with the margin of victory in a close national election. Underlying their votes were the faith traditions that informed and shaped their values: These same exit polls demonstrate a strong correlation between churchgoers and "values" voters.[5]

The values debate, in fact, has taken a highly partisan turn. While polling data shows that Democrats were viewed by American voters in the 1970s and 1980s as "the party of traditional family values," in the last two decades, Republicans have taken the moral high ground in these partisan battles. Polls from the first years of this century reveal that the GOP is overwhelmingly viewed as the values party and the party most friendly to religion, while Democrats are seen as being dominated by an anti-religious, morally relativist, liberal faction.[6]

Today's values debate, however, has strayed far from the core teachings of Hillel and Jesus. Most political discussions about moral values usually do not draw upon the key spiritually significant values of love and compassion for others. Indeed, the human emotions most associated with the values debate are just the opposite: anger and fear. And instead of focusing attention on God's powerful instructions to show compassion to society's most vulnerable, typical political discussions about moral values nearly always involve discussing consensual sex or its consequences. Abortion and gay rights dominate the political conversation, and former President Bill Clinton has emerged as the poster child for America's alleged moral decline, due to his highly publicized sexual affair while in office. As former Moral Majority leader Cal Thomas argues, talk of sexual sin "goes to the gut" and, as a bonus, allows us to argue about changing someone else's behavior, rather than our own. Further, as prominent Christian minister and sociologist Tony Campolo notes, it is easier to rally people around a common enemy than around a set of common beliefs.[7]

Values voters generally are described as evangelical Christian conservatives who feel marginalized by the American culture's indifference to moral values. They see amorality in the degradation of popular culture through sexual and violent imagery in the media, the discouragement of public religious expression, and the legal authorization of practices traditionally deemed sinful, such as abortion and same-sex marriage. They fear that a polity that does not formally acknowledge God's presence—indeed, a polity that often seems hostile to expressions of faith—has allowed our democracy to become morally ambivalent and ethically corrupt.

Some of these same voters believe that many libertine values that are manifestly immoral and anti-religious pervade American culture. By worshipping the false gods of greed, achievement, power, selfishness, and licentiousness, American cultural and political forces are undermining and contradicting God-centered moral values. As the Apostle Paul wrote, to be Christian, you must imitate Jesus and "do nothing from selfishness or empty conceit, but with humility of mind, regarding one another as more important than yourself; do not merely look out for your own personal interests, but also for the interests of others." Selfishness that results in the degradation, oppression, or exploitation of others is deemed universally to be contrary to God's will.[8]

This reveals one of the most disturbing ironies of modern American politics. Over the past decade, the national agenda has been hijacked by special interest groups that have focused their policy attention on their own short-term economic self-interest. Elected officials, swayed by large campaign contributions, have promoted tax cuts and deregulation that primarily benefit wealthy individuals and powerful corporations, leaving future generations with record budget deficits. Instead of focusing on good public policy, many politicians of both parties emphasize the three P's—power, patronage, and pork projects—in their single-minded quest to seek reelection merely for the sake of reelection. I call this "the politics of self-interest," and it is precisely what our religious traditions would scorn.

Yet many of these same politicians have married the politics of self-interest with compelling, value-laden rhetoric on hot-button social issues. The strategy has worked: Religious conservatives have been credited with delivering victories to candidates in many recent elections.

Unfortunately, while religious conservatives receive symbolic gestures and lip-service attention to their moral concerns, the Robin Hood-in-reverse economic policies rob this largely working- and middle-class constituency of critical educational and economic opportunities. Worst of all, the morally offensive failure of American policymakers to deal substantively with poverty in America—a direct result of the politics of self-interest—correlates precisely with our failure to achieve meaningful long-term reductions (and in fact, we have seen short-term increases) in the national rates of abortion, disease, crime, and divorce.[9]

In 2004, I traveled to some of the poorest counties in Kentucky—among the poorest counties in the United States—to campaign for state legislative candidates. I ventured into the Appalachian "hollers"—valleys of substandard houses and trailers without running water or indoor plumbing—to talk about educational opportunity and affordable health care. I was met time after time with one question: "What is your position on gay marriage?"

Polling in Middle America by the Democracy Corps think tank found much the same phenomenon. Interviews revealed that most voters were largely unable to distinguish among Democratic and Republican candidates on issues involving health care, jobs, and education. However, many drew the assumption that if a candidate agreed with them on cultural issues such as abortion, gay marriage, and the role of faith in public life, that candidate likely would share their views on other issues.[10]

Other studies demonstrate that voters are willing to vote for a candidate with an expressed moral code, even if they happen to *disagree* with many of the politician's positions on key issues. One respondent eloquently articulated this mindset: "President Bush won on values, yes, but not hatred of gays or any other stereotype you have in your head about Bush voters like me. He won because he *has* values, and even though I agree with little of what he believes, at least I know *what he believes*. At least I know that *he really does believe in something*."[11]

Perhaps in the midst of an ever-coarsened culture, Americans yearn for an honest and open conversation about what is right and wrong for their families and communities. And the public-values debate has been hopelessly one-sided: discussions of moral values are ignored, or even rejected, by those on the left who are reluctant to discuss faith, criticize any aspect of a free culture, or impose a majority morality on a diverse citizenry.

When politicians talk about jobs, education, and health care in a morally neutral context, the message often appears to reflect entitlement, rather than the social justice and mutual responsibility that underlie these public policies. The cerebral approach used by many politicians to explain policy options often misses its intended target: Too often, they take aim at the head, when they should be aiming at the heart. Their failure to convey compassion is sometimes interpreted as a lack of conviction. Debating the subtle nuances of policies opens them up to charges of "flip-flopping." And ultimately, many values voters abandon the candidate who refuses to speak their language, to embrace the candidate who says the right words while producing the opposite results.

THE COMPASSIONATE COMMUNITY

Politicians from both parties reacted swiftly to the lessons learned from the 2004 elections. Conservative Republicans tried to exploit their values advantage by amplifying their rhetoric, accusing liberals of demeaning people of faith in policy disputes and judicial nomination battles. Liberal and moderate Democrats began to inject more discussions of faith and values into their public pronouncements and made best-sellers of authors such as Jim Wallis and former President Jimmy Carter, both of whom argue that the right is wrong in its interpretation of God's teachings.[12]

No one, however, has attempted to design a coherent vision for American public policy that is rooted in and informed by the true core values embraced by our religious and democratic traditions. More significantly, we have not tried to develop a values-based policy agenda that transcends labels and could unite Americans of all faiths and political persuasions. Instead, the current values debate is marked by the use of inflammatory fear tactics designed to rally partisans at the ideological extremes, while ultimately serving to further polarize and divide our "red" and "blue" nation.

That's why I offer *The Compassionate Community*. It has a simple theme: "Love your neighbor as yourself." When Americans put aside our own selfish desires and instead act on the behalf of the greater good, we create a compassionate community, a society that provides everyone who works hard and assumes personal responsibility an opportunity to share in the American Dream. It reflects our aspirations, our ideals, our better angels, in contrast to the selfish ambition scorned by the Apostle Paul. It appeals to our hearts, instead of our fears.

In the ten chapters that follow, I discuss ten essential American values that emanate from this core theme, and that will, if enacted, lead us to a more united nation. The ten essential values are:

1. Opportunity
2. Responsibility
3. Work
4. Family
5. Freedom
6. Faith
7. Justice
8. Peace
9. Respect
10. Life

I discuss some of my own life experiences—both personal and political—to demonstrate the universality and current relevance of each of these values. More importantly, I draw from some of the lessons I have taught to teenagers in Sunday School for almost a decade, illustrating each of these values with the story of a hero from the Hebrew Bible. The tales of great biblical figures such as Abraham, Moses, David, and Esther do more to animate these values than would thousands of policy white papers.

But this is not simply a rhetorical exercise: Policy matters. Merely trying to "reframe" the debate by using more politically palatable, poll-tested language will do nothing to bring the country together. The time-honored values discussed in these pages can be realized only if our political leadership implements programs that reflect these values. This is why each chapter also discusses major initiatives that policymakers can implement to ensure that these values become part of our culture. While some national efforts will be necessary, our primary focus must be on local initiatives because they not only reach the public in the most direct and intimate manner, but—in the words of former

Supreme Court Justice Louis Brandeis—states and localities also can serve as "laboratories of reform," providing federal policymakers with proven examples of our values in action.

The proposals that follow do not endorse today's "anything-goes" culture. True compassion embraces what pop-psychologists refer to as "tough love." It requires individuals to sacrifice and work hard. Our love for our neighbors is conditioned on their acceptance of personal responsibility, as we assume it for ourselves. But at the same time, Americans should not deny respect to those whose own responsible search for truth and fulfillment may follow a path different than ours.

In this vision of America's future, the compassionate community would require society to reflect the values of its citizens, not the coarsening of our culture brought to us by the economics of self-interest. Our moral outrage, resources, and energy would be directed to the stark reality that in the United States, the richest country in the history of the world, nearly 36 million of our neighbors live below the poverty line. And we would require our institutions, particularly our governmental bodies, to be responsive and accountable to the people they represent, and to refine and reform themselves in a constant quest for excellence.

The policies outlined in this book, framed by our enduring values, should enable politicians and policymakers to broaden the definition of "morality" in today's political culture. Too often, a discussion of moral values is limited to personal private behavior. But morality means so much more. As the respected psychologist Lawrence Kohlberg has argued, the highest stage of moral development is when an individual accepts universal principles of justice, the reciprocity and equality of human rights, and respect for the dignity of human beings.[13] In this context, Martin Luther King, Jr., was one of the greatest moral leaders of the twentieth century: his willingness to sacrifice his life to pursue justice for all overwhelms any personal, human faults that have been exposed in recent years.

The primary focus of public policy, therefore, should not be the private morality of individuals. It should instead be the public morality of the nation. Taken individually, each of us is a flawed work in progress. But as a community, working for the mutual benefit of all, we have the potential for true greatness.

In the pages that follow, I discuss how these shared values are deeply embedded in the American political experience, and find great support from the political philosophies that inspired the Founders of our nation. More profoundly, they are grounded by religious instruction, faith, and tradition. The Bible—and its interpretations, as embraced by Jews and Christians—serves as the primary text, but an examination of other world religions demonstrates that these values are universal to the human experience.

I approach this subject with great sensitivity. Talking about the Bible, or faith in general, has lately become the "third rail" of politics. Many Americans—in particular, many liberals—view the injection of faith into political dialogue as the first step on a slippery slope to a fundamentalist Christian theocracy. Many are not aware that most religious Americans reach their positions on issues through honest, selfless reflection and fidelity to Scripture, not the self-important, paternalistic manipulation by some of the more familiar right-wing spokesmen.

I believe that any legitimate analysis of American values must involve some discussion of religion. Just as secular thought and political philosophy certainly played, and continue to play, important roles in the creation and development of our republic, the Judeo-Christian ethic animates much of what we claim as our shared American values. More significantly, the language of faith unites many Americans by grounding our values and public policies in traditions that have informed, guided, and inspired so many people for so many centuries.

But we must also recognize that the suggestion that the state should be exclusive in its recognition of faith can be extraordinarily divisive and hurtful. Any attempt to employ the language or the values of our faith traditions must be nonsectarian and inclusive of all Americans. That's why the compassionate community must stand strongly for the proposition that government should never define or prescribe a certain set of religious beliefs for its people. The devout should not be forced to moderate their faith, nor should nonbelievers be required to adapt to a religious standard.

In designing a book about faith, values, and politics, I do not pretend to be a theologian, a grizzled political operative, or an expert in policy minutia. I do, however, offer a unique perspective on the values debate.

For six years, I have served as state treasurer of Kentucky, a "red" state in middle America. Despite a recent Republican trend in our region, I have been elected twice statewide as a Democrat, winning each race by comfortable margins. And while I am proud of my partisan affiliation, I am even more passionate about the need to work in a bipartisan manner once the election season concludes. In each of the major policy initiatives I have pursued while in office, I have actively sought and secured the cooperation and input of my colleagues on the other side of the aisle.

My political perspective is shaped by two central forces. I am a devoutly religious Jewish man, and I take seriously the Biblical tradition of *tikkun olam*—which means literally "to repair the world"—and holds every Jewish adult responsible to help make the world a better place. As a native and resident of an overwhelmingly Christian community, I have also developed a deep appreciation and understanding of Jesus, his teachings, and followers. This unusual background provides a more nuanced outlook on the great church/state divide that has polarized our nation. As a religious minority, I am acutely sensitive to fears about religious oppression. However, as a public official representing a large and growing conservative Christian constituency, I am also aware that freedom of religious expression should not be muzzled in the guise of political correctness.

My second guiding force is my family. In the pages that follow, the reader will grasp the deeply important role my parents and my wife have played in the development of my ideas. But the most profound influence on my politics comes from my children. As the father of two pre-teen girls, I am extremely interested in providing them with the opportunity to share in the American Dream, while I am acutely concerned about protecting them from the predatory cultural and societal influences that have arisen precipitously in recent years.

Whether my own political path will allow me to affect the changes I outline in this book, I cannot pretend to know. But I hope that *The Compassionate Community* will provide a vision of America's future that can be embraced by other elected leaders, grassroots activists, and ordinary voters of all political stripes. I believe these values can help politicians formulate a set of principles and policy ideas that will enable them to connect more effectively with the hearts of disaffected voters. If religious Americans understand the moral grounding that informs public policy, perhaps they will reject the undelivered promises and the harsher economic realities provided by the politics of self-interest. Further, with an appeal to our shared American values, candidates could demonstrate that their leadership would bring a hastier demise to the cultural trends that so many Americans of all religious beliefs find so toxic.

I want to emphasize that this is not a partisan political exercise. From my experiences in state and federal government, I have learned one consistent lesson: Only those public policy measures that receive bipartisan support and cooperation can have a lasting positive impact on the American experience. If elected officials left their partisan agendas outside the halls of government, and brought the notion of the compassionate community into the corridors of power, to develop plans that respect the values of all Americans, our nation would be strengthened.

Indeed, *The Compassionate Community* is not about moving the country or the political system to the left or the right. In a political culture where those who run up the national credit card through budget-busting tax cuts call themselves "conservatives" and those who advocate the conservation of our natural resources are deemed "liberals," these terms have lost any real meaning. Nor does the notion of the compassionate community mean moving the nation toward a morally relativist "center," where all Americans are asked to compromise their core beliefs and values to establish a watered-down uniformity of political viewpoints. Instead, I seek to move the political debate "up"—away from the debased and corrupted culture created by the politics and economics of self-interest, toward the values upon which our democracy was framed, toward common higher ground on which Americans can be united.

If our elected leaders could challenge the rest of us to become more engaged and to make the small selfless sacrifices necessary to build stronger communities, our democracy would be stronger. In his influential essay, "A Return to National Greatness," conservative columnist David Brooks argues that democracy "has a tendency to slide into nihilistic mediocrity if its citizens are not inspired by some larger national goal."[14] Our leaders missed out on a golden opportunity to engage the nation in the days following the 9–11 terrorist attacks; instead of encouraging shared sacrifice to promote the common good, Americans were plied with tax cuts and urged to go shopping. However, when elected officials at all levels failed to respond promptly and sufficiently to the damage caused by Hurricane Katrina in the Gulf Coast region in

September 2005, the American people demonstrated their nature to show compassion for their fellow human beings, volunteering and donating money in record numbers. For a short period of time, the compassionate community emerged instantaneously, on its own. With committed leaders, we can make it a permanent reality.

Our challenge is burdened by the simple reality that the politics of self-interest are very compelling. When a candidate or a party promises that individual success does not rely on mutual cooperation or sacrifice, that message can be very persuasive to an electorate already made cynical by our poisoned political culture. But these easy political promises come with an enormous societal cost—the race to enact spending hikes and tax cuts for wealthy contributors and special interests continues to run up our deficits and mortgage our future.

I hope that *The Compassionate Community* enables our political leadership to make the case that public policy that serves the public interest ultimately will lead to a better society for all of its individual members. Through public-private partnerships that embrace the compassion for others that is central to our religious teachings, we can build communities that ultimately are less dependent on government largesse.

This is not simply a feel-good prescription for the nation's ills. Indeed, today's economists and business leaders recognize that our country's future fiscal health will depend on policymakers understanding that the global economy has fundamentally changed, and that collaboration and mutual understanding are not simply a moral goal, but a practical necessity. As IBM's Irving Wladawsky-Berger notes: "This emerging era is characterized by the collaborative innovation of many people working in gifted communities, just as innovation in the industrial era was characterized by individual genius."[15] Benjamin Franklin's words at the signing of the Declaration of Independence are fitting: "We must, indeed, all hang together or, most assuredly, we shall all hang separately."[16]

In fact, as former Czech President Vaclav Havel eloquently decreed at a July 4th celebration at Independence Hall in Philadelphia, it is the recognition of the interconnectedness of all individuals that can address today's great popular sentiment of uncertainty and selfishness that foment so many of our modern struggles. Havel discussed new scientific discoveries that demonstrate that we are all connected to the broader cosmos, and argued that a study of world religions offers a sense of God's compassion and unity that transcends all of our differences. He concluded: "The Declaration of Independence, adopted 218 years ago in this building, states that the Creator gave man the right to liberty. It seems man can realize that liberty only if he does not forget the One who endowed him with it."[17]

The compassionate community lies at the intersection of old, enduring values—those that informed our Founders and can still inspire us today—and new, modern technologies that have the capacity to bring greater opportunity, justice, and equality to all of us. With a look back to the traditions of our faith, and a look forward to the brave new possibilities being brought to us by the digital technologies of the new economy, we can develop policies, implement programs, and build communities that enhance everyone's quality of life and give every citizen a stronger voice in their democracy.

Our challenge is similar to Hillel's. The time a person can stand on one foot is approximately the time politicians have to articulate a vision in campaign commercials and news sound bites. It is simple to develop a pithy message of self-interest, or one that uses fear or hatred of others to spur political action. It is far more complex, and strategically risky, to explain how sacrifice and concern for others can lead to long-term progress. But by employing the language and the values that have been embraced by humankind for centuries—and by implementing sound public policies that reflect these values—we can all be reminded about our real moral obligations and then can begin the journey to true compassion for all citizens.

The Compassionate Community has a simple message: If we can all come up with public policies that reflect the fundamental moral value of compassion for others, and that abandon the politics of self-interest, we can, together, build a stronger America. It's a message that can help candidates win elections and elected officials win public support for policies that result in progress for the people. It's a message that can lift people's hearts and make them more optimistic about the country's future.

All the rest is commentary. Now go and learn it.

Table 1 The World's Religions and Spiritual Traditions on The Universal Value of Compassion for Others

JUDAISM: Rabbi Akiva taught that the commandment, "Thou shalt love they neighbor as thyself" was "the great principle of Torah." Offenses against a fellow human being are a denial of God himself. Talmud, Sifre on Leviticus 19:8.

CHRISTIANITY: The Apostle Paul taught, "Through love, serve one another, for the whole law is fulfilled in one word, in the statement: 'You shall love your neighbor as yourself.'" Galatians 5:14

Paul also taught: "For this, 'You shall not commit adultery,' 'You shall not murder,' 'You shall not steal,' 'You shall not covet,' and if there is any other commandment, it is summed up in this saying, 'You shall love your neighbor as yourself.'" Romans 13:9.

ISLAM: "Not one of you is a believer until he loves for his brother what he loves for himself." Forty Hadith of an-Nawawi 13.

Islam views itself as systemizing Jesus' teachings on brotherly love. Ameer Ali, *Spirit of Islam*, 1902.

CONFUCIANISM: "Try your best to treat others as you would wish to be treated yourself, and you will find that this is the shortest way to benevolence." Mencius VII.A.4

"What you do not wish done to yourself, do not do to others." *The Analects*.

HINDUISM: "One shall not behave towards others in a way which is disagreeable to oneself. This is the essence of morality. All other activities are due to selfish desire." Mahabharata, Anusasana Parva 113.8.

Vyasa, who wrote the major Puranas—the fountainhead of Hindu religious thought—announced the gist of all his 18 Puranas thus: "Helping others is merit, hurting others is sin!"

BUDDHISM: "Comparing oneself to others in such terms as 'Just as I am so are they are so am I,' he should neither kill nor cause others to kill." Sutta Nipata 705.

Buddha's message was subtitled "a religion of infinite compassion." Huston Smith, *The World's Religions*.

JAINISM: "A man should wander about treating all creatures as he himself would be treated." Sutrakritanga 1.11.33.

NATIVE AMERICAN: "Do not judge your neighbor until you walk two moons in his moccasins." Northern Cheyenne Proverb.

AFRICAN (TRAD): "One going to take a pointed stick to pinch a baby bird should first try it on himself to feel how it hurts." Yoruba Proverb (Nigeria).

ONE

NOAH AND THE VALUE
OF OPPORTUNITY

God said to Noah, "I have decided to put an end to all flesh, for the earth is filled with lawlessness because of them: I am about to destroy them with the earth. Make yourself an ark of gopher wood; make it an ark with compartments, and cover it inside and out with pitch. This is how you should make it: the length of the ark shall be three hundred cubits, its width fifty cubits, and its height thirty cubits. Make an opening for daylight in the ark, and terminate it within a cubit of the top. Put the entrance to the ark in its side; make it with bottom, second and third decks."

—Genesis 6:13–16

I imagine most parents have a difficult time explaining to their young children what they do for a living. But I also know that having a parent with a political career is particularly bewildering to a young child. During my first statewide political campaign, I had a breakfast conversation with my then five-year-old daughter, Emily, which made quite an impression on me. Emily understood that I was asking the voters of the Commonwealth to elect me to the position of Kentucky's state treasurer. But then she confounded me with an unusual question: "Daddy, does that mean we get to ride a big boat?" When I asked her what she meant, she exclaimed: "To search for the hidden treasure!"

Knowing that my daughters were confused by the concept, I instead have tried to illustrate what I do by telling them a story involving

a subject that always piques their interest—a famous horse. This particular horse, that just happened to be Kentucky's most famous early-twen-
tieth-century native, was named Seabiscuit.[1]

Seabiscuit was a thoroughbred that everyone thought was too
small, and no one gave him a chance to become a champion in the
"sport of kings." He had a jockey that everyone thought was too tall,
and no one gave him a chance to win the big races. He had a trainer
that everyone thought was too old, and no one gave him a chance to
work with the most talented thoroughbreds.

Then one day, one man came along—Seabiscuit's owner, Charles
Howard—and gave them all a chance. Howard empowered each of
them with the resources, equipment, facilities, and public show of confidence they needed to succeed. And Seabiscuit became a champion.
Howard provided Team Seabiscuit with the tools they needed to
achieve unparalleled racing success. Their success also empowered
Howard; not simply to win renown and money, but, more importantly,
to complete the grieving process for his deceased son.

What is most interesting is that Seabiscuit ran and won during a time
in the nation's history when there were millions of Americans who were
struggling just to get a chance. It was the Great Depression, and hope was
scarce amid unparalleled economic hardship. And then one man came
along and gave them all a chance. One man arrived on the scene and empowered millions of Americans with the tools they needed to work hard
and build a good quality of life for their families. And because of that
man—President Franklin D. Roosevelt—the United States, in time,
emerged as the strongest economic power in the history of the world.

My kids know that FDR is one of my political heroes. And while his
mission and mandate were far, far greater than mine, we share the same
value: opportunity. I go to work every day trying to provide more and
more Kentuckians the chance to realize their own personal dreams.

These lessons for my children are not limited to politics. In fact, I apply
them on the softball field.

My own baseball career peaked at the age of eight, when I completed an extremely rare feat during a T-ball game: an unassisted triple
play. The achievement can be credited not to any special athletic ability,
but to the fact that the umpire and I were the only people on the field

who knew what was going on at the time. However, that did not prevent my father from bragging about the incident for the next 25 years.

My involvement with the sport now consists of rooting for the Cincinnati Reds and the Boston Red Sox (until recently a miserable preoccupation), "playing" in two fantasy baseball leagues, and, most importantly, coaching my daughters' Pee Wee softball teams. While I initially signed up to spend more time with my own daughters, coaching young girls for five years has been one of the most rewarding—and downright fun—things I have ever done. Teaching the fundamentals, making out lineups, and watching the girls grow, improve, and sometimes even win are the best parts of my summer.

Coaching has also helped me apply and demonstrate to the girls my vision of the moral value of opportunity. Unlike some coaches who focus on winning and winning only, playing the best athletes at the critical positions, I constantly rotate my lineups and fielding positions to give each girl a chance to learn, grow, and have fun. This strategy may have been the leading reason we always ended up with losing records during our first four years.

In 2005, however, my luck changed. In the last inning of the deciding game, we were up 7–4 with the chance to clinch our first winning season. It was Kayla's turn to play the key position on the field—pitcher. Kayla was one of my all-time favorites, but with the winning record on the line, I briefly considered substituting my best fielder, Cassi, at pitcher. I left Kayla in. With the lead narrowed to 7–6, and the bases loaded, Kayla made two heads-up plays to make the final two outs and win us the game. Kayla's entire extended family—who attended every game—couldn't hold back their tears when I awarded Kayla the game ball. I gave Kayla a chance, and she delivered all of us a victory.

NOAH AND THE GREAT FLOOD

I also believe that we all must witness the value of opportunity in action. When my daughter Emily turned six, I took her to attend Sunday services at the Historic Pleasant Green Missionary Baptist Church in Lexington. The minister, Rev. L. F. Peeples, had offered to introduce me to his mostly African American congregation.

I wanted to introduce Emily to Christianity. African American churches like Pleasant Green offer the most spiritually inspiring church experiences I have witnessed. The sounds, the rhythms, and the dancing in the aisles enthralled Emily. Fortunately, the place was loud enough so that only those sitting closest to us could hear Emily when she asked loudly, "Daddy, who is Jesus?"

I also brought Emily along because we had the very rare chance to listen to the guest preacher, Jesse Jackson. While Rev. Jackson and I part ways on a number of political and policy issues, I find him one of the most stirring and accomplished orators alive today. And Jackson is perhaps the most eloquent advocate of the value of equal opportunity for all Americans. Little did I know how relevant his talk would be.

Jackson's sermon focused on one of the most popular Bible stories—particularly among children of Emily's age—the story of Noah, found in chapters six through nine of the Book of Genesis. With his fluid delivery and rhythmic cadences, Jackson recounted how a grieving God despaired of the wickedness of man and chose to cause a great flood to destroy nearly all of His creation.

Of course, Jackson reminded us, there was one righteous man, Noah, and God decided to spare him, his family, and two of each species of living animal, so that the Earth could then be repopulated. This was a second act of creation—my daughters would call it a "do-over"; my grandfather, an accomplished golfer, would claim that God took a mulligan.

But then Jackson parted from the Biblical text. It was an election year, and he wanted to make a political point from the pulpit. This was the late 1990s, a period when right-wing politicians were making a resurgence nationally through piercing critiques of the federal bureaucracy. Speaker of the House Newt Gingrich was trying to dismantle Lyndon Johnson's "Great Society," anti-tax zealot Grover Norquist was drawing up plans to shrink government so that it could be "drowned in a bathtub," and radio personality Rush Limbaugh was challenging his listeners to name a single federal government program that actually worked.[2]

Jackson asked the congregation to envision Noah's predicament had the Gingriches and Limbaughs ruled the heavens. Jackson imagined that they would have advised Noah to do push-ups. Like a prehistoric John Wayne, Noah should have picked himself up by his bootstraps (or sandal-straps, in his case), built up his muscles, and be prepared to swim—after all, the rain would only last for 40 days and 40 nights!

I found Jackson's critique of laissez-faire, do-nothing government to be compelling. Government has a vital role to play in society and in public policy, and the mythic notion of an entirely self-reliant populace, operating as wholly distinct and detached individuals, is not an appealing nor realistic vision of society in my mind.

Yet I also do not find the converse to be true. While government is not the problem in itself, it is also not the solution to all of our challenges. Indeed, there is a middle ground—the so-called third way—that was made famous by former President Bill Clinton and has proved around the globe to be an effective alternative to the politics of the left and the right. The fundamental principle of the third way is that government's role is to empower able-bodied individuals to help themselves. (Of course, direct government assistance will always be required for those who cannot help themselves: the young, the very old, the disabled, etc.) Policymakers are best suited to develop programs that equip people with the tools they need to solve their own problems.

Noah's Ark, in fact, is an appropriate symbol for the third way. God did not create a massive shelter, stocked with food and supplies (the "big government" approach). Nor did God adopt the laissez-faire attitude lampooned by Rev. Jackson. Instead, God provided direction to Noah on how to survive the impending natural destruction.

God gave Noah very detailed instructions on how to build an ark that would ensure the propagation of the human race and the animal kingdom. From the construction materials to the size specifications to the architectural design, God provided a blueprint for Noah's life raft—and charged Noah with the work. God equipped Noah with opportunity—the tools he needed to survive the storm—and empowered Noah to save his family.

OPPORTUNITY:
A MORAL VALUE, AN AMERICAN VALUE

Opportunity, indeed, is a critical value of the compassionate community. World religious tradition instructs us that providing others with an opportunity to realize their own dreams is one of the most powerful ways to demonstrate love for your neighbor.

For society's most vulnerable, this means providing the opportunity to, at the very least, secure the basics: food, clothing, and shelter. Jesus instructed his followers to lend assistance to those who were struggling on their own to make ends meet: "Give to him who asks of you, and do not turn away from him who wants to borrow from you." Jewish Rabbinic law called for the creation of communal agencies to assure the minimum needs of survival for those who are destitute. And Eastern religious figures ranging from Mohammed (Islam) to Confucius (Confucianism) to Vivekanada (Hinduism) consistently advocated that society must provide for those who have the greatest needs.[3]

But access to opportunity should not be limited to the destitute and the disabled. These same religious traditions promote equal opportunity for all of humanity. And while making charitable gifts is considered a universal virtue, the most noble of all charitable practices is empowering others with the opportunity to provide for themselves and their own families. You are probably familiar with the ancient proverb: "If you give a man a fish you feed him for a day; if you teach him how to fish, you feed him for a lifetime." While the source of the quote is unknown, its philosophy is consistent with the teachings of most renowned world religious leaders. For example, the great twelfth-century rabbi Maimonides proffered that the highest form of charity was not giving money—but rather helping someone get a job to strengthen his own hand.

Our nation was built on the value of opportunity. The first waves of Europeans to settle our lands came for the opportunity to practice their religion without persecution. More recently, immigrants have traveled to the United States from all over the globe for the opportunity to earn a higher standard of living. Much like with Noah, the boats these brave men and women boarded to the New World represented their dreams of safety, security, and opportunity.

Not coincidentally, the value of opportunity occupies the core of the country's mission statement—the Declaration of Independence. In drafting the document, Thomas Jefferson relied heavily on John Locke's *Two Treatises on Government* in declaring that "all men are created equal, that they are endowed by their Creator with certain unalienable Rights." But in defining the key rights, Jefferson departed from Locke's formulation of "life, liberty and property," by listing them as "life, liberty and *the pursuit of happiness*" (emphasis added).

By substituting "happiness," Jefferson was not proposing an amorphous, lighthearted concept often identified with the term today. Instead, he was enlisting the definition of the Greek philosopher Aristotle, who declared that the "final cause," or purpose in life, for all individuals was happiness, a well-being or human flourishing that could only be achieved through the pursuit of reason, combined with the opportunity to reach one's highest potential. Accordingly, Aristotle argued that it was the state's preeminent obligation to provide every individual with an opportunity to pursue his or her own version of happiness.

This political philosophy also influenced the framing of the country's governing document, the U.S. Constitution. During the constitutional conventions, future Treasury Secretary Alexander Hamilton unsuccessfully argued that because the masses were "turbulent and changing" and "seldom judge or determine right," it was vital to give the rich "a distinct permanent share in the government" by structuring a formally class-based government as had been the case in Great Britain. While early American history indeed was marked by a concentration of power in the "enlightened few," the Framers created a Constitution and a Bill of Rights that provided opportunity to the masses, and a political process by which the nation has moved much farther in that direction over the past two centuries.[4]

Today, every American should expect an equal opportunity to pursue happiness. This means that every individual, who works hard and plays by the rules of society, should have the opportunity to share in the American Dream. People who are responsible for themselves and their communities should have the opportunity for a good job, the opportunity to live in their own home in safety and good health, and the opportunity to retire with financial security.

For those who are able-bodied, this does not necessarily mean a hand out, but a hand up. As the story of Noah illustrates, the ideal role of government is to empower individuals to help themselves, to give them the tools they need to build their own dreams.

Ultimately, the most vital guarantor of equal opportunity is education. Even in the early years of the Republic, our nation's leaders realized that universal public education was critical to the premise of equal opportunity for all. And in designing his roadmap to create a vibrant middle class in the wake of the Great Depression, President Franklin D. Roosevelt recognized the need to ensure that all American children received a free, quality public education through high school. By the end of World War II, the opportunity to earn a high-school diploma was all most Americans needed to secure a good factory job, buy a home, and raise their children in prosperity.[5]

Today, however, a high-school degree is not enough for most Americans. Without higher education—college, vocational or technical school—it has become increasingly difficult to escape a life of poverty. The factory jobs of the post-war era are disappearing due to a sharp decline in the manufacturing sector, free trade agreements that have shifted many manufacturing jobs overseas, and the emergence of the new information-based economy. Since the 1970s, the American manufacturing sector has lost over six million jobs (more than three million have been lost since 1998 alone), due to new technologies and cheaper overseas competition. Further, the market value of those left unemployed has declined precipitously, forcing millions of formerly middle class, blue-collar American workers closer to the poverty line.[6]

This trend is expected to continue and accelerate. With rapid advances in technology linking the globe digitally, and with the impending retirement of the disproportionately large baby boom generation, industry employment projections predict that the fastest job growth will occur in the high-tech and health-care sectors, both of which usually require higher education. High-school graduates (and dropouts) will be forced to fill the remaining service-related jobs offered by low-wage, low-benefits employers such as Wal-Mart and McDonald's. Those Americans without higher education will earn far less money than their peers; studies show that on average, a higher education degree could make a difference of nearly one million dollars over the course of a lifetime.[7]

Young people who fail to earn a higher education degree are not the only projected losers in the new economy. Communities with fewer college graduates have a much harder time competing economically with neighboring areas in which a greater percentage of the workforce is more highly educated. Between 1929 and 1998, the per capita output of the national economy grew by 240 percent—and the most significant growth was specifically located in regions where there had been an increasingly educated workforce. The data is clear: A state's economic success is directly related to the higher education attainment of its children. The information-based industries of the new economy will locate in communities where a highly educated workforce is put in place to handle the critical responsibilities.[8]

And the communities that are fortunate enough to retain the industries and jobs of the new economy might not ultimately reside within the borders of the United States. A 2005 study by the nation's leading academies on science, engineering, and medicine revealed their deep concern about the future prosperity of the United States due to the fact that the "scientific and technical building blocks of our economic leadership are eroding at a time when many other nations are gaining strength."[9] Asian universities are producing eight times as many science-related bachelor's degrees than the United States, and Mexico is graduating more engineers every year. The study concluded that unless we reverse these trends, our lead in science and technology could disappear, and the majority of high-paying, high-tech jobs of the twenty-first century could be lost forever to India, China, and Japan.

The answer to these daunting forecasts is simple: We need to ensure that more American children have the opportunity to graduate from college or technical school to acquire the skills needed for our modern economy. But here the challenge is also great. Too few young Americans are entering college, and even fewer are graduating. If current trends hold, for every 100 ninth graders in the United States, only 40 will enter college, and only 18 will graduate.[10]

There are a wide variety of reasons why so many American children are denied the opportunity to a college degree. Sometimes the cause is cultural; when a child is raised in a family or a community where there are few college graduates, an assumption from childhood develops that college is not an option. Other times, there is a social explanation—some parents in rural areas do not want their children to leave home out of fear they will lose them and their help forever.

But clearly the most influential factor is economic. As the need for higher education increases, its affordability has become a much more acute problem, particularly in tough economic times. Tuition at state colleges and universities has skyrocketed in recent years—far outpacing inflation and average income growth—as state legislatures have reduced their investments in higher education due to tighter budget circumstances and competing policy priorities. Further, state and federal financial aid programs have fallen far short of the escalating need for their resources. And not only are many families unable to send their children to college, a large and fast-growing number of college students are forced to drop out before graduation. College dropouts are becoming one of the largest and fastest-growing groups of young adults in America: almost one in three Americans in their mid-20s fall into this group, up from 20 percent in the late 1960s. The leading cause of college dropouts is financial. Only 41 percent of low-income students entering a four-year college managed to graduate within five years, but 66 percent of high-income did, according to Department of Education report.[11] Credit-card debt is a growing culprit, particularly when students or their parents use credit cards to pay tuition and are unable to keep up with the expensive interest payments.

Furthermore, those students who are able to acquire financial aid often do so in the form of student loans: Almost half of the country's college students depend on federal loans. By the time their education is complete, many of these young men and women have built enormous personal debt, posing severe economic hardships and forcing some to choose professions because of higher salaries instead of personal fulfillment or social benefits. To make matters worse, in 2006, Congress made the largest cut to the federal student loan program in history, resulting in significantly higher interest rates and greater debt for participating students. Ironically, the cut was made just one day after President Bush called for an American Competitiveness Initiative to strengthen the nation's ability to compete internationally.[12]

CRADLE TO COLLEGE:
IMPLEMENTING OPPORTUNITY

The subject of access to affordable higher education and the opportunity it provides is one very close to my heart. In fact, I focused most of my early career in public service on the notion. My initial bid for state treasurer was built around a simple premise: to bring to Kentucky a pre-paid college tuition savings program to help make it easier for parents to afford a college education for their children.

By my third month in office, the General Assembly unanimously passed legislation that created KAPT—Kentucky's Affordable Prepaid Tuition. KAPT guarantees tomorrow's tuition for colleges and technical schools once a parent or grandparent locks in their child's higher education payments at today's lower rates. The family need not pay all of the tuition up front; indeed, two-thirds of KAPT participants choose one of our many monthly installment payment plans that start at as little as around $2 a day. And since the program was created under Section 529 of the Internal Revenue Code (hence this is why many state-sponsored college savings plans are referred to as "529 plans"), all of the investment growth is retained by the family completely tax-free.

In four short years, nearly 9,000 families have invested more than $100 million in the KAPT. And this beacon of opportunity is not limited to Kentucky: Every state in the union now has a 529 plan. Together, more than seven million children are enrolled across the country, with over $67 billion invested.

But despite the success of KAPT and its sister plans across the country, millions of American children remain deprived of the oppor-

NOAH AND THE VALUE OF OPPORTUNITY   25

tunity of higher education. I have found that when many families from the more rural areas of the state are made aware of KAPT, they assume they cannot apply because of their economic circumstances. Further, those who live in poverty may not be able to afford even the minimal payment of $2 a day. For the cultural and economic reasons I have discussed, too many children are falling through the cracks of our leaky opportunity boat.

Fundamentally, our student financial-aid system in this country needs a complete overhaul. We have to find a way to ensure that every child in this country, no matter what obstacles the family's background, circumstance, or income present, can take that first step toward fulfilling the American Dream through access to higher education. We need to determine how to provide every young Noah with the educational tools he needs to build a successful career and to provide for his family.

We need a new paradigm. Kentucky's Secretary of State Trey Grayson and I have come up with a new idea. In 2004, we developed a concept that we call "Cradle to College." Under Cradle to College, every child born in the state would be provided a 529 college savings account on the day of her birth. Ideally, the account would be funded so that families could afford at least a community- or technical-college education. Parents and grandparents could then supplement these funds by making monthly or lump-sum payments, to guarantee that tuition would be available at a four-year college. Private employers could also make contributions, and designate them for young scholars who promise to develop the skills necessary to become employed in a particular twenty-first century industry.

Cradle to College helps overcome the traditional obstacles to higher educational opportunity. The financial incentives would ensure that some form of higher education will be affordable for every family. And the knowledge that every child will be guaranteed at least a community-college education at birth will help address the cultural and social concerns that intellectually and emotionally eliminate the potential for college for many American children. Instead of giving up hope for a college education, these families will assume at their child's birth that higher education is part of their future.

There is an important "catch." With opportunity, also should come responsibility. As a result, every high-school senior who uses his or her Cradle to College account to attend college must first provide a year of full-time community or military service in Kentucky. Through their work, these young people will "pay back" the money the state has provided for their higher education. But more importantly, the community-service experience will give these young people a greater sense of civic responsibility. This tradeoff is emblematic of the third-way approach illustrated in the story of Noah. Cradle to College is not a new entitlement, but a hand up that provides hard-working, community-minded children an opportunity to reach their higher-education dreams.

Cradle to College can be tweaked in other ways to bring long-term benefits to a state or to the country. For example, to plug the "brain drain" that robs smaller rural states of their best and brightest young workers (seeking to earn more money at jobs in the big cities), we can build in incentives for graduates who stay in state to pursue their careers. Further economic incentives can be developed to benefit those college graduates who pursue lower-paying, but socially beneficial professions—such as teaching, law enforcement, social work, and the military.

This type of initiative offers a win-win-win scenario for economically struggling states. The college savings component provides the state's children and their parents a new opportunity for affordable higher education and the better job prospects it presents. The state also wins because a higher-educated workforce will attract more tax-paying businesses and industries. And communities win with more of their youth participating in community-service projects, both by filling gaps left by scarce public resources, and by instilling a greater sense of civic engagement in our next generation of leaders. It is the type of program that can demonstrate to a skeptical public that morally virtuous shared sacrifice and compassion for others can produce much greater long-term benefits than the politics of self-interest. And in so doing, it can help restore public credibility for our systems of government.

Cradle to College is just one of many programs emerging across the globe that introduces the concept of universal children's savings accounts. The most comprehensive, mature model can be found in Great Britain. In 2003, under the leadership of Prime Minister Tony Blair, the British Parliament enacted the Child Trust Fund, which establishes a savings account for every child born in that country. The system is based on the principle of "progressive universalism," under which every British child receives an endowment, while those in lower-income families receive a larger lump sum. The initial deposits range from £250 to £500 (approximately $360 to $720). Additional contributions could be made by parents, relatives, or friends, to the tune of up to £1,200 a year, for a total of £22,000 by the time the child reaches 18 years of age. A limited number of investment options are available for these accounts, including money market, bond, and stock funds. When the fund matures, the savings will be released to the teenager free of income or capital-gains taxes and without any restrictions on how the cash is spent.[13]

Politicians in the United States of both parties already have discussed adopting some version of the British model. As early as the 1990s, former U.S. Senator Bob Kerrey developed the concept of KidSave, whose purpose was to create individual retirement savings accounts for American children. One version of his proposal would have permitted a child to borrow from her account temporarily in the form of a ten-year loan in order to pay for higher-education expenses. In another version, the Social Security Administration would have been required to open and endow an account for every newborn.[14]

While KidSave never progressed past the discussion phase, the idea was reintroduced in another form in 2004. That year, Pennsylvania Republican Senator Rick Santorum and former New Jersey Democratic Senator (now Governor) Jon Corzine introduced the America Saving for Personal Investment, Retirement, and Education (ASPIRE) Act, under which every child born in the United States would automatically receive a $500 deposit into a Kids Investment and Development Savings Account ("KIDS Account"). Children from lower-income households would receive a supplemental deposit at birth and would be eligible to receive dollar-for-dollar matching funds up to $500 per year for voluntary contributions to the account, which could not exceed $1,000 per year. American children, in conjunction with their parents and financial educators at school, would participate in investment decisions and watch their money grow. Assuming modest but steady contributions, a typical child from a low-income family could accumulate about $20,000 by age 18, at which point the KIDS Account might be used to go to college, buy a home, or build up a nest-egg for retirement. To signal that the KIDS Account was not something for nothing, the accountholder must begin at age 30 to pay back the $500 which was initially deposited at birth. Over ten years, the accounts are projected to cost $40 billion; but in the long run, as participants pay back the initial investments, the program's expenses will diminish significantly.[15]

To date, the ASPIRE Act has remained bottled up in the legislative process. With the considerable taxpayer investment up-front, there is an absence of political will in lean budget times. However, pilot projects like Cradle to College are emerging on the local and state level across the country that might ultimately provide federal policymakers with a model and a justification for developing a national child savings account program. Indeed, the Saving for Education, Entrepreneurship, and Downpayment (SEED) Policy and Practice Initiative had been formed specifically to provide "seed" funding for these local initiatives. SEED is a 20-year national policy, practice and research endeavor to develop, test, inform, and promote matched savings accounts and financial education for children. Organizers aim to set the stage for a universal, progressive American policy for asset-building among youth and families.

There are dozens of SEED-sponsored child savings account initiatives across the country. Each program provides children with a savings account, seeded with money from foundations and, sometimes, local businesses and governmental entities. Some use a state-sponsored 529 plan as the financial platform; others use the Individual Development Account (IDA) format that has been authorized by federal law to enable individuals to build assets (often with monetary matches from private or public sources) in a tax-preferred vehicle. Each asset-building initiative provides matching funds from a variety of sources that correspond to family savings and/or to the achievement of particular benchmarks. Among the more exciting programs emerging across the country are:

- The Boys & Girls Clubs of Delaware initiative, which involves 71 children in an asset-building program with economic incentives for parents and children to participate in financial education programs;
- A Cherokee nation project involving 75 tribal children in a college savings account program that requires that young participants maintain good grades, learn about tribal history, complete career counseling, and participate in community service;
- Fundación Chana Goldstein y Samuel Levis, a community development program in Puerto Rico that provides economic incentives for good grades, financial planning, and extended family participation;
- People for People, a faith-based Philadelphia community economic development organization with an affiliated charter school and credit union, which involves 75 nine and ten year-olds, and provides financial incentives for student achievement, attendance, behavior, and participation; and
- The Jim Casey Youth Opportunities Initiative that provides an "opportunity passport" for foster children in 11 communities,

that includes a funded debit account and "door openers," who provide participants job and interviewing skills and help them with critical life skills, such as finding an apartment and affordable health-care insurance.

With so many different models, and with varying structures and incentive systems, the SEED-sponsored initiatives truly serve as a laboratory of reform, offering federal policymakers proven experience for developing a national program within the next several years. It is the hope of those of us who advocate for children's savings accounts that some day every American child will have a savings account, providing for better financial management and literacy, more efficient delivery of social services, and the true ideal of an "ownership society," where every American has control of his or her economic destiny. Noah needed God's guidance in building the ark; otherwise the project would have been too daunting. Similarly the children's savings account asset building initiatives can outfit all of our children with the tools, advice, and opportunity they need to pursue their vision of happiness.

But as Congress explores the idea of universal children's savings accounts, it should pay close attention to the lessons learned by the existing pilot programs. For example, it is essential that policymakers reduce barriers to enrollment—such as excessive paperwork—to avoid discouraging skeptical applicants. Further, the more successful programs provide for automatic enrollment; families must voluntarily opt-out to avoid participation in the program. And administrators should offer a variety of account options—Great Britain, for example, involves 70 different financial providers—to reduce political influences and eliminate distrust of any particular institution.

I also suggest that whatever model is chosen that it should include the same, third-way condition we have established with Cradle to College: a community-service requirement. Joining opportunity with responsibility not only makes any proposal more politically palatable and more cost-effective in the long run, it will encourage greater civic engagement in our young people, preparing our next generation for leadership.

The community-service requirement should be included even where the children's savings account is geared toward retirement instead of college. There is no reason why able-bodied retirees could not perform meaningful community service projects to "cash in" their publicly supplemented savings accounts. As Senator Tom Carper of

Delaware has argued, the impending retirement of the baby boom generation will leave this country with the "best educated, healthiest, and most active group of elders the world has ever seen." Local public-private partnerships are demonstrating a new approach that enlists retired baby boomers in service projects that will help tackle the social and economic problems their increasing numbers create.

One such program is Experience Corps, which since 1995 has grown to include more than 1,000 service members in 12 cities. The program recruits senior citizens to serve at least 15 hours per week tutoring in their local public schools, focusing their time on at-risk children and using intensive one-on-one mentoring to improve educational performance.[16]

BUILDING BOATS

When the Great Flood receded, God made a covenant with Noah that no such natural calamity would ever threaten all of humanity again. However, even today, millions of Americans are drowning in the metaphorical flood that is created by a lack of opportunity. Too many children—who believe that a college education and a good, fulfilling job are not attainable—are sinking in a sea of poverty. Too many seniors—who have no supplemental savings in addition to Social Security—are submerged in an ocean of hopelessness. And too many working families—who believe that their share of the American Dream is beyond their reach—are drowning in a torrent of low expectations.

So it is the task of the compassionate community to build boats—to ensure opportunity for all. Through partnerships combining public experience with private know-how, we must empower all Americans and equip them with the tools they need to build their own boats and steer their families through rough waters. Only through a united community effort can we ensure that the value of opportunity—and the boat that it represents—is secured by all Americans. As Martin Luther King, Jr., so eloquently stated, "We may have all come on different ships, but we're in the same boat now."

So in the end, there is wisdom in youth. My daughter Emily was right. I did run for state treasurer to build a boat. And to search for the hidden treasure. I believe that it is just beyond the rainbow that God provided as the token of his covenant with Noah. And together, as a compassionate community, we can row, sail and steer our mighty boat until we reach the end of that rainbow.

TWO

ABRAHAM AND THE VALUE
OF RESPONSIBILITY

Some time afterward, God put Abraham to the test. He said to him, "Abraham," and he answered, "Here I am."

—*Genesis 22:1*

On September 14, 2001, I was driving home from an engagement in western Kentucky when I heard on the radio that the governor had called for a service that day to commemorate the National Day of Prayer and Reconciliation.

It had been a particularly difficult year for me. While none of my friends had perished in the 9–11 terrorist attacks (although a few had close calls), I shared with most Americans a deep sense of loss and regret.

But I had a much deeper crisis closer to home. Earlier that year, my father had been diagnosed with stomach cancer, and was forced to undergo radical treatment and surgery. Many of my weeks consisted of shuttling back and forth between my home in Lexington and the Cleveland Clinic.

My dad's battle with cancer took a devastating toll on me—emotionally and physically. As I took on new responsibilities for my parents, my responsibilities to others were suffering: I found myself distracted at work, and as I struggled to be a supportive son, my roles as husband and father were marginalized. I was hardest, however, on myself. I have been quite fortunate to have good health most of my life, but the stress and anticipation of grief manifested themselves in back problems and crippling sinus infections that kept me in bed for days at a time.

I turned to a book with which I had some familiarity, but of which I had never developed a great understanding—the Bible. My parents had imbued me with a strong Jewish identification and a robust sense of pride in my religious heritage. I was active in religious youth groups, following my father to serve as president of a national organization, and I attended a religious camp, where I met my future wife, Lisa. But aside from my pre-teen education for my Bar Mitzvah service, my Judaism was less about prayer and ritual, and more about a shared sense of culture and—significantly to my politically active parents—a mandate to perform acts of charity, compassion, and social justice.

But when my father became sick, I embarked on a desperate quest for meaning and understanding. I read voraciously, and I shared my personal quest with my Sunday School students and my largely Christian political constituency. I found comfort in many traditional rituals: Still to this day, I have eliminated pork and shellfish from my diet, as observant Jews have done for thousands of years to make their bodies more kosher or holy.

During this period, I experienced a spiritual awakening. I began to understand more deeply that most of the values that my parents had imparted in me came directly or indirectly from the lessons in the Bible and other Jewish texts. My early training to engage in social justice had come from the Jewish tradition of *tikkun olam* (the mandate, literally, to "repair the world"), and I was humbled to learn that my core social, political, and cultural beliefs had emerged—directly, though without my conscious knowledge—from a more than 5,000-year religious tradition.

Most significantly, my religious studies allowed me to reexamine my responsibilities and priorities. In a time of crisis, I was able to clarify my duties as son, husband, father, and public servant. Most importantly, I was reminded that beyond our responsibilities to others, there remains a responsibility to self and to God. Without this, it is impossible to show true compassion toward our neighbors.

THE *AKEDAH:* ABRAHAM'S SACRIFICE OF ISAAC

In my studies, I had devoted particular attention to struggling with one of the most interesting and most complex father-son relationships in the Bible—that of Abraham and Isaac's journey to Mount Moriah in Chapter 22 of Genesis. Known as the *Akedah* (the binding), the passage is one of Judaism's most important and sacred texts, and is read during the Rosh Hashanah (New Year) service, one of the holiest days of the Jewish year. (The story is also very important to the Muslim tradition and is celebrated in their holiday, the Feast of the Sacrifice, with one significant difference: Abraham travels to Mount Moriah with his other son, Ishmael, who is seen in Islam as Abraham's legitimate heir and father of the Arab people.)[1]

When I entered the state Capitol on the National Day of Prayer and Reconciliation, I was surprised to be escorted immediately to the front row. I looked at the program's agenda, and I noticed that it featured a talk from representatives of each major religion. I was especially pleased to see that my friend Kathy Stein, a spirited and very articulate state legislator, would be representing the Jewish community.

I soon found out why I had been rushed to the front. The emcee, former Governor Julian Carroll, explained that Kathy was caught in a traffic jam, and they were unsure if she would make it. As the only other Jewish elected official in Frankfort, I was asked to fill in if she did not show. I told him I was glad to read whatever they had prepared. "No, Jonathan," said the governor, "we need you to deliver a speech." It was five minutes until the service was to start; ten until my part.

When the time approached, it looked like the governor was giving me a reprieve; he announced Kathy's name. After a seeming eternity of silence, however, he introduced me.

As I approached the microphone to address a packed Capitol and a statewide, televised audience, I turned to Abraham for inspiration.

I told the story of how Abraham and Sarah had waited years, even decades, to have a child. Finally, God blessed them with a baby boy. They named him Isaac, *Yitzhak* in Hebrew, which literally means, "and he laughed" because they were so happy at his birth.

Then God put Abraham to the test. He told Abraham to sacrifice his only son, to kill him with his own hands. Abraham's response? He simply said "Here I am!"

Abraham took Isaac with him and prepared to sacrifice him because of his strong faith in God. God rewarded Abraham's faith. He sent down an angel who told him to stop. He found a ram to sacrifice instead. Because of Abraham's strong faith, because he believed in God, because he said "Here I am," we now have three of the world's most influential religions, Judaism, Christianity, and Islam.

In the aftermath of 9–11, God had put us to a test. The incidents of terrorism had been beyond any of our comprehension. But in the following days, millions of Americans said "Here I am!" When help was needed for the injured in New York and Washington, Americans ran to their blood banks, said "Here I am," and gave a record amount of blood. When help was needed in clothing and feeding the displaced and the injured, Americans came forward, said "Here I am," and gave out of their own pockets to help the people of these communities. And when thousands of souls in New York, Washington, and Pennsylvania needed our help, Americans said "Here I am," and prayed and joined together in their churches, synagogues, and mosques.

A week was closing that many of us would have soon preferred to forget. But I believed that if we looked at this very dark cloud, composed of ash and soot—which not only covered New York, but covered all of us—we could see a silver lining. In fact, we could see a rainbow, with this renewed spirit of community, with this renewed patriotism in this, the greatest country in the history of the world. Millions of us had come together to say, "Here I am!"

I concluded the address that day with the words of Genesis: "And God tested Abraham. And Abraham said 'Here I am!' Today, God has tested us. Together, we join to say, 'Here I am!'"

RESPONSIBILITY: THE HILLEL TEST

While the tale of Abraham and Isaac raises many complex—some painful—issues and questions, I used the story to illustrate an essential value of the compassionate community: responsibility.

A society that values responsibility encourages its citizens to be accountable for their own actions. Just as Abraham refused to complain, or point fingers elsewhere, responsible individuals say "Here I am," and take ownership of their everyday lives. Responsible individuals also recognize that they are part of a community. By virtue of their citizenship, they are duty bound to serve others around them.

The revered first-century rabbi, Hillel the Elder, summed up this multi-tiered philosophy of responsibility eloquently: "If I am not for myself, who will be for me? If I am only for myself, what am I? And if not now, when?"[2]

Hillel thereby imparted a three-part test for the value of responsibility: responsibility to self; responsibility for community; and the virtue of immediate responsible action. Indeed, Hillel demonstrated that the value of responsibility is the embodiment of the all-encompassing spiritual injunction to "love your neighbor as yourself."

The first part of the Hillel test, responsibility to self, is a critical value inherent in all of the world's religions. Judaism teaches that human rights are considered by God to be only part of God's promise; these rights must be reciprocally supplemented by a clear manifestation of human responsibilities. Similarly, Jesus taught, "Do not judge so that you will not be judged. For in the way you judge, you will be judged, and by your standard of measure, it will be measured to you." St. Ignatius of Loyola concluded: "Pray as if everything depended on God; act as if everything depended on you." Many Americans subscribe to the Eastern concept of karma—a critical doctrine for Hindus and Buddhists—which serves as the moral law of cause and effect, whereby each individual is wholly responsible for her condition and will experience the future that she is now creating.

The second part of Hillel's test, responsibility to community, is an equally compelling and universal religious value. The Jewish concept of *tikkun olam* arises from hundreds of Biblical and historical examples of the idea that only when people work together as a community can progress be achieved. Community is such a powerful value that Jews can atone for their sins through acts of loving kindness to their neighbors. Community has great resonance in the New Testament as well; Christians are told: "Give and it will be given to you"; "The congregation of those who believed were of one heart and soul; and not one of them claimed that anything belonging to him was his own, but all things were common property to them"; "Do not neglect doing good and sharing, for with such sacrifices, God is pleased"; and "Let us not love with word or with tongue, but in deed and truth." A survey of the major world religions reveals that this value is embodied in every prominent culture.

The third test brings the first two together in a pressing call for responsibility and social justice. The Christian pastor, author, and lecturer Tony Campolo tells a powerful story that illustrates this urgency. During World War II, Nazi troopers had rounded up hundreds of Bulgarian Jews in a barbed-wire enclosure, preparing to send them to the Auschwitz death camp. When they were ready to load the Jews into a train, Metropolitan Kyril, a local church leader, appeared. Kyril went to the entrance of the enclosure, surrounded by his supporters, and pushed aside the Nazis and their guns. He went in among the Jewish men and women, raised his hands, and quoted the Biblical heroine, Ruth: "Wherever you go, I will go. . . . Your people shall be my people, and your God my God." With that one act of personal risk and courage, not a single Bulgarian Jew ever died in a Nazi concentration camp, even though Bulgaria was under Nazi control. The Nazis understood that the Bulgarian Christians were taking responsibility for their Jewish neighbors, and that any move against the Jewish people could lead to a popular uprising.[3]

The value of responsibility also underlies the political philosophies that inspired the American Revolution and later helped to define the democratic experiment. In *Two Treatises on Government*, John Locke wrote that "men are naturally in . . . a state of perfect freedom to do and say as they wish, limited only by the law of nature, without having to ask permission of anyone." In that state of nature, humans have both right and responsibility: the right to take whatever actions are necessary to preserve their own freedom, but also the duty of helping preserve the rights of other people. John Stuart Mill, who wrote after the American Revolution, built on this notion; he argued that every individual has the responsibility to map out for himself his plan of life that will promote the spirit of progress.

The political philosophers who wrote around the time of the American experiment also placed great emphasis on responsibility to community. John Stuart Mill advocated democratic systems in the nineteenth century because he felt that they would build better interpersonal relationships, and ultimately, they would develop a broader conception of the common interest. Jean-Jacques Rousseau believed that when citizens participate in their communities, they become more socially aware and feel more connected to their fellow citizens.

A "HERE I AM" SOCIETY

Both our faith and our political experience instruct us that responsibility must be a key part of the compassionate community. This is the notion of "tough love": We will love our neighbor as ourselves, but each of us must act in a responsible way. That means all three parts of the

Hillel test must be fulfilled: responsibility to self, responsibility to community, and immediate responsible action.

Over the past few decades, policymakers have applied this "tough love" approach to individuals. Responding to a perceived decline in this ethic, political leaders ranging from Ronald Reagan to Bill Clinton developed policies to reflect personal responsibility, bipartisan efforts that emphasized work instead of welfare, and provided more accountability into the criminal justice system.

At the same time, however, the politics and economics of self-interest turned a blind eye to the issue of responsibility among our institutions—corporate America and government. That's why we need a "Here I Am" Society—echoing Abraham, the father of Judaism, Christianity, and Islam—requiring personal responsibility, corporate responsibility, and government responsibility. We would ask individuals, as well as institutions, to abide by all three elements of Hillel's test.

1. Personal Responsibility

In the compassionate community, personal responsibility means that able-bodied men and women should be encouraged to work whenever jobs are available, instead of simply relying on government largesse. Welfare programs should have the participation only of those who are sincerely needy—the abject poor, the physically or mentally disabled, the very young or very old—and those who simply cannot find a job. We fail to love our neighbor when we enable and perpetuate a cycle of dependency or when we misallocate funds that could be more appropriately directed to society's truly vulnerable.

Personal responsibility also means that violent criminals should receive appropriate prison sentences for their crimes, both to deter illegal conduct and to protect our law-abiding neighbors. We must also provide our law-enforcement officials with the tools they need to enforce the laws, especially an adequate number of police on the streets and within our neighborhoods. America's criminal-justice system must be rooted in and responsive to the communities it serves.

Most of all, parents must be responsible for their own families. Nothing provokes more moral outrage in me than parents (usually fathers) who fail to provide child support. More government resources need to be invested into cracking down on deadbeat dads and ensuring that they live up to their financial obligations. And just as we heap public scorn and embarrassment on sexual predators and drunk drivers, we should also target deadbeat parents. Many states have put the names and pictures of the state's leading deadbeats on the Internet—a "most wanted" list of child-support evaders. States and local governments should shame deadbeat parents into upholding their personal responsibility.

As for the second part of the Hillel test, it will be essential that we look to tying new major government initiatives and entitlements with community involvement—that is, tying opportunity to responsibility. That's why an initiative like "Cradle to College," which (as discussed in Chapter One) would provide every newborn with a partially funded college-savings account, insists that only young people who participate in meaningful community service activities could claim public funds. If every child in this country were exposed to community service before they entered the workforce, the more likely they would be to involve themselves in the civic activities of their communities when they are older. No generation has been more devoted to their community than our "Greatest Generation," who, at an early age, either fought for American freedom in World War II, or served their country by supporting the war effort at home.

The timing is right for this approach. Sociologists have noted that our youngest generation of Americans—termed by some the "Millennial Generation" (children born in the last two decades of the twentieth century who are coming of age during the new millennium)—is very similar in attitude to the "Greatest Generation." With 9–11 and its aftermath the central moments in their memories, these youth are unusually motivated to participate in civic involvement, community volunteering, and political activism.[4] Policymakers should say "Here I am," and seize their enthusiasm in order to establish more programs that instill and reward the value of community.

2. Corporate Responsibility

Judeo-Christian teachings strongly rebuke improper and criminal business practices, and protecting society against theft by the wealthy and powerful is a common injunction of the world's major religions.[5] Still, the past few decades have seen significant reductions in the regulation and oversight of corporate America. Most businesspeople are ethical and honorable, but recent corporate scandals—such as the Enron,

Worldcom, and Tyco debacles of the early twenty-first century—have brought disrepute to our economic system and have served to reduce public confidence in the markets. Capitalism is essential to our free economy, but when left unchecked, it can corrupt society's core.

Martin Peretz, publisher of *The New Republic*, identifies what he calls a new "rapacious capitalism [that] is demoralizing and punishing [and] threatens its own ethical foundations."[6] It is manifest in the recently exposed actions of financial institutions and mutual funds that were manipulating their accounting records and favoring preferred customers to gain financial advantages. And it is evident in actions of the accountants and lawyers who helped these businesses achieve their deceptions and cover their tracks. The recent corporate scandals demonstrate that it was not one person or even a group of people, but rather a culture that has encouraged cutting ethical corners, insider-dealing, and withholding information from the public.[7]

The recent wave of corporate scandals has hit many Americans hard. Accounting ruses, management corruption, and self-enrichment schemes have driven the stock prices of several major publicly traded companies downward, some to bankruptcy. The net uncertainty drove down public confidence and reduced the value of the entire market, even for those companies that had a healthy bottom line. As the stock market plummeted, thousands of families witnessed a dramatic reduction in their retirement savings and 401(k) plans. Some seniors were forced by stock market losses to interrupt their retirements to find a job.

At a time when lawmakers of both parties have developed a consensus over the need for the law to reflect the value of personal responsibility, it is essential that we hold corporate America to the same standard. Fortunately, a few modern-day Abrahams have stepped forward, said "Here I am," and worked to ensure corporate responsibility in the marketplace. The most prominent of these Abrahams is New York Attorney General Elliot Spitzer, whose efforts to police corporate abuses have received broad national attention. A series of investigations from Spitzer's office have led to a fundamental revolution in America's financial markets. By cracking down on insider deals among brokers, analysts, and Wall Street firms, Spitzer publicly revealed scams that had robbed small shareholders of equity. Of the ethics changes Spitzer has brought to Wall Street, *Time* magazine chose a comparison with another Bible hero, stating—with a bit of hyperbole—that "there has not been such an affirmation of what's right since Moses and the Ten Commandments."[8]

A less visible, yet just as influential modern Abraham, is North Carolina Treasurer Richard Moore. Moore has used his position as the sole trustee of one of the nation's largest pension funds—and thus a major shareholder in most significant public companies—to place pressure on corporate chieftains to reform their actions and promote accountability and responsibility. While Spitzer used the stick of regulation and litigation, Moore used the carrot of the power of the purse to demand accountability from the corporations in which his fund had invested. By 2002, Moore joined with pension fund leaders from 15 states, representing over $1 trillion combined in institutional capital, to place even greater pressure on corporate America to reform its governance. The mission was to use their leverage to reform corporate America from the inside, as major shareholders of the nation's largest companies. In so doing, they hoped to ensure more corporate accountability, protect the retirement funds of their citizens, and help restore confidence in the stock market. Under Moore's leadership, pension fund leaders have used this leverage to force more equitable executive pay arrangements, promote more public disclosure and transparency, and encourage more ethical business behavior.

Professionals also must say "Here I am" and take more responsibility for their own contributions to the compassionate community. The ever-expanding health-care crisis is an example. Physicians and hospitals must do a better job of policing and preventing medical errors and malpractice, instead of simply seeking legislation to deny the sacred, constitutional right to a jury trial and to cap the legal damages for their actions. Attorneys, in turn, should crack down on frivolous lawsuits which, when highly publicized, serve to undermine public confidence in the legal system.

But while the public, political fight over malpractice insurance is being waged by doctors and lawyers, the true culprits have escaped responsibility. The real cause of high malpractice rates has not been runaway juries—jury awards have actually declined over the last three decades—but rather, the insurance industry's practice of increasing premiums every time the economy sours and their stock prices fall. The insurance industry refuses to accept responsibility for the spiraling costs of health care; instead, the industry funnels millions of dollars into lobbyists and political contributions to protect every dollar of profit and shareholder value.[9]

Accordingly, where self-policing does not work, government must step in to ensure responsible behavior by all of these entities, in order to promote a society in which health care is available and affordable to every American. Attorneys general and state insurance commissioners should crack down on abuses in the insurance system. Additionally, states should look to California for an example. There, voters approved a health-insurance premium freeze by referendum, and premiums dropped more than 20 percent, while three of the state's largest malpractice companies returned more than $69 million to physicians and hospitals. Finally, states should look to e-health technology to help them create an electronic health network, which would serve to reduce medical mistakes and improve the standard of care by allowing doctors, hospitals, and pharmacies to share medical information about patients via computer, while still protecting individual privacy.[10]

Government action and regulation will always be necessary to promote cooperation and discourage and punish the unethical and illegal behavior of corporate "bad apples." Accordingly, policymakers on the state and federal level must fight back attempts of the so-called Constitution in Exile movement, whose mission is to declare that a corporation's economic rights are inviolable and that the work of regulatory institutions such as the Environmental Protection Agency, the Securities and Exchange Commission, and the Federal Trade Commission be deemed unconstitutional. Advocates of this approach seek the virtual repeal of Franklin D. Roosevelt's New Deal, with Michael Grieve of the American Enterprise Institute arguing that "the modern, vibrant, mobile and global economy of the twenty-first century is competitive enough to regulate itself in most areas." The Constitution in Exile movement represents the politics and economics of self-interest in the extreme, and has lost many more political battles than it has won in recent years. Unfortunately, the movement's focus now is on the judiciary, through the appointment of judges who promote this philosophy on local, state, and federal benches.[11] We need more Abrahams to be vigilant in preventing the return of this country to the 1920s, a period whose rampant, unchecked self-interest led directly to the Great Depression.

Ultimately, corporate responsibility will only manifest itself in its complete form when more corporate chieftains understand that the ethic of the compassionate community is not only the right thing to do, but also the right thing to do for the bottom line. Leo Hindery, formerly the CEO or chairman of five multinational corporations, writes that the current "race to the bottom" among some U.S. firms may have short-term benefits for shareholders, but in the long run, the costs to society are devastating—not only to the national economy, but to the bottom lines of these very same companies.[12]

Indeed, as journalist Thomas Friedman notes, a "growing number of companies have come to believe that moral values, broadly and liberally defined, can help drive shareholder values." Quoting General Electric CEO Jeff Immelt—"If you want to be a great company today, you have to be a good company"—Friedman argues that being a better global citizen, through social activism, environmental promotion, and worker protection, can produce long-term economic benefits, while avoiding short-term pitfalls such as investor lawsuits and stock market dips.[13] If "Compassionate Capitalism" becomes the wave of the future, the whole global economy will benefit.

3. Government Responsibility

Finally, government responsibility must be promoted and encouraged. Since the early 1990s, the "reinventing government" movement has called for ensuring results-based policies that give citizens the services they want at a price they are willing to pay. By promoting consolidation of programs, competition among vendors, customer choice, and a steadfast focus on results, these initiatives have been able to save taxpayers millions of dollars while improving public services at all levels of government. Reinventing government ultimately forces government to transform the bureaucratic model into a more entrepreneurial approach, whereby every level of organization is encouraged to improve performance, customer service, and the bottom line. Purchasing departments, for example, learn to use their leverage as major buyers to drive down the cost of government supplies and services; while personnel offices enable all employees to have their voices heard, often leading to efficiencies and better public service.[14] The compassionate community must continue to pursue a government on all levels that works better for less.

Most of all, our political leaders must say "Here I am" and ensure fiscal responsibility. The politics of self-interest lead legislators to rush and compete to bring home pork projects for their districts and tax breaks for their special-interest contributors. On both the state and federal level, deals are continually struck behind closed doors, as votes are traded on major pieces of legislation for the promise of a local project or program. On crucial, close votes, the support of undecided legislators is many times bought through expanded government largesse in their districts. And powerful incumbents often try to demonstrate their influence to their constituents by obtaining funding for major projects back home, sometimes with little public value—the most infamous recent example being federal funding for the "Bridge to Nowhere" that Alaskan Senate Appropriations Chair Ted Stevens vocally, but ultimately unsuccessfully, attempted to secure in 2005 in the face of national public outrage.[15]

When politicians of both parties do what is in the best interests of their reelection campaigns, and not the best interests of the nation, massive budget deficits result. In states where balanced budgets are required by their constitutions, the politics of self-interest result in compromising cuts to the most vital human-service programs. Mutual back-scratching and deal-making leads government into a race to the bottom, a phenomenon whereby scarce public resources are directed toward marginally useful activities, away from the programs that truly embody responsibility and the other values of the compassionate community.

Balanced budgets and fiscal responsibility ensure the optimal long-term economic health of the country. By contrast, massive budget deficits impair confidence in the markets, discourage investment in U.S. industries, drive up interest rates for corporations and individuals, and leave future generations footing the bill.

We cannot afford to enact massive cuts of social programs that truly benefit society's most vulnerable without violating the very core moral values of our religious traditions and our nation's founding documents. That's why our leaders must pursue deficit reduction plans that target the waste and abuse created when our government institutions act irresponsibly.

This would include massive cuts to corporate welfare programs that benefit the bottom lines and share prices of large political contributors but do not promote economic growth to the economy at large. Legislatures should also establish budget caps and "pay-as-you-go" rules to restrain government spending and eliminate the deficit, so that politicians are prevented from using excess funds to buy votes on bills and help their colleagues win elections. In addition, as economist Paul Weinstein suggests, we should deny bonuses and pay increases to state legislators and governors in years when their budgets are in deficit, or when they use phony accounting methods to produce structurally imbalanced budgets that will require a taxpayer bailout in future years. As Weinstein argues, there is no greater deterrent to irresponsible spending than to threaten to pull money out of the pockets of politicians.[16]

One particularly egregious practice that should be eliminated is the so-called legislative earmark, a device that allows one legislator to set aside a special pork project into a larger spending bill, without having to expose the project itself to an up-or-down vote. To the surprise of many American citizens, earmarks are tacked on in the last minutes of closed-door conference committees, as part of deals cut to secure the passage of legislation or to help a particular incumbent in a close re-election bid. Abrahamic state legislators should follow the lead of U.S. Representative Jeff Flake of Arizona, who has proposed federal legislation to provide more transparency in the process and prohibit last minute insertions of pork projects. Even better, legislators can propose complete moratoriums on earmarking, such as that proposed by Kentucky Congressman Ron Lewis, who suggested that the $30 billion in Congressional earmarks in 2005 should be allocated to Hurricane Katrina relief.[17]

Further, Congress and state legislatures should fundamentally diminish their role in providing funding for local construction projects. Local projects should be the province of local governments; municipalities and counties generally should have the legal capability, as well as the responsibility, to raise local revenue to fund these projects, and to seek public buy-in through a referendum process. Congress and state legislatures should play a funding role only when a particular project has a significant economic impact on a state or region, or where the municipality or county is suffering economically and needs state or federal assistance. Shifting responsibilities directly to local voters provides more accountability in our representatives and more ownership on the part of taxpayers.

In a "Here I Am" society, state governments must also be more open and honest about the budgeting process. Colorado provides a good model. In 2004, the state faced a significant budget shortfall, and at the same time was required to return about $500 million in mandated tax refunds required by an irresponsible constitutional amendment enacted in 1992. For several years, state leaders had applied short-term patches and accounting gimmicks to maintain the state's fiscal solvency. As job growth and the economy declined, businesses fled. By 2005, new Colorado leaders dedicated to accomplishing real reform introduced a smart, transparent, and forward-looking budgeting process—one that held departments and agencies accountable for the way that they spend taxpayer money, replacing gimmickry with honest budgeting.[18] By taking responsibility and making tough choices, Colorado legislators of both parties secured a healthier economic climate for the state and prepared Colorado for a much brighter financial future. They demonstrated a key principle of the compassionate community: Mutual sacrifice in the short term can mean long-term progress for all.

"HERE I AM"

In the compassionate community, our leaders must understand that responsibility is not a one-way street. Efforts to promote personal responsibility have been critical to our nation's economic growth and have helped restore confidence in our democracy. But we cannot give our institutions a free ride: Avarice and power must be constantly checked by imposing requirements of responsibility on all of society's participants in our "Here I Am" society, including corporate chieftains and government officials.

The Book of Genesis tells us that God asked Abraham to make the ultimate sacrifice: the loss of a child. His response was an immediate and unconditional acceptance of responsibility: "Here I Am."

We will never ask our society's leaders to make such an awful choice. But every American, particularly those who share power and influence over our nation's future, must understand that the Biblical injunction to "love your neighbor as yourself" means that each of us is ultimately responsible for our own behavior, as well as that of our communities. In each action we take, we must be responsible stewards of the public's well-being. And while sacrifice might temporarily mean a leaner wallet, a lower share price, or a tighter reelection bid, we must understand that these sacrifices add up to a healthier economy and society for all Americans.

The moral value of responsibility is transparently absent in today's politics and economics of self-interest. Only when both our citizens and our institutions follow Abraham's example, say "Here I am," and accept responsibility for their actions, will our compassionate community be truly realized. And the responsible time to do so is right now. If not now, when?

THREE

JACOB AND THE VALUE OF WORK

Jacob left Beer-sheba, and set out for Haran. He came upon a certain place and stopped there for the night, for the sun had set. Taking one of the stones of that place, he put it under his head and lay down in that place. He had a dream; a ladder was set on the ground, and angels of God were going up and down on it. And the Lord was standing beside him and He said, "I am the Lord, the God of your father Abraham and the God of Isaac: the ground on which you are lying I will assign to you and to your offspring . . . All the families of the earth shall bless themselves by you and your descendants. Remember, I am with you; I will protect you wherever you go and will bring you back to this land."

—Genesis 28:10–15

M y dream of being a rock star ended when I turned 14. While I had taken up guitar a few years before, the onset of adolescence left me unable to hit the high notes—or many notes on key, for that matter. While I continue to pick and strum, my office staff has banned me from performing in public—I have a voice only my daughters can love.

My passion for music, however, is unabated. As a teen, I rejected the heavy-metal and synthesizer-driven pop of the 1980s for the "classic rock" of the previous generation. Listening to Kruser spin records on WKQQ-FM in Lexington,[1] I became a fan of The Who, the Rolling Stones, and, most of all, Bruce "The Boss" Springsteen. The Boss's evocative lyrics spoke to my youthful restlessness and yearning for love and freedom. More significantly, Springsteen's working-class heroes were my own: Average men and women struggling to make a living to take care of their loved ones.

When I entered elective office, my chief of staff introduced me to country music, which had already captured most of my constituents. To my surprise, I found a new love. Every morning on the ride to school, my daughters and I sing along with the country radio stations—from old standards like Johnny Cash and Dolly Parton to the modern country of Shania Twain and Tim McGraw. From Lonestar's "From My Front Porch Looking In," a rousing ditty celebrating the everyday happiness of raising a family, to Willie Nelson's plaintive ballad "Always on my Mind," which speaks of the imperfections of love and relationships, it is hard for a father and husband not to find something with which to identify.

But during my father's last days, I turned to an old friend for comfort. Bruce Springsteen had just released *The Rising*, his ode to the firefighters, police officers, and everyday working men and women who lost their lives in the 9–11 terrorist attacks. I doubt that any poet has ever captured the language and emotions of grief so eloquently. While my daughters obliviously made up hand motions and dance routines in the back seat of my car, I silently cried as the Boss waxed poetic about my father's influence in my life: Springsteen's songs spoke to his strength, his faith, his hope, and his love.

My father did not live the life of a vibrant extrovert; he never reached the high corridors of power. He never sought the spotlight. Instead, he lived a life of quiet dignity. Like all of us here on earth, he was not perfect. But he tried to do what was right and good. He demonstrated integrity and character. He had class and principles. His accomplishments were not part of any attempt to impress the outside world. Instead, he had a strong moral compass that guided his actions. He led, not through strong words, but through his soft-spoken example.

My dad threw himself into the Civil Rights movement of the 1960s, and proudly helped organize Martin Luther King, Jr.'s, historic March on Washington in 1963. Back home in Lexington, he drafted the charters of the local Urban League and Human Rights Commission, and served among their first directors. But what's amazing is that his two children, who loved and admired him more than anyone else, did not know the level of his involvement in the Civil Rights movement until we dug around his papers in the weeks before his death. This act of humility illustrates my father's character—what was important was that he did his job, not that he got credit for doing what was right.

To me, my dad was like one of Springsteen's heroes, or the subject of many a country song: a working man who cherished family, faith, and justice.

JACOB'S LADDER

My wife Lisa helped me connect this musical inspiration with my growing religious studies by giving me a book to help put my father's death—and more importantly, his life—in proper perspective. Rabbi Harold Kushner's book, *Living a Life that Matters: Resolving the Conflict between Conscience and Success*, tells the story of a biblical figure whose life really mattered. Surprisingly, the book is not about Abraham, whose great faith ensured the vitality of monotheism; Moses, whose great leadership freed the enslaved; nor Solomon, whose great wisdom was legendary. Kushner contends it was Jacob—Abraham's grandson; Isaac's son—who lived a life that mattered.

Our early introduction to Jacob—in chapter 27 of the book of Genesis—is not very favorable. Seeking to win his family's valuable birthright, traditionally given to the first born, Jacob disguised himself as his older brother Esau, deceiving his blind father into blessing him.

But the turning point in Jacob's life came when his furious brother was made aware of the deception, and began to pursue Jacob. Jacob ran away from home, went to sleep in the desert, and had a dream. He dreamed of a ladder reaching from the earth up to heaven. At the top of the ladder, he sensed God, who assured him that everything would be all right, that he would go on to do great things and be a special person.

This lesson was strongly reinforced a few years later. In the Bible's first example of romantic love, Jacob fell head over heels for the beautiful Rachel. When Jacob asked her father, Laban, for her hand in marriage, Laban offered a deal: If Jacob would tend Laban's flock for seven years, he would be allowed to marry Laban's daughter. Unfortunately for Jacob, after seven years of hard work, he soon learned that *he* was the victim of a deception. Jacob had been tricked into marrying Laban's *older* daughter, Leah. Only after another seven years of hard work was Jacob permitted to marry the woman of his dreams, Rachel. And soon after, Jacob worked hard for another six years (for a total of 20) to build up his own flocks and herd.

God did not put Jacob at the top of his ladder. Instead, God empowered Jacob to climb his own ladder, and through his hard work, he climbed from isolation and poverty to family and prosperity.

As Kushner explains, Jacob learned what it means to live a life that matters. You do not need to achieve fame or fortune to really matter. You do not need to win competitions or gain credit for your good work. Instead, Kushner writes, Jacob came to understand that "everyone who puts in an honest day's work, everyone who goes out of his or her way to help a neighbor, everyone who makes a child laugh, changes the world for the better."[2]

Jacob's ladder led him to an awareness that simple acts can provide great meaning. He may have been the Bible's wealthiest man—not measured by gold and riches, but in self-satisfaction and the great love of friends and family, particularly, his second wife, Rachel.

The Hebrew Bible is filled with stories of remarkable men and women—people who led great armies, demonstrated extraordinary bravery, and accumulated tremendous riches. But it was Jacob's softspoken example, an average working man who loved his wife and children above all, that may provide the Old Testament its greatest hero. And Jacob is certainly a modern example for us all.

THE MORAL VALUE OF HARD WORK

The story of Jacob illustrates another key value of the compassionate community: work. Millions of Americans go to work every day. We may work to seek justice, to help others, or simply to put food on the table. We work for what is right and good—whether for our communities, our families, or both.

Far beyond Jacob's example, the Judeo-Christian tradition celebrates the value of work and the contributions of everyday working people to society. The prophet Isaiah talks about the nobility of hard work in a passage important to both Christians and Jews: "No more shall there be an infant or graybeard who does not live out his days. . . . They shall build houses and dwell in them, they shall plant vineyards and enjoy their fruit. . . . My chosen ones shall outlive the work of their hands. They shall not toil to no purpose."[3]

The value of hard work is also embodied in the *Pirkei Avot*, the Jewish laws of ethics compiled by the rabbis of the Middle Ages. In an oft-quoted text, the great second-century Rabbi Tarfon stated that, "The day is short, and there is much work to be done. You are not required to complete the work yourself, but you cannot withdraw from it either." Eastern religious tradition also confirms that the value of hard work is universally shared by all of humanity.

Because of the great emphasis we place on the value of hard work, the Judeo-Christian tradition strives to protect workers from mistreatment by employers. The Mosaic law requires a wage earner to be paid after every day's hard work because he is deserving "and urgently depends on it." When these laws were broken by oppressive bosses, the prophets of the Hebrew Bible protested, condemning the employer "who makes his fellow man work without pay, and does not give him his wages."

The Judeo-Christian tradition is also clear that average workers should enjoy the fruits of their labor, and that wealth should not be accumulated by a powerful elite. As the Christian author, minister, and public servant Roy Herron explains, the Biblical intent is unambiguous: the Torah and the prophets declare that society should be structured so that wealth and power do not flow permanently into the hands of a landed gentry.[4] Jesus took this a step further, teaching Christians not to succumb to the temptation to accumulate wealth and power, because they might ultimately sacrifice their own salvation: "It is easier for a camel to go through the eye of a needle than for a rich man to enter the kingdom of God." The New Testament scolded with indignity those who horde their riches: "Come now, you rich, weep and howl for your miseries which are coming upon you. Your riches have rotted and your garments have become moth-eaten. Your gold and your silver have rusted; and their rust will be a witness against you and will consume your flesh like fire."

The Bible's admonitions against greed, oppression, and sloth rang true with many of the men who conceived and developed America's democracy. Benjamin Franklin, the gray eminence of the Constitutional Convention, listed "industry" and "frugality" among the 13 virtues he included in his famous public project to attain "moral perfection." And despite the wishes of some Framers to model the new United States after the class-based systems of England and much of the rest of Europe, egalitarians like Franklin and his protégé Thomas Jefferson ultimately prevailed. A rejection of European hereditary aristocracy and the extraordinary wealth inequalities among the classes within society was at the core of their democratic philosophy.[5]

Still, as historian Sean Wilentz explains, many of the key political battles of the first half of the nineteenth century revolved around the struggle between the elite landowners who sought to preserve their wealth, and the growing popular movement to establish hard work and merit as the guideposts for success. Emblematic of this conflict was the debate over the Bank of the United States in the 1830s, during which President Andrew Jackson railed against "a few monied capitalists," who he claimed were trading upon the public revenue to "enjoy the benefit of it, to the exclusion of the many." While Jackson was successful in his effort, 30 years later, President Abraham Lincoln viewed the Civil War as an effort "to save the principles of Jefferson from total overthrow" by forces whose objective was "supplanting the principles of free government, and restoring those of classification, caste, and legitimacy."[6]

By the end of the nineteenth century, the industrial revolution was creating greater disparities of wealth in the United States, and the Progressive movement emerged to restore the value of hard work in public policy. Toward these ends, many Progressive Era reforms were implemented during the first two decades of the twentieth century, including child labor laws and the establishment of a progressive income tax. But it was the implementation of the estate tax that truly signaled that our American democracy would value hard work more than inherited wealth. As Franklin D. Roosevelt later argued, "Great accumulations of wealth cannot be justified on the basis of personal and family security. . . . Such inherited economic power is as inconsistent with the ideals of this generation as inherited political power was inconsistent with the ideals of the generation which established our government."[7]

Almost a century later, however, the estate tax—the linchpin of Progressive Era reform—is under assault. Many wealthy Americans wished to pass their entire fortunes to their children without taxes, and urged the Republican president and Congress to overturn nearly a century of progressive public policy. In 2001, Congress responded, and passed a broad tax-cut bill that slowly phases out the estate tax (reducing the tax rates on a graduated basis) until 2009. By 2010, the estate tax will be repealed entirely.

However, due to the peculiar nature of legislative compromise, most of the tax cut legislation passed in 2001 expires ten years later, and as a result, the estate tax comes back to life in 2011. This has left proponents of eliminating the estate tax (which they call the "death tax") urging for a permanent repeal. Unfortunately, these advocates distort the facts to claim that it is aimed at protecting farmers and owners of small businesses. (Placing reasonable caps on the estate tax would accomplish that objective more narrowly.) In fact, behind the wizard's curtain lie the politics of self-interest: an entire industry of lobbyists, political consultants, and think tanks, funded by some of America's richest families, including the Gallo (as in wine) and Mars (as in candy) families.[8]

What's worse, some of the more prominent advocates of these changes are the visible leadership of the so-called Christian right. The Christian Coalition of America proclaimed in 2004 that its top legislative priority would be "making permanent President Bush's 2001 federal tax cuts." Further, when conservative Republican Governor Bob Riley proposed a tax hike in Alabama to dig his state out of a fiscal crisis and put more money into its school system, routinely ranked near the bottom of the nation (arguing that it was Christian duty to look after the poor), 68 percent of the state voted against it. The opposition was led by the Christian Coalition of Alabama, whose president John Giles stated, "You'll find most Alabamians have got a charitable heart. They just don't want it coming out of their pockets."[9]

We need to rethink the process of reforming our tax laws. Just as policymakers have placed incentives on hard work in the welfare system, we must reflect that same value in the tax code. When policymakers make changes—whether tax increases or cuts—they should do it in a way that rewards hard work instead of inherited wealth. One good example has been proposed by economist Paul Weinstein. His "Family-Friendly" tax reform would eliminate 68 redundant, unnecessary, or special-interest tax breaks and give Americans four simple tax incentives: a $3,000 per year college tax credit, a universal home mortgage deduction available both to those Americans who itemize and those that do not, an expanded family tax credit for couples with children, and a universal pension that replaces 16 IRA-type accounts with a single, portable retirement account for all workers.[10]

A currently existing model for tax reform is the earned income tax credit (EITC)—started under Gerald Ford and expanded by Ronald Reagan and Bill Clinton. The EITC benefits lower-income working families and embodies the value of hard work. In practice, the EITC refunds payroll taxes paid by lower-income workers, allowing them to keep more of their paycheck for more pressing needs. The average family may receive a $1,700 refund check or credit, but some could receive as much as $4,000. For a parent earning the minimum wage, the benefit can be the equivalent to $1.92 an hour—a 36 percent pay hike.[11] Several states have started their own version of the EITC, and it would make good public policy for every compassionate community to do so as well.

FINANCIAL LITERACY EDUCATION: A LADDER TOWARD FINANCIAL PROSPERITY

Unfortunately, many hard-working Americans who can benefit from the EITC never access these credits. Studies by the Internal Revenue Service reveal that 25 percent of Americans who were eligible under the EITC did not claim what they were owed under the law.[12] Many deserving and eligible Americans are unaware of such government programs that are currently available to help them build and invest assets. And too often, those that cannot afford a tax advisor to identify these funds are among the neediest and hardest working of our citizens.

This ignorance is largely a symptom of a growing plague in this country: that of financial illiteracy. Today's popular culture celebrates consumption. Through mass-media advertising, Americans are bombarded with messages to live beyond their means, to spend money on luxuries, instead of saving for necessities like higher education or retirement. The economics of self-interest promote a culture of debt and fiscal irresponsibility. And while a small percentage of Americans are quite proficient at personal financial planning, there are too few opportunities for them to share this knowledge with those who really need it.

Our education system is, in many ways, the envy of the world. Yet the same schools that have produced brilliant scientists, physicians, and poets have also produced generations of financially illiterate Americans. We teach our children to master such difficult mathematics concepts as trigonometry and algebra, but we do not teach them how to balance a checkbook. Many young people can discuss with great insight the history of ancient civilizations, but are not cognizant of their own credit histories or the significance of their credit reports. And while admission to college requires good grades and high scores on standardized tests, no specific knowledge on how to use—or not use—a credit card is required. Financial illiteracy is a major contributing factor to a growing demographic trend: Nearly 60 percent of young adults between 18 and

34 are struggling for financial independence, their wages not keeping pace with health care and housing costs and loan repayments.[13]

It is important to note that financial illiteracy is not simply a problem faced by our youngest generation of Americans. In fact, it is an epidemic. When the country's national savings rate during a period of unprecedented prosperity dips below 1 percent, and when 12 percent of Americans have no retirement savings whatsoever, we realize that financial illiteracy could leave many American seniors desperately needing financial assistance. And when the total household debt reaches $7.3 trillion, with the average credit-card holder having over $8,000 in debt, we realize that financial illiteracy has a devastating effect on our nation's economy.

There are many organizations and individuals across the country trying to combat the growing problems posed by financial illiteracy. Groups such as Junior Achievement and the National Council on Economic Education have developed excellent curricula for promoting financial literacy among students of all ages. The Consumer Federation of America and Cooperative Extension have joined to create "America Saves," a national program that promotes sound personal financial practices in several large cities. These valuable programs, however, only reach a small minority of our population.

In order for the compassionate community to truly embrace the value of hard work, it must ensure that hard-working Americans are provided with the tools they need to achieve financial self-sufficiency. While by no means a solution to the economic problems faced by many Americans, good financial education can help working Americans keep more of the fruits of their labor, enabling them to reap more from their hard work. In so doing, financial education can serve as a ladder for society's Jacobs to provide them with the comfort that everything will be all right.

One of America's most able "ladder assemblers" is Delaware Treasurer Jack Markell. In 2002, Markell launched the groundbreaking "Money School," which provides low-cost, convenient, and comprehensive financial education to Delaware residents. The Money School covers a wide variety of topics, ranging from debt management, home ownership, day-to-day budgeting, and retirement planning. The school has been very successful, with broad participation across the state, offering more than 90 classes, all of which are taught by volunteer analysts, financial planners, and other financial professionals. Markell's approach is a great validation of the value of hard work, empowering Delaware citizens to help themselves and their families reach their economic and financial dreams.

Every state should follow Markell's lead. There are four specific areas in which financial literacy training can help assure that average, everyday working men and women can climb their own ladders toward greater financial security in today's financially disparate economy. These areas, as discussed below, are credit cards on college campuses, predatory lending, marriage and money, and identity theft.

1. Credit Cards on College Campuses

Every fall, tens of thousands of young men and women across the country leave the protections of home and enter college. The first few weeks of college have always presaged many rites of passage: choosing a major, attending your first football game, rushing a fraternity or sorority.

But a new rite of passage has emerged recently for college freshmen on campuses across the country: applying for your first credit card.

The opportunities are endless. If you have been to a ball game or a public event, you likely have been barraged by credit-card companies offering some gift or service in return for filling out an application. For college students, this is almost an everyday occurrence. Students are tempted by unavoidable offers from dozens of different credit-card companies, and they are bombarded by credit cards at freshmen orientation, at activities fairs, in student unions and lunchrooms, in the campus bookstore, and even in the privacy of their dorm rooms. On average, they will receive eight offers during the first week of college alone. It is rare to find a bulletin board on campus that is not covered with card offers.

The sales pitches can be irresistible. Thousands of dollars of "free money" if you just fill out a form. (And by the way, a T-shirt or a chance to win an enticing vacation are also offered.) The offer might come from a friend who needs your help in completing his quota of completed applications. The card might come with a so-called teaser rate—a low introductory interest rate that looks too good to be true—unless, of course, you read the fine print and find out that the rate balloons dramatically within a few months. As the General Accounting Office (GAO) reported in 2001, some credit-card vendors "created a carnival atmosphere with loud music and games . . . mask[ing] the responsibilities of owning a credit card, especially since there was no discussion of the consequences of misusing a credit card."[14]

In some circumstances, the solicitation turns ugly. In 2001, a commission that I appointed on personal savings and investment held a hearing on the issue of credit cards on college campuses. A University of Kentucky student testified that one credit-card marketer pushed his way into her freshman dorm room and would not leave until one of her roommates filled out a credit-card application. This young woman, for obvious reasons, felt violated. The GAO study revealed that this example is not unique: Students reported that vendors followed them around campus when their initial sales pitches were rejected. Sometimes students are even manipulated into revealing personal information in exchange for gifts.

The economic incentives that encourage these types of aggressive credit-card solicitations are enormous. Many universities, struggling to fund vital programs because of state budget cuts, have signed multi-million dollar contracts to give a particular company exclusive rights to market its credit cards on campus. Student organizations raising funds to pay for their expenses have been recruited as sales agents by credit-card companies—these groups are often compensated $25-$200 a day to table the student union and are paid $1-$5 for every completed application. Peer pressure has become an invaluable sales tool.

For many college students, owning and using a credit card does not pose any serious problems and offers some advantages. For instance, in an emergency situation, where cash is not available, a credit card can be invaluable. Credit cards can be a useful way to learn about personal finance and budgeting if students are properly educated about their use. Credit cards can also offer a vehicle, albeit an imperfect one, for young people to develop a positive credit rating. For the majority of students, credit-card debt is not a problem: The GAO study revealed that almost 60 percent of students pay their credit-card balances in full every month.

However, for a significant and growing minority of college students, credit-card use and misuse can be devastating. Without proper education on credit-card use, and with only self-serving, on-campus promotions instructing them, students often sign up for numerous credit cards, making purchases up to the credit limit on each. In a telling study, the Public Interest Research Group (PIRG) revealed that students who obtained credit cards at student union tables had more cards and higher debt balances than those that signed up elsewhere.[15] Instead of the false promise of "free money," students wind up building mountains of credit-card debt before they even have an income stream to pay for it.

College students are more likely than other credit-card customers to accumulate significant debts. That is why companies that sign up cardholders with higher risks of default—in exchange for higher interest rates—often target college students. Students see low, seemingly easy minimum payments, but don't realize they could spend much of the rest of their lives repaying their debts.

Here is an example: Suppose a student today built up a credit-card balance of $3,000 on a credit card that charged a typical 19.8 percent interest rate. If that student never made another purchase, and dutifully made the minimum payment each month, it would take her 39 years to repay that debt. In this example, the student would have to pay out over $10,000 in interest—on only a $3,000 balance.

This is not an uncommon experience. Various studies reveal that the average student credit-card debt ranges from $500 to more than $3,000. Meanwhile, in 1999, a record 100,000 Americans under the age of 25 filed for bankruptcy.

The impact on students can be more than financial. The stress of credit-card debt has significant emotional, even physical effects on these young adults, compounding the stress of leaving the security of home and family. One administrator at Indiana University reported in the GAO survey that they "lose more students to credit card debt than academic failure."

With many college graduates already facing significant student-loan debts, the added burden of growing credit-card balances can leave many young men and women entering the workforce with seemingly desperate debt problems. As a result, many young people are forced to choose jobs solely on the basis of the starting salary offered, without regard to suitability or personal satisfaction. This leads to further economic problems for the young worker when the job situation worsens, increasing the cycle of debt and credit-card dependency. It also appears to have the effect of shrinking the pool of otherwise eligible and willing applicants for socially important, but less lucrative entry-level jobs in fields such as education, social work, law enforcement, and the military.

This problem was exacerbated by bankruptcy "reform" legislation passed in the spring of 2005. The new law makes it harder for debt-ridden people to wipe clean their financial slates by declaring bankruptcy. The big winners were the credit-card companies who lobbied aggressively for the change. Travis B. Plunkett of the Consumer Federation of America noted: "This is particularly ironic because reckless and abusive lending practices by credit-card companies have driven many Americans to the brink of bankruptcy." The credit-card companies argued that the "reform" was necessary to cure the growing problem of credit addiction—individuals who spend beyond their means. However, recent studies clearly demonstrate that about half of all Chapter 7 filers do so because of major new *medical* expenses. Meanwhile, bankruptcy filings have increased 17 percent since 1997, and credit-card company profits have increased by 163 percent. Further, the bill did nothing to crack down on wealthy debtors who use loopholes to shield income from bankruptcy claims, nor did it do anything to prevent scandal-prone companies such as Enron and Worldcom from entering bankruptcy to escape the burdens of legal claims made against them.[16] Again, public policy—influenced by special interest contributions—favored the value of wealth over hard work.

It would be too easy, however, to pin the entire blame for this growing phenomenon on the credit-card companies and their representatives. While some regulation of credit-card marketing is necessary, the problem is much greater than this. Indeed, credit-card misuse on college campuses is just a symptom of the much greater problem—as discussed above—of financial illiteracy. The hard work of our students is being erased by the lack of financial education we provide them.

State governments should engage in a comprehensive financial education project—beginning in the public schools and culminating on college and university campuses. It should be implemented through a public-private partnership that brings together government and industry to develop curricula and train teachers. Financial literacy should be taught in every elementary, middle, and high school classroom in the states. Moreover, mandatory, meaningful financial literacy courses should be also offered during freshman orientation of every college or university.

Credit-card companies, moreover, should be required to register with colleges and universities in order to solicit on campus, and to abide by a Code of Conduct that governs solicitation methods. This code should promote full disclosure of credit-card terms and prohibit the more egregious marketing practices. Universities would be charged with guaranteeing the best interests of their students, and ensure that every student is able to capture the full value of their hard work.

Further, because credit-card companies are national, sometimes multinational conglomerates, for any regulation to be effective, the U.S. Congress must take action. These corporations have few ties to the university communities they target, and, as a result, they are often unresponsive to local concerns. Congress can and should impose a real code of conduct covering the actions of credit-card companies on all of the nation's college campuses—prohibiting incentives such as gifts, and banning the more aggressive sales practices such as the recruitment of student groups that use peer pressure to complete applications. Credit-card companies should be forced to determine before approving a card whether the student could afford to pay off a balance. Teaser rates should be restricted. All credit-card materials should provide clear examples of how long it will take to pay off the maximum debt permitted when the cardholder makes only minimum payments, and examples of how much will be paid in interest by the cardholder maintaining a balance over time. This common sense type of information is currently provided by banks to borrowers obtaining a home mortgage, and it helps inform borrowers of the true long-term cost of their debt.

We must challenge all credit-card companies to join us in our national effort to protect college students from credit-card debt and to promote financial literacy. Today's college students rarely review educational brochures and Web sites sponsored by the credit-card companies, no matter how well-meaning or comprehensive they may be. We must ask the companies to make a substantial monetary commitment to the development of mandatory financial curricula for our nation's schools and colleges and to train teachers to provide effective instruction on these issues. We do not need to re-invent the wheel; we simply should build on existing resources provided by the outstanding organizations that have been working on these issues. Funding can help us produce and publish materials that young people will read, understand, and apply to their financial behavior.

Ultimately, credit-card debt is an issue of personal responsibility. Once given proper education on credit-card use and misuse, college students can learn to be accountable for their own financial behavior.

And by empowering our citizens with the skills to manage their finances effectively, we can help reduce our national reliance on social welfare programs and personal bankruptcy.

And maybe, a decade or so from now, there will be some new rites of passage for our nation's college students. A rite of passage for every third grader to learn about the magic of compound interest and the importance of savings. A rite of passage for every eighth grader to study the stock market and American financial institutions. A rite of passage for every high-school senior to take a course on family budgeting and income management. And finally, in some future September—before the football games, before the fraternity rituals—a rite of passage for every college freshman to be given solid instruction on credit and debt management to prepare them, as they leave their parents' nest, to build their own nest eggs. In so doing, these young Jacobs can truly realize the value of their own hard work, as they build ladders toward financial prosperity.

2. Predatory Lending

While the Bible does not weigh in on the subject of credit cards (Moses and Jesus both preceded the invention of plastic by thousands of years), the Judeo-Christian tradition is very specific about the problems inherent in the practice of lending. The Torah forbade Jews from charging interest to fellow Israelites, particularly the poor, even requiring a creditor to return a neighbor's garment that had been pledged for a debt. Indeed, Mosaic law commands that every seventh year—the "sabbatical" year—the land should rest and all debts be forgiven. When these laws were broken by lenders who charged exorbitant interest rates that drove people to poverty, the prophets decreed that they presented a "social plague" that incurred God's wrath.[17]

Even today, this social plague infects many Americans. For many of us, borrowing money for a home or other personal expenses can be a daunting challenge—or even a nightmare. The value of our hard work can disappear, with little notice.

By the 1990s, a whole new fringe loan industry had emerged—ranging from check-cashing firms to home improvement contractors to other short-term lenders. With many lower-income Americans unable to borrow money from traditional sources such as banks or savings and loans, these institutions provide lending services to nearly all who walk in their doors. As our credit-card culture encourages many Americans to spend well beyond their means, lenders looking for healthy profit margins have found a very convenient target.

While some of these companies provide a legitimate service, particularly in lower-income communities, some cross the line into what is known as "predatory lending." Predatory lending occurs when a lender engages in practices that involve fraud, deception or the manipulation of a borrower through aggressive sales tactics. Generally, a borrower is duped by a scheme promising easy, immediate cash, only to find out much later there is a catch: it might be extremely high interest rates, prohibitively expensive administrative fees, or unnecessary insurance policies or other obligations. The fruits of the borrower's labor are denied through this chicanery.

One common predatory lending scheme can be found in the home mortgage business. Many times the predatory lender's intent is to tie borrowers to loans they cannot pay, and then ultimately foreclose on their homes. Often the victims of this type of predatory lending are poor, elderly, and from minority groups. Recent studies demonstrate that African Americans—regardless of income level—have been hit hardest by these practices. The Federal Reserve found that African Americans were about three times as likely to borrow through high-interest mortgages. Among low-income households, 39.2 percent of African Americans took out high-priced mortgages, compared to 12.9 percent of white families.[18]

Unfortunately, current federal law rewards lenders who charge excessive fees. Homeowners usually do not pay these fees in cash; instead they borrow more to cover the costs, resulting in larger loan balances. The original lender usually is not concerned about the borrower's ability to make monthly payments because it can sell the loan on the secondary market. Instead, the original lenders profit from fees collected at the time of closing, so they focus on trying to make as many loans as possible. Accordingly, their incentive is to repeatedly refinance loans, which drains the wealth of homeowners who see their home equity decrease over time. Further, up to 80 percent of high-interest home loans contain significant prepayment penalties that cost families when they refinance or pay off their loans early. To make matters worse, many of these contracts require borrowers to give up their right to go to court if any legal problems arise.[19]

Another common example of predatory lending can be found in the payday lending industry. Many Americans live paycheck to paycheck.

When unexpected expenses must be incurred, many families look to emergency loans to offer a solution. Unfortunately, this often propels them into a further cycle of debt.

Payday lending businesses have popped up all over the country, in nearly every shopping center and retail strip. They advertise themselves extensively, offering to provide ready cash in emergency situations. These operations have very few occasional customers; 99 percent of payday loans go to repeat borrowers. In fact, borrowers with five or more loans a year account for 91 percent of the payday loan business.[20]

To qualify for a payday loan, all you need is a bank account and a steady paycheck. Customers write a post-dated check, and receive cash from the lender. Typically, lenders allow two weeks for repayment of the loan, plus a fee at a specific interest rate. Many customers, however, do not make on-time payments. If their bank accounts do not have the required funds, the customers may be assessed fees by their bank for a bounced check, or even run the risk of being prosecuted for issuing a bad check. To avoid default, many borrowers agree to renew the loan and pay the interest fee again. With typical interest rates of 400 percent, the average payday borrower will pay $800 to repay a $325 loan.[21]

Men and women of our armed forces are often victimized by these practices. A 2003 National Consumer Law Center Report found that "scores of consumer-abusing businesses directly target this country's active duty military men and women daily." Using deceptive names such as "Force One Lending" and "Armed Forces Loans," they charge interest rates of 100, 500, even 1,000 percent.[22] When I travel around the Fort Knox and Fort Campbell bases in Kentucky, I see a higher concentration of these businesses than in any other part of the Commonwealth.

The problem of predatory lending must be tackled on three fronts to ensure the value of the hard work performed by prospective borrowers. First, legislation is needed to crack down on firms that send people into the homes of vulnerable Americans to sell them loans they do not need and cannot afford. Federal law should be dramatically revised to eliminate the incentives to engage in predatory lending. Check-cashing companies should be prohibited from charging interest rates that would make Tony Soprano blush. Reasonable limits on up-front fees and prepayment penalties on home loans can help prevent borrowers from seeing their equity drained from their homes. And no borrower should be asked to waive her constitutional rights to seek redress in the courts to remedy an unfair lending scheme.

Second, government should work with existing organizations that have already begun efforts to educate lower-income Americans about the practice of predatory lending, and to empower them to resist plans that could drive them into significant debt. (Appendix 2 lists dozens of groups that are providing free financial services in areas such as avoiding predatory lending schemes.)

The third and most important issue to address is the economic instability of the working poor, who are unable to finance their American dreams. To experience a true "ownership society," every American needs to be able to build up sufficient assets to finance their American Dream. Currently, there is only one federal savings incentive program designed for lower- and middle-income households—the Savers' Credit—but even it is unavailable to the 40 percent of Americans who do not earn enough to have a tax liability. Meanwhile, the federal government spends over $150 billion a year on tax incentive programs that encourage savings among primarily the affluent: 70 percent of the tax breaks go to the top 20 percent of American earners.[23]

As I discussed in Chapter One, universal children's savings accounts would enable Americans of all incomes to build assets; save for major expenses such as college, home purchases, and retirement; and prepare themselves for emergencies, such as a health-care crisis. Until that dream is fulfilled, however, states should develop legislation to promote programs such as Individual Development Accounts (IDAs) that enable the working poor to develop and build assets in order to pay for a home, afford higher education, or start a small business.

One effective model is the Connecticut IDA Initiative that facilitates self-sufficiency and economic stability through financial education and asset development. Lower- and moderate-income Connecticut residents can contribute their own money into an IDA, knowing some of their investment will be matched by a community-based organization that administers the fund. These groups also provide participating families with extensive financial education so that they understand how to save wisely and build assets in order to reach their own financial dreams. Corporations, foundations, and wealthy individuals are provided tax incentives to contribute to the community-based organizations in order for them to administer these programs and match participant contributions. Ultimately, IDA assets can be used for education, job training, homeownership, small business capitalization, lease deposits on primary residences, and vehicle purchases for obtaining or maintaining employment.

Another worthy idea, advanced by the Brookings Institution, would be to encourage more employees to contribute to their firm's 401(k) tax-deferred savings plan. Currently, many employers offer 401(k) plans to their employees, and some provide generous matches for the pre-tax salary deductions that are taken out of their paychecks. These prove to be excellent asset-building vehicles, and they provide a means to reduce income-tax liability. However, less than half of the employees eligible for a 401(k) plan take advantage of it. Worse, the 401(k) participation rates for women (30 percent participate), Latinos (19 percent), and those with incomes under $20,000 (13 percent) fall well below the mean.[24]

The Brookings Institution suggests that federal law be changed to make it automatic for employees to be enrolled in their company's 401(k) plan, requiring the employee to actively contribute the program, unless they affirmatively choose not to participate. The Brookings study estimates that if automatic 401(k) enrollment were the default option, 30 percent more employees would enroll, and therefore more Americans would build a nest egg for their families' future.[25] In the long run, due to their involvement in these plans, these Jacobs will discover that their hard work will provide a more secure retirement.

3. Marriage and Money

Complicating the value of hard work is the fact that many financial decisions are made by committee: a husband and a wife. In today's world, often both a husband and a wife are contributing to the household finances through their employment, and each must have a say in how the fruits of their labor should be allocated.

While the political debate on marriage recently has focused on whether outside cultural forces may menace the institution, the real power and responsibility to strengthen a marriage comes from within the couple itself.

Every marriage is wholly unique. If the formula for calculating success in marriage were universal, publishers would stop putting out thousands of self-help titles on improving marriage, and Dr. Phil would likely be out of business. Still, there is one factor that resonates in the discussion. And it is a factor that seems to reverberate in the discussion of every significant problem we desperately need to address. It's money.

A married couple that has not fought about money is probably still on their honeymoon. (And even then, many are already anxious about paying off the bills incurred during their wedding reception.) Many marriage counselors will tell you that friction over money and household spending generates a great deal of tension in the modern-day marriage. It would seem logical that the less money a couple shares, the greater the opportunity there is for conflict, as it becomes more difficult to determine how to allocate the scarce resources. This may help explain why some sociologists suggest that divorce rates correlate to socioeconomic status, and why some of the highest divorce rates in the country are seen in lower-income Southern states, despite our reputation for strong family values. (Indeed, a study by the National Center for Health Statistics revealed that so-called red states—those that voted for Republican President George Bush in 2004—have a 27 percent higher divorce rate that the blue states won by Democrat John Kerry.)[26]

Policymakers cannot change the human heart. Nor should we assign new bureaucracies to treat problems that are much better served by our religious leaders and health-care professionals: There are too many other significant issues—spiritual, stress-related, family—that they should help to remedy. However, we can—as a compassionate community—diminish one of the common root causes of troubled marriages. And we can do it by using existing resources, existing curricula, and existing alliances among the government, private industry, and faith-based institutions.

Every state should attempt what Kentucky developed through a Marriage and Money task force that I convened in 2004. We brought together leaders in the fields of education, business, marriage counseling, academia, and the clergy to study how and where we can intervene with financial education to help couples build a stronger foundation for their unions. With such a task force, leaders can gather examples of tried and tested financial literacy curricula and discuss how to apply it to the modern marriage—for richer and for poorer. And ultimately, the task force can determine how to develop and disseminate financial advice and information to couples at the four critical stages of marriage: (1) during the engagement when life plans are first discussed; (2) in the first months of marriage when financial independence is often a novelty; (3) after children are born and financial pressures mount exponentially; and (4) when marriage turmoil leaves couples at a breaking point.

The end goal would not be to replace the many existing resources that provide counseling to married couples. Rather, the goal should be to provide new assets—such as easy-to-read financial tool kits—to assist clergy and counselors in their important work. We can also bring to their attention the many unique opportunities already available for parents: child-care support for full-time workers or students; tax credits and other asset-building opportunities for the working poor; and community-based programs that provide free financial advice to couples trying to survive on a shoestring budget. Further, we can shine a spotlight on outstanding local initiatives, such as those that provide mentors to young dads who may have grown up without a role model for a father and husband.

We need to stop paying mere lip service to family values. If we can change a few lives by empowering couples with the tools they need to form a healthy and lasting marriage—a more perfect union—then our engagement in marriage will be well worth the effort. When we value the hard work of each spouse in a marriage, we can ensure healthier families and stronger communities.

4. Identity Theft

Jacob's deception of his father—disguising himself as his brother to win the family's birthright—may be history's first example of a growing crime plaguing working families and robbing them of the fruit of their hard work: identify theft. Today, personal information, especially Social Security numbers, bank account or credit card numbers, and telephone calling card numbers are being used by identity thieves to personally profit at your expense. An identity thief will reap the rewards of your hard work, while you are left trying to repair the damage.

In recent years, nearly one million Americans have reported that unauthorized persons have taken funds out of their bank or financial accounts; or, in some extreme cases, taken over their identities altogether, running up vast debts and committing crimes. In some instances, a victim's losses may include not only out-of-pocket financial arrears, but also substantial additional costs associated with trying to correct erroneous information for which the criminal is responsible, or to restore credit ratings and financial reputation in the community.

In one extraordinary case, a convicted felon not only incurred more than $100,000 of credit-card debt, obtained a home loan, and bought homes, motorcycles, and handguns in the victim's name, but he also called his victim to taunt him. The felon claimed that he could continue to pose as the victim for as long as he wanted because identity theft was not a federal crime at that time. Ultimately, he planned to file for bankruptcy, also in the victim's name. While the victim spent more than four years and more than $15,000 of his own money to restore his credit and reputation, the criminal served only a brief sentence for making a false statement to procure a firearm. No restitution was paid to the victim for any of the harm the thief had caused. This case, and others similar to it, prompted Congress to establish identity theft as a federal crime in 1998.[27]

There are several steps that every American should take to protect themselves from becoming a victim of identity theft. First and foremost, you should immediately obtain a copy of your credit report. The federal Fair Credit Reporting Act, passed in 2004, requires each of the three major nationwide consumer reporting companies to provide you with a free copy of your credit report, at your request, once every year. By simply perusing this document on an annual basis, you can determine whether expenditures have been made or debts have been incurred on your accounts without your permission. To order this report, simply go to my Web site, www.TheCompassionateCommunity.com, where we provide a direct link to the free service. Be wary: The "free" credit reports offered in television or radio commercials often have a catch—you can receive a free report only if you sign up for their paid "monitoring" service. The reports we connect you with on our Web site are free.

It may sound obvious, but another way to avoid risk is to create unique passwords for your credit card, bank, and phone accounts. When coming up with a password, many Americans use easily available information like a mother's maiden name, a birth date, or the last four digits of a Social Security number—these are far too easy for an identify thief to obtain. We must also make sure that personal information in our homes is secure. Even in today's digital world, the most common way identity thieves access your personal information is by going through your garbage, outside of your home, or at a public landfill.

Further, some entrepreneurial identity thieves have posed as representatives of banks, phone companies, and government agencies to get people to reveal their personal information. Always be wary when asked for personal information on the phone or the Internet unless you have initiated the communication. Also, double check the Web address of any business or organization with which you are making purchases or sharing identifying information. Some identity thieves will purchase a

Web site with a name similar to a popular site to trick careless spellers into providing them with personal information.

If you believe that you are a victim of identity theft, there are some immediate steps to take. Contact the fraud departments of reputable credit-reporting companies, and ask them to place a "fraud alert" on your credit report. This will notify creditors to contact you before opening any new accounts or making any changes to your existing accounts. Second, close all of your accounts that you know or believe have been used improperly. Third, file a report with your local police or the attorney general of your state. Make sure to obtain a copy of the report to submit to your creditors that may require proof of the crime. Additionally, file a complaint with the Federal Trade Commission, which maintains a database of identity theft cases used by law enforcement.[28]

"Credit freezing" is another way to protect yourself. A credit freeze goes a step further than a fraud alert. With a credit freeze, no one can open any form of credit in your name. Your credit file is placed off limits to potential lenders, insurers, and employers. This does not mean that you will not be able to get credit for yourself or allow potential lenders or employers to check your credit. When you freeze your report, the credit bureaus assign a password to you, and using this password, you can lift the freeze when necessary. Even if an identity thief has your personal information, it will not matter: No credit will be issued to him.

Unfortunately, as of 2006, only five states permit credit freezing: California, Louisiana, Texas, Vermont, and Washington. This common sense consumer protection should be enacted by every state legislature. Better yet, Congress should pass federal legislation mandating the right of consumers to freeze credit anywhere in the country.

Ultimately, it is up to each of us to remain vigilant about protecting our own personal information and encouraging our elected representatives to provide us additional protections against the crime of identity theft. When your hard-earned finances are stolen through this or any other means, the fundamental American value of hard work is severely undermined.

THE RISING

What I have learned most in my experiences at promoting financial education is that there are already hundreds of groups and thousands of individuals who provide these services—or would be willing to do so—

free of charge to the neediest and most deserving working families. Many of the most effective financial education organizations are listed in appendix 2. A more comprehensive resource bank is available on my Web site. There, you can access a wide range of national resources—from broad financial advice to very specific instruction on personal financial needs. Further, through modern blogging software, we can enable two-way communication between those who need financial advice and those who are willing to offer it for free. Once laptops and broadband access are available to all Americans, the Internet will serve as a virtual ladder of sorts, empowering all American citizens—no matter their location or circumstances—with the opportunity to develop the knowledge that they can couple with their hard work in order to enjoy a higher quality of living.

Through new technology and partnerships between government and the private sector, we can help create a compassionate community, of the sort that Bruce Springsteen imagines: where the work of everyday Americans is valued, honored, and respected.

Indeed, the title track to Springsteen's Grammy-winning *The Rising* provides a beautiful coda to the compassionate community he creates in his album. Describing the simple heroism of our firefighters, Springsteen portrays these brave men and women climbing their ladders higher and higher, joining their hands to save those whose lives are in danger.

The analogies to Jesus and the resurrection are obvious. But a more subtle reading of Springsteen's poetry reveals that the job of saving others from distress is not the sole province of God. It is incumbent on each of us to reach out our hands to lift up our neighbors. It is incumbent on each of us to empower others to live more fulfilling lives.

As Rabbi Kushner suggests, it is essential that we recognize those lives that matter. Everyone who puts in an honest day's work—like Jacob—is a living embodiment of American values. None of us should live in poverty. Each of us should be empowered with the ability to manage our finances.

Through daily, often thankless, efforts, Americans climb their own ladders—like Jacob, and like the 9–11 firefighters—and in doing so, give meaning to our lives. And it is up to the compassionate community to help all Americans build their ladders and promote greater self-sufficiency.

FOUR

JOSEPH AND THE VALUE OF FAMILY

When Joseph's brothers saw that their father was dead, they said, "What if Joseph still bears a grudge against us and pays us back for all the wrong that we did him?" So they sent this message to Joseph, "Before his death your father left this instruction: So shall you say to Joseph, 'Forgive, I urge you, the offense and guilt of your brothers who treated you so harshly'" . . . And Joseph was in tears as they spoke to him. His brothers went to him themselves, flung themselves before him, and said, "We are prepared to be your slaves." But Joseph said to them, "Have no fear! Am I a substitute for God? Besides, although you intended me harm, God intended it for good, so as to bring about the present result—the survival of many people. And so, fear not, I will sustain you and your children."

—Genesis 50:15–21

My renewed and revitalized faith was not the only gift my father left me in death. I watched my sister's noble sacrifice in uprooting her life, delaying her own sparkling career, to be by my father's side in his final months. I witnessed my parents' deep love, demonstrated by my mother's constant care and attention. And knowing that our time together was dwindling, my dad and I were finally able to express to each other the things often left unsaid between fathers and sons.

But most of all, I realized how much I had taken for granted, both as a son and a father. I held my daughters a bit tighter, doted on them a bit longer. I was reminded that, whatever direction my career took me, the most important title I would ever claim was "Daddy."

I had learned very quickly that parents have the toughest, most challenging, most rewarding, most dignified, most important job in the world. Fortunately, I had a partner for whom it all came naturally. I could not have been luckier: The fellow camp counselor with whom I fell in love not only turned out to be my best friend, but also the most powerful influence in my life. With her love, advice, and guidance, I was inspired to grow into a more responsible adult. And this growing process was rapidly accelerated by the birth of our two children.

Even for someone like me—who writes and delivers speeches for a living—it is difficult to articulate the special love a parent has for a child. While landfills are littered with novels, poems, and verses describing the romantic love of a spouse, or the reverence and gratitude for a mother, a father's love for his daughters is often overlooked.

Suffice it to say that every day my daughters bring me unexpected joy. Watching Emily turn into a young woman before my eyes—while sometimes quite scary—brings me renewed confidence for the future. Abby's joyful innocence (as well as the cute dimples she inherited from Lisa) reminds me of what is truly important in life.

Parenting is a life-changing experience—changing our focus, our priorities, and our values. And our role as parents is not significant simply for our children's well-being. The entire compassionate community is strengthened by our actions toward our own children. Every one of our neighbors has a stake in our success. Society—and our government—should celebrate good parenting when we do our job well. As sociologist Barbara Dafoe Whitehead points out, when people become parents, they become more closely connected to their neighborhood community, more involved in their houses of worship, and more likely to vote and be involved in civic affairs. Further, they have a greater ownership stake in good schools, safe neighborhoods, and a healthy environment.[1]

While our responsibilities toward our children are limitless, there are three special duties that take priority over all others: keeping them safe from harm and illness; providing them a loving home with all of life's essentials; and teaching them right from wrong. While these responsibilities are simple to understand, in today's coarsened culture—brought to us by the economics of self-interest—they sometimes can be extraordinarily difficult to implement.

JOSEPH AND HIS BROTHERS

Of course, raising kids has never been easy. History's most dysfunctional family might be found more than 4,000 years ago, as depicted in chapters 37 through 45 of Genesis.

Of all of his 12 sons, Jacob "loved Joseph best of all." That did not sit too well with many of the others. Things reached a boiling point when Jacob gave his favorite son a special silk garment, a "coat of many colors."

After debating among each other whether to kill Joseph, the brothers decided to throw him into a pit, from which a group of traders seized him and sold him into slavery in Egypt. Despite Jacob's intense grief about Joseph's apparent death, the brothers did nothing to attempt to return him home.

More than two decades passed before they met again. Joseph had risen to become the pharaoh's influential right-hand adviser, while his brothers struggled to feed their families during an intense famine. When they approached Joseph to plead for food rations, they did not recognize this powerful Egyptian figure. But Joseph recognized his brothers.

Joseph logically could have been expected to seek revenge on his oppressors. Based on his own horrifying experience, as well as the history of sibling conflict in Genesis—Cain killing Abel; Jacob fighting with Esau—we might have even expected violence.

But Joseph's commitment to his family—particularly to his elderly father, Jacob—transcended his feelings of revenge. Once his brothers passed a series of tests that demonstrated to Joseph that they had truly repented for their transgression—and that their love of Jacob too was real and true—he embraced them. Joseph set up his brothers and his father in a fertile region of Egypt where they lived in comfort.

Joseph's noble and selfless decision—and his brothers' moral transformation—reveals that blood is indeed thicker than water. Joseph's greatest regret—and he wept more often than any male Biblical figure—is the loss of time he had to spend with his family, particularly his father, during the forced separation. (It is telling that immediately upon revealing his true identity to his brothers, the first thing Joseph does is inquire about Jacob's health: "I am Joseph; is my father still well?") Rabbi Joseph Telushkin concludes that "in the deepest sense possible . . . the brothers have learned that the answer to Cain's question 'Am I my brother's keeper?' is yes, yes, and again yes."[2]

THE FUNDAMENTAL
HUMAN VALUE OF FAMILY

The story of Joseph and his brothers, of course, is the embodiment of an essential value of the compassionate community: family. The family is the fundamental building block of society; there are literally hundreds of instructions in the Bible concerning the sacred responsibilities among parents and children and husbands and wives. It is instructive that the first of 613 *mitzvot* (commandments) in the Hebrew Bible is to "be fertile and increase" (sometimes translated as "be fruitful and multiply"), which Jewish tradition understands as a mandate for marriage and procreation. Every Sunday School student is aware that "Honor your mother and your father," is one of the Ten Commandments brought down from Mount Sinai by Moses. And the relationship between husband and wife is sacrosanct: The New Testament teaches that each man "is to love his own wife even as himself, and the wife must see to it that she respects her husband."[3]

In fact, the family unit is a central focus of nearly every world religion. Islam believes that the family is the very basis of the community, while the *Bhagavad Gita* celebrates the Hindu child's duty to his parents, the love and attachment parents must show to children, and the mutual respect to be displayed in marriage. In China, family relationships are at the heart of the Confucian tradition, with the five cardinal relationships in Confucianism being that parents should be loving, children reverential; elder siblings gentle, younger siblings respectful; husbands good, wives listening; elder friends considerate, younger friends deferential; rulers benevolent, subjects loyal. Confucius taught that a good family dynamic promoted a good society; the stronger the family, the lower the crime rates and the higher the educational achievement.[4]

While U.S. democracy—influenced by Aristotle, John Locke, and Thomas Jefferson—employs a more central role for representative government than did Confucius, American politicians have been paying homage to the central role of family since the beginning of the Republic. Lincoln, the great emancipator, wrote that family is the "strongest bond of human sympathy"; while Jefferson, the ultimate accomplished Renaissance man, wrote that "the happiest moments of my life have been the few which I have passed at home in the bosom of my family."[5] Today, every politician and political organization tries to claim the mantle of family to justify their candidacy or cause: from the Working Families Party on the labor left to James Dobson's Family Research Council on the far right. Indeed, the slogan "family values" has been used for so many different political purposes, that it has lost any substantive meaning. But for our society to function effectively and appropriately, the compassionate community must place a higher priority on valuing families.

ESCAPING THE PARENT TRAP: THE FAMILY TIME-SHARING PLAN

In today's society, there is a new, pernicious kind of "parent trap." As parents struggle to provide their children with the basics—security, sustenance, and moral values—they feel trapped by three destructive outside forces.

First, as I have discussed in previous chapters, the politics of self-interest in Washington and state legislatures across the country have resulted in cutbacks to the most essential programs that give working families a leg up. In today's economic and political environment, it is becoming increasingly difficult for parents to afford good childcare, accessible health care, safe housing, and a sound education for their kids—from preschool to college.

Second, the economics of self-interest have generated a coarsened culture: Our children are exposed to negative, corrupting influences far beyond our control. New technologies that are more difficult for parents to monitor have provided novel avenues for predators to reach, influence, and harm our children. Further, the explosion of new media—especially elements that sensationalize drugs, sex, violence, and crime—have confused the boundaries of what is right and wrong for too many children. As Whitehead argues persuasively, "the culture is getting ever more violent, materialistic and misogynistic, and [parents] are losing their ability to protect their kids from morally corrosive images and messages."[6]

These two forces are compounded by the third: the lack of family time. With two parents working full time in many modern families, and with all of the competing activities available for children, it is often quite difficult for spouses and parents to carve out the requisite time to spend with their families. Parents—who are challenged by the many obstacles in society to earn a sufficient living to raise their family—often do not have sufficient time and energy to address their children's spiritual needs, to help them build a moral framework to distinguish right from wrong. In addition, some children are so overloaded by activities by their overly anxious and competitive parents that they rarely have quiet, quality time to reflect, relax, and simply enjoy each other's company.

What is needed is a comprehensive effort to empower families with the gift of time—the absence of which Joseph lamented in his later years. I call it the "Family Time-Sharing Plan." And in the compassionate community, the Family Time-Sharing Plan would involve the five components outlined below.

1. Time for a More Perfect Union

The marriage of Jacob and Rachel, Joseph's parents, is the Bible's first example of romantic love. Today, it has become an ideal. We recognize that a child living in a happy home with two married parents is more likely to thrive—financially and emotionally. While we should celebrate the extraordinary support so many single parents across the country provide for their children (I will discuss this below), the data clearly demonstrates that children with single parents are more likely to grow up poor.[7] That's why we must strengthen the institution of marriage by arming couples with the tools for a more successful union, such as the "money and marriage" initiative I discussed in chapter three.

But money clearly is only one factor in the dissolution of marriages. Divorce has many causes, and many Americans view it as a serious national problem. That's why states should take a look at emulating the Oklahoma Marriage Initiative (OMI), launched by former Governor Frank Keating. OMI provides marriage and relationship education to couples and individuals, both married and unmarried, through skills-based workshops that are offered in communities across the state. Hundreds of workshop leaders are trained to provide couples with a stronger union by providing relationship, financial, professional, and mental-health expertise. OMI is not about marriage counseling, but simply providing practical tools and skills to help couples connect, communicate, and process anger effectively. Forming a more perfect union must be a priority in formulating policy.

The Family Time-Sharing Plan must also focus attention on helping new moms and dads understand and grapple with the responsibilities of parenthood. A whole industry has emerged in the past few decades offering assistance to parents in the birthing process, but other than a library of self-help books, less training is available on what actually happens after the child is born. I can tell you from personal experience that the first few months of a child's life—while certainly won-drous—can also be the most difficult for a new parent, particularly when a family support base is not readily available. States should invest in ef-forts that directly empower new parents for this challenging experience.

2. Time to Be a Mom

While we celebrate marriage, the Family Time-Sharing Plan must also show compassion toward single-parent families, particularly because they tend to face more economic hardships. Further, we must under-stand that, in today's real world, the "ideal" family—a married mom and dad raising children—represents less than a quarter of American families, down from nearly half of American families in 1960.[8]

Special public attention must be placed on the issue of adequate child support in situations where a couple has divorced or never were married. So many times, one spouse—usually the mother—ends up the sole financial and emotional provider for a child. As discussed in chapter two, our political leaders must insist on stronger laws that crack down on deadbeat parents. In turn, we must continue to reform the judicial system so that well meaning, non-abusive divorced fathers have appro-priate custodial rights and adequate time to spend with their children.

Difficulties are not limited to single moms. Recent polls show that 70 percent of *all* moms find motherhood "incredibly stressful," with 39 percent of mothers of young children reportedly suffering from depres-sion. The journalist Judith Warner suggests that today's mothers "take on the Herculean task of being absolutely everything to children, sim-ply because no one else is doing anything at all to help them. Because if they don't perform magical acts of perfect Mommy ministrations, their kids might fall through the cracks and end up as losers in our hard-driv-ing, winner-take-all society."[9]

While the popular press and some politicians like to frame the debate as a choice between working and stay-at-home moms, the distinctions these days are not that clear. The Department of Labor revealed in 2000 that 64 percent of American moms worked, but only one-third of mar-ried women with children under six worked full time. Similarly, the *Washington Post* reported that although most of the women polled in its region identified themselves as "working mothers," one of every four worked only part-time, while half of the "stay-at-home mothers" in fact worked since having children. And a recent study that analyzed the career paths of an elite group of working women showed that 44 percent of those moms left work voluntarily at some point during their careers.[10]

Some mothers work full- or part-time because it brings them personal fulfillment—indeed, it is their pursuit of happiness. For some moms, however, particularly single moms, there simply is no choice: They have to work to provide for their family. On the other hand, Warner notes that there are some women who have no choice but to stay at home; because of the lack of any child-care alternatives, they are "effectively put in the situation of *having* to stay home—either because their now sixty-hour workweek was incompatible with family life or because their husbands' seventy-hour workweek meant that if they didn't stop working there would literally be *no one* at home with the kids."[11]

Policymakers need to understand the varied circumstances of being a mom, and state and local governments would be wise to examine a number of different policy prescriptions as a means to provide more time for all types of moms, and therefore better respect the value of family.

We should provide moms (and some dads) with more adequate family-leave time after a child is born or when the family is in the midst of a health-care crisis. Washington state has considered the creation of a statewide, paid family-leave insurance program run through the unemployment compensation system. Employees who agree to a small payroll deduction could take time off under this plan for family emergencies, and they still would collect 50 percent of their salaries.[12]

Other countries boast mandatory paid parental leave. In 2001, Canada expanded its parental-leave benefit to almost a full year. New mothers and fathers, including adoptive parents, can collect as much as 55 percent of their weekly pay, for as many as 50 weeks per couple. After their leave is finished, parents are guaranteed their jobs back. In the program's first year, parental-leave claims filed by fathers in Canada soared by 80 percent, while total claims surged nearly 25 percent. Overall, the average parental leave grew from 6.5 months to more than 10 months.[13] Clearly, the costs of such an initiative—to productivity and to employers—could be prohibitive. But with the first year of a child's life so critical to her development, the general concept should be explored by state legislatures, think tanks, and business groups.

There are, of course, less comprehensive and less costly measures that will free spouses and parents and enable them to spend more time with their families—the time so cherished by Jacob and Joseph. A simple but obvious idea: a new focus on easing traffic congestion through improvements in the computer synchronization of traffic signals. Innovations in this technology, such as in King County (Seattle), Washington, have proven to be very effective in reducing the time motorists spend in traffic, freeing up time for their families.[14]

Technology that encourages affordable and productive telecommuting would also give working parents more freedom. Using the Internet and other modern technologies to provide more "quality time" and "quantity time" for families should be a priority of state policymakers.

Further, states should provide tax subsidies to encourage corporations to adopt family-friendly policies. Businesses should be rewarded for providing more liberal leave, on-site day care, and a corporate policy that acknowledges the important role that their employees play in the rearing of their children. This is not only compassionate, but it makes good business sense. Economists are now discussing the notion of a female "brain drain" emerging in the United States. Women are graduating in record numbers from elite universities and graduate schools, and they are eager to enter the workplace, but most still want to raise children.[15] Companies that can reform their practices and make them more family-friendly could enjoy a considerable competitive advantage.

States and localities should also provide incentives to make flexible, affordable, high-quality day care more available. This would not only help working parents, but it would also help stay-at-home moms maintain an appropriate emotional balance and be more effective parents when they are with their children.

Moreover, government-mandated standards and quality controls should be implemented on child-care providers. Many parents today both fear and dread leaving their children in day care. With a system of standards guaranteeing a sufficient level of experience and care, parents will feel more comfortable leaving their children with strangers. Studies show that a standardized system of public regulation for child care, plus subsidies to lower-income families, could help promote their children's social and intellectual development, providing long-term benefits for the economy. Unfortunately, bills in support of child-care regulation have come before Congress at least five times since the 1970s, but the only bill that passed was the weakest one of all of those proposed, offering improvements for only about 220,000 children.[16] We need to make it a priority for our elected representatives to allow all working parents the comfort and security of knowing their children are in good hands.

3. Father Time

Initiatives in the Family Time-Sharing Plan to promote effective, engaged parenting by fathers can provide the most help to moms—both single and married. One means is through public-private partnerships, such as former Indiana Governor (now Senator) Evan Bayh's Fatherhood Initiative in Indiana, that provide mentoring to young fathers, particularly those young men who had no male role model growing up. As Bayh's research discovered:

> Children who aren't in contact with their fathers are five times more likely to live in poverty and ten times more likely to live in extreme poverty. They're more likely to bring weapons and drugs into the classroom. Children without fathers are twice as likely to commit crimes and drop out of school. They're more than twice as likely to abuse drugs and alcohol. Children without fathers are also more likely to commit suicide and to become teenage parents. The overwhelming majority of violent criminals—including 72 percent of adolescent murderers and 70 percent of long-term prison inmates—are males who grew up without fathers.[17]

Bayh's colleague, U.S. Senator Barack Obama, in a powerful 2005 Father's Day address, noted that these problems are particularly acute in the African American community:

> One of the difficulties that African American men in particular face is that many of us grew up without fathers. . . . As a consequence, there are a lot of 30-, 40-, 50-, even some 60-year-olds who never quite grew up, who still engage in childish things, who are [more] concerned about what they want than what's good for other people, who may not treat their women the way their women deserve to be treated, who may not engage their children and nurture their children in the way their children need to be engaged.[18]

What can a state do to enable modern day Jacobs to take more time and responsibility with their children? The experience in Indiana and other states suggest four strategies that recognize the essential role of fathers, and promote responsible fatherhood in a cost-efficient manner.

First, state programs should require dads to work so that they may become more financially responsible for their children. The economic independence of a father is essential to his ability to provide for his children. The Texas Fragile Families Initiative offers assessments of each father's educational level and acquired job training in order to develop a career goal and an attainable path toward that goal. It also offers training in skills such as interviewing techniques, resumé preparation, job retention, and money management skills. Additionally, fathers enrolled in this program may take advantage of a job-referral service, using the skills they obtained to land a job.[19]

Second, fatherhood initiatives should address emotional connections between fathers and their children. The bond needs to be more than financial. A Charleston, South Carolina, project called "Father to Father" promotes anger management, self-esteem development, and communications skills. Barriers between divorced or unmarried mothers and fathers can be burdensome on fathers who wish to form relationships with their children. These skills are strengthened through the offering of mediation services and individual counseling, as well as couples counseling. Similarly, Massachusetts' Office of Child Support Enforcement pairs fathers who have not paid child support with social-service workers who help them access services and enroll them in peer support groups.[20]

Third, states should award grants to private programs that already promote responsible fatherhood and related causes. For example, more than 20,000 Indiana families have been helped in programs such as "Security Dads," a group of fathers who patrol high-school hallways and let students know that there are adult men who care about the school. Participating fathers also provide reassurance to their own children that they are engaged in their development and care about their safety.[21]

Finally, states should fund continuing research on the best practices in the field. Since this is a new policy area, research and evaluation are essential in determining which ideas work most effectively. Fatherhood programs should be aimed at producing measurable results in improving the lives of the children they serve, in ways that can be replicated elsewhere. In fact, a wide variety of state fatherhood programs can serve as "laboratories for reform" for potential federal action in the future.

The role of a father in a child's life is too important to ignore, or be allowed to deteriorate: As the Bible suggests, Joseph's greatest regret was the loss of a substantial relationship with his father. It is not only essential for the child's welfare; I can say from personal experience how rewarding, fulfilling, and meaningful it is for the dad himself. States should take an active role in promoting this essential bond, both for the families and the entire compassionate community.

4. Time for Kids to be Kids:
"Let Them Be Little"

One of my favorite new songs addresses my greatest complaint: My daughters are growing up much too fast. Country singer-songwriter Billy Dean reminds us that it is a parent's duty to maintain the innocence of childhood for as long as possible, and urges parents to "Let Them Be Little."

The compassionate community stands fervently for the proposition that we must afford children the opportunity to be children. Our wired culture—today's "coat of many colors"—offers many advantages, but it also poses many threats to the innocence of youth. A recent Kaiser Family Foundation report revealed that "young people today live media-saturated lives, spending an average of six and a half hours a day with media. . . . Across the seven days of the week, that amount is the equivalent of a full-time job, with a few extra hours thrown in for overtime." TV and music are the dominant media, with young people spending an average of three hours a day watching TV and about two hours a day listening to the radio or to CDs, tapes, or MP3 players. Interactive media come next, with young people averaging more than one hour a day on the computer outside of schoolwork, and less than an hour playing video games. The six and a half hours a day devoted to media compares to about two hours spent with parents and about one and a half hours spent in physical activity.[22]

This media saturation poses many challenges. Parents are fearful of predators being able to reach our children through e-mails, text messaging, and Internet chat rooms, and are concerned about their access to explicit content. Further, media and video game glorification of violence has made crime and aggressive behavior more common. Research consistently finds an increase in aggression and a decline in pro-social behavior among kids who are exposed to media violence. Millions of parents are feeling that they are fighting a losing battle with the coarsening culture for influence over their children's values and habits.

The economics of self-interest produces another set of casualties. Glorification of ideal body images—combined with the increased sedentary nature of our children's lives—causes great health and emotional tolls (and sometimes physical threats) to our children, particularly our daughters. Combating these forces on behalf of our daughters, as well as on behalf of the local community, is my wife Lisa's special mission. Relying on her own experiences with our daughters and her own childhood struggle with body image and self-esteem, Lisa established Girls Rock!: Healthy Body Image, Self-Esteem and Empowerment for Girls and Mothers. Through workshops, publications, school presentations, and curriculum development, Lisa brings together professionals from a wide variety of health-care fields—as well as impressive healthy teen mentors—to empower kids and moms alike with the tools they need to navigate the minefield of the body image war in today's culture.

One of Lisa's pet peeves is the growth among young girls of the destructive valuing of appearance over the development of inner character and health. Today's popular culture projects an extremely unrealistic sense of body image to girls and women, leading to loss of self-esteem, depression, risky plastic surgery, and sometimes, serious eating disorders. Parents must attend to and cultivate healthy habits in the home. Lisa teaches that parents not only must sit down regularly with their children to communicate the facts of psycho-social pressure, but they also must find the time to monitor the effect of media messages upon children that are so pervasive both within and outside the home.

Protecting the innocence of children is the parent's responsibility, but the Family Time-Sharing Plan can help. When we arm parents with tools such as the V-chip on televisions, school uniforms (which Lisa believes can ease peer pressures caused by explicit fashion trends), and effective parental ratings on entertainment, we can make that job a bit easier. States should examine Illinois Governor Rod Blagojevich's proposal to ban sales of violent video games to minors, and this can be expanded through requiring a uniform rating system of all entertainment media. At the same time, policymakers and community leaders should expose parents to the new wave of entertaining, yet educational, video and computer games, which allow children the opportunity to have fun while developing their own intellectual and social skills. Further, increased public and private support of after-school programs not only helps parents balance their own commitments, it helps keep kids off the streets, promotes better student behavior, and also offers opportunities to enhance learning, particularly for struggling students.[23]

Corporate America must also be held responsible. Too often when called to task for gratuitous violence or explicit marketing tactics, industry lobbyists claim that it is not their role to protect the innocence of children—that is the parents' responsibility. Our elected officials must take on these cultural forces that make it more difficult for parents to teach their kids how to distinguish right from wrong. While censorship is not the answer, and regulation is not always necessary or appropriate, politicians should use their "bully pulpit" (as Senators Joe Lieberman and John McCain have done) to shame these marketers into protecting our children—to make clear that a media company's earnings need to take a backseat to the moral health of young America. And government needs to play a more prominent role in building a zone of protection for children and providing more wholesome alternatives that will empower parents to protect their innocence. This can partly be achieved by giving the Federal Trade Commission (FTC) more power in regulating the conduct of marketing to children. The FTC should closely monitor the content of advertisements played during children's programming. States should further curtail marketing in public schools, by establishing professional review boards to monitor and regulate the type and scope of advertising practices used in today's classrooms and lunchrooms.[24]

But the most significant way to give many kids the time to be kids is to make sure they have parents, or adult mentors who can provide them with the love, support, and sustenance all children desperately need. We should bring to bear all of the resources of government, the faith community, and the private sector to promote adoption and foster care. In Kentucky, many families have found the adoption process so burdensome and slow that they have chosen to either give up or pursue other options. State Auditor Crit Luallen has wisely launched a performance audit of the state's adoption process to determine if there are ways to make it work better. Each state should use all of its resources to make it easier to unite orphaned children with loving parents. Legislators also should replicate California's Foster Youth Mentoring Program, which encourages collaboration among social-service agencies, school districts, and community organizations to pair foster children with adult mentors.[25] We can only let our children "be little" by reminding them that there are grown-ups around to nurture and protect them.

5. Time for Home, Safe Home

Perhaps the most significant component of the Family Time-Sharing Plan is to better ensure that the home offers a zone of protection from violent crime and abuse. As was the case with Joseph and his brothers, too often an assault or murder victim is harmed at the hands of a loved one. And with the Internet bringing new forms of communication into most households, parents are less able to block predatory influences from reaching their children.

Until just a few decades ago, domestic violence was considered a private matter. But, fortunately, as women gained more equality in society, spousal and child abuse have become socially and legally unacceptable. Studies demonstrate that domestic violence knows no boundaries: It occurs in families regardless of race, religion, culture or socioeconomic status. Research indicates as well that merely witnessing domestic violence can have profound effects on children: from increased aggression, to depression and anxiety, to poor academic achievement. Childhood exposure to family violence also creates a vicious, violent cycle by significantly increasing the likelihood of either perpetrating or being the victim of violence as an adult.[26]

Domestic violence is a significant and growing health-care problem in the United States. Nearly 25 percent of all American women are abused by their partner at some point in their lives; and every year, women make close to 700,000 doctor or hospital visits as a result of physical assault. More than one in three women who come to emergency rooms for violence-related injuries were harmed by a family member. More than 300,000 pregnant women are battered each year—indeed, homicide is the leading cause of death for pregnant women.[27]

We must accept nothing less than zero tolerance for domestic violence. Law enforcement must treat domestic violence as any other crime; and the court system must apply appropriate prison sentences to perpetrators and supply necessary protection for victims. Protective orders against abusive spouses must be strictly enforced by police officers, and violations should result in severe punishment. Shelters to protect victims and their children must be adequately funded and equipped to deal with the physical and emotional needs of the residents.

The entire compassionate community indeed must be enlisted to identify and treat victims of domestic violence. Utah has a creative program that solicits the assistance of hair-care professionals in identifying victims of domestic abuse who might be too frightened to come forward through other venues. In 2005, Utah Attorney General Mark Shurtleff launched "Cut it Out," a program that provides domestic-abuse training for salon students and professionals in Utah. The curriculum teaches how to recognize domestic abuse and how to safely refer potential abuse victims to local authorities. Additionally, Utah officials believe that simply placing a "Cut it Out" poster at a salon might provide a victim with a safe, comfortable place to find and access help.

States and communities should also examine innovative initiatives to provide long-term support for victims of domestic abuse. One successful approach is the Domestic Violence and Mental Health Policy Initiative (DVMHPI), a Chicago-based project designed to address the unmet mental-health needs of domestic violence survivors and their children. DVMHPI engages over 75 different domestic violence, mental health, and substance abuse agencies, in a holistic effort to address the mental-health impact of domestic violence. DVMHPI also works with local and state agencies to establish appropriate standards of care for dealing with victims of ongoing domestic violence. Significantly, the program works with policymakers to develop a political agenda that promotes both early intervention and prevention of abuse in future generations.[28]

Domestic violence is becoming a pervasive public-health problem in poorer, rural communities. It is essential that state and local governments provide appropriate training for rural health-care providers, particularly with mandatory reporting requirements for abuse, awareness of assistance programs for victims, and an integration of health services into the community response to domestic violence.[29]

Of course, violence in the home is not limited to adults. Every day in the United States, four children die as a result of child abuse in the home; more than 75 percent of these victims are under the age of four. Nearly three million cases of child abuse are reported every year, but authorities estimate that three times as many incidents go unreported. The impact on children is devastating: Studies of prisoners demonstrate that they have suffered child abuse at a significantly higher rate than the general population, and there is a clear nexus between abuse as a child and vulnerability to substance abuse as an adult.[30]

Child sex abuse is a particularly disturbing and growing crime. One in five girls and one in ten boys are expected to be the victims of sexual assault during their childhood. Two-thirds of all reported victims of sexual assault are minors, and one out of every seven is under the age of six. Among victims younger than 12, 90 percent knew the offender, who most of the time was a family member or a close family friend. Victims of child sexual abuse suffer long-term psychological damage, including fear, guilt, anxiety, depression, anger, poor self-esteem, mistrust of others, and a tendency toward substance abuse and eating disorders. Adolescents with a history of sexual abuse are significantly more likely than their counterparts to engage in sexual behavior that puts them at risk for HIV infection; indeed, in a study of prostitutes, 95 percent reported sexual abuse as a child.[31]

Abusers must be identified and prosecuted immediately. Steps must also be taken to ensure that perpetrators do not attack again once the criminal justice system's punitive measures have taken their course. When released back into society, repeat offenders should be required to undergo pharmacological treatments and therapy, which have proven to be effective in decreasing sexual thoughts and urges by reducing testosterone levels. Further, while all states and the federal government have enacted versions of Megan's Law that require community notification and sex offender registration, lax registration requirements in some states have made it easy for some sex offenders to avoid detection. Registration evaders must be subject to significant jail sentences, and all families should have ready access to lists of sex offenders in their homes via the Internet and through toll-free hotlines. Further, state laws that reduce or eliminate jail sentences when the perpetrator is a parent should immediately be repealed.[32]

With early detection and treatment, the cycle of violence can come to an end. One successful program can be found in Vermont: Stop It Now addresses child sexual abuse systematically by using social marketing and public education to emphasize prevention. Through public service announcements and community events, the program challenges sexual abusers to take responsibility for their behavior; helps family members and neighbors understand and question inappropriate sexual behaviors; and encourages all members of the community to educate themselves about the warning signs for abusive behaviors and victimization.

While most child sex abuse is committed by a family member, there is a growing and pernicious variety being perpetrated by strangers using the new technologies of the Internet. One method utilized by sexual predators has been to pose as teenagers on Internet chat sites, where they solicit, manipulate, and ultimately, sexually assault children at designated meeting places. When Nebraska Attorney General Jon Bruning became aware of the practice, he immediately tried to take remedial action. With the assistance of New York Attorney General Eliot Spitzer, Bruning secured a settlement with Yahoo, under which they agreed to monitor and shut down chat rooms that promote sex with minors, restricted all chat room use to adults only, prioritized the investigation of complaints made online about child sex abuse, and donated $175,000 to the National Center for Missing and Exploited Children.[33] More state and federal officials should take strong legal action to deny sexual predators the easy access to our children that the Internet provides.

Fundamentally, it is up to us parents to be vigilant. Every mom and dad should closely monitor our children's Internet use. And for help, we should access monitoring software and educational information made available by the Federal Bureau of Investigation (FBI) and local authorities. (See appendix 1 for contact information)

OUR BROTHERS' KEEPERS

In every world culture, but particularly in the United States, family has been the building block of society. However, the new economy and the technologies it has produced have imposed serious burdens on the modern family. And as the story of Joseph and his brothers illustrates, some of the most difficult challenges arise from within the family unit itself. Jacob's sons realized before it was too late; we too must overcome every obstacle to allow our families to thrive.

The health of individual families reflects directly on a community's progress and vitality. When parents are provided with the time and resources to take responsibility for producing healthier, better educated, emotionally supported children, the entire society benefits from lower crime rates and increased productivity. It is incumbent on each of us to insist that our elected representatives understand that it is in everyone's interest to promote strong families and attentive parenting.

The key component is time. Implementation of a Family Time-Sharing Plan will enable parents to play a more effective role in their children's nurturing and development, and help protect them from the predatory forces emerging in the modern world around them. When government understands this notion, and makes it easier for parents to protect and raise their children, then family values can be a reality, instead of merely a political slogan. In the compassionate community, we are all our brothers' and sisters' keepers.

FIVE

MOSES AND THE
VALUE OF FREEDOM

*Moses and Aaron went and said to pharaoh, "Thus says the Lord, the God
of Israel: Let My people go, that they may celebrate a festival for Me in the
wilderness."*

—*Exodus 5:1*

For a few days as a young adult, I was a refusenik. A few months
after graduating college, Lisa and I were married in her hometown outside of Toronto, Canada. Lisa was a native and citizen
of our neighbor to the north, but it had never really made any difference to us. Except for pronouncing worlds like "about" and "house"
funny, and ending many sentences with "eh?," Lisa seemed like a typical American. In the weeks before our wedding, we consulted with an
immigration lawyer and prepared for her ultimate naturalization as a
U.S. citizen.

The morning after the wedding, we drove to the U.S. border on
the way back to Kentucky for a reception my parents were throwing.
Once we reached customs, the agent asked our relation. Proudly, we
showed him our new rings.

After a brief consultation with his supervisors, he turned us
around. Apparently, our attorney was mistaken. Lisa's student visa to
attend Boston University was nullified by our marriage; under U.S.
immigration law, married couples require a permanent visa.

With our reception, our honeymoon, and potentially our first year of marriage in jeopardy, we started making phone calls. I phoned the senator for whom I had worked on Capitol Hill; my dad called a Kentucky senator; and my best friend's father called his close friend who was a congressman. By the time we arrived at the U.S. Consulate in Toronto, we were rushed to meet the consulate-general. He was shocked to see that it was two 22-year olds (who looked more like teenagers) who had caused such a political storm.

Ultimately, my "on-the-lam" new wife was granted "parole" to enter the United States and complete her immigration paperwork. We arrived home in Lexington to a big sign on my parents' house proclaiming: "Welcome Home Refuseniks," the term referring to thousands of Soviet Jews who at the time were being refused freedom to emigrate. While the difficulties we faced pale in comparison, our journey to freedom gave us a small taste of the immigrant experience.

We were able to enjoy our reception and honeymoon; and three years later, I proudly watched Lisa be sworn in as a U.S. citizen. Since then, every time a friend has complained about customs searches or having to take his shoes off at airport security, I have a great story to tell.

MOSES AND THE EXODUS

No Biblical story better illustrates the value of God's gift of freedom than the story of Moses and the Exodus from Egypt, found in the Book of Exodus. From Charlton Heston's portrayal in *The Ten Commandments* to depictions in our children's Sunday School curricula, Moses has become—next only to Jesus—the world's most well-known and beloved Biblical figure.

Moses had been adopted as a baby by an Egyptian princess, and had watched the Hebrews struggle in slavery—forced to work under excruciating circumstances and endure physical cruelty at the hands of their captors. With each incident of abuse, Moses's indignation rose against these injustices.

Moses's sense of injustice culminated when he killed an Egyptian overseer who was beating a Hebrew slave. Still, when God first approached Moses, he was very reluctant to lead the effort to seek freedom for the enslaved Jewish people. In Chapter 3 of the Book of Exodus, God confronted Moses through a "burning bush" and ordered him to appeal to the pharaoh on behalf of the Hebrews. Yet five times,

Moses refused God's mission, afraid that he was not strong enough a leader, speaker, or motivator to accomplish this awesome goal.

Moses finally accepted the mantle of leadership, and, with his brother Aaron's help, approached the pharaoh with the powerful words, "Let my people go!" When the pharaoh did not consent, God punished Egypt with ten plagues, each more horrific than the last. Most of the plagues consisted of environmental calamities: turning the Nile River into a sea of blood; swarms of frogs, lice, and insects; and heavy downpours of hail and locusts. None impressed the callous pharaoh, until the last—the killing of every first-born Egyptian child. (The Hebrews placed lamb's blood on their home's entry to ask God to "pass over" their homes—giving American Jews the English name of the holiday during which they celebrate the Exodus.) With his own first-born son the most prominent victim, the pharaoh submitted, and he granted the Jewish slaves their freedom.

Unfortunately, the pharaoh changed his mind, and sent 600 chariot drivers to chase after the fleeing slaves and press them back into service. As the pursuing troops trapped the Hebrews at the Red Sea (actually "the sea of reeds"), Moses lifted his rod to part the sea, leaving the middle land dry for the Jews to escape. The pharaoh and his troops continued their chase, but once the Israelites made it to the other side, God forced the waters back to their original status, drowning the pharaoh and his army.

Within the Torah's text, God defined the true meaning of freedom. The Bible's most dramatic words, "Let my people go," are followed by another Hebrew word: *ve-ye-av-duni*, "that they may celebrate a festival for Me." Moses's goal was not simply to achieve liberty from physical slavery for the Hebrew people, but also to free them spiritually to follow God and His commandments, so that they could later enter into covenant with God at Mount Sinai. The story of the Exodus shows that freedom is accompanied by responsibilities to ourselves, our community, and our God.[1]

FREEDOM AND SECURITY: THE MOSES-MILL BALANCE

The story of Moses and the Exodus from Egypt has been used for generations to illustrate a value inherent in the compassionate community: freedom.

Even today, Moses's struggle against injustice is embedded into the conscience of every young Jewish child. Every Passover, when we read the story of the Exodus of the Hebrew people from Egypt, we are reminded that our passion for social justice must be fueled by our own experience with slavery. Citing the book of Deuteronomy, the Passover *Haggadah* (prayer book) instructs: "Remember that you were slaves in Egypt."[2] Moses's dramatic words—"Let my people go"—have been used many times by modern freedom fighters: from Martin Luther King, Jr., to advocates for the Soviet refuseniks.

Indeed, there is a strong obligation under both Christian and Jewish law to secure freedom for all men and women. The prophet Isaiah declared that he was sent by God to "free the captives"; while the Talmud's rabbis taught that there was an obligation to do everything in one's power to help release people who are trapped in some way. The religious scholar Karen Armstrong wrote that "The right to liberty is crucial: it is difficult to find a single reference to imprisonment in the whole of rabbinic literature because only God can curtail the freedom of a human being."

Moreover, as with the case with Moses and the Israelites, our tradition teaches us that with freedom comes responsibilities. The New Testament, for example, instructs that "you are called to freedom . . . only do not turn your freedom into an opportunity for the flesh, but through love, serve one another." Indeed, the blessings of freedom demand that we embrace a compassionate community.

Accordingly, since Biblical times, rulers, religious leaders, and political philosophers have struggled with a perplexing dilemma: How much freedom is necessary or indeed desirable? As we have learned, freedom is accompanied by responsibilities: How do we weigh them against each other? More specifically, with the prospects of war with other nations always on the minds of government leaders, how does the state balance the competing values of individual liberty and collective security?

The Chinese were among the earliest to enter this debate. The third-century B.C. Confucian scholar Hsun Tzu argued that all human nature is evil, and that goodness is only acquired through moral instruction. He therefore concluded that the state must emphasize rules and public obedience to them.

By contrast, Mencius—second only to Confucius in Chinese tradition—suggested that human nature was fundamentally good. Mencius contended that rulers should appeal to the people's best instincts by creating a just society, with broad liberties. Indeed, Mencius argued that since government derives its power from the consent of the governed, the people had a natural right to overthrow an unjust ruler who had denied them essential freedoms.

Thomas Hobbes famously entered the debate in the seventeenth century. While Hobbes argued that human nature was amoral, his conclusions were similar to those of Hsun Tzu. Hobbes believed that life was "solitary, poor, brutish, and short," and that every individual had the right of self-preservation in the state of nature. To preserve your life and prevent others from hurting you, humans created a contract with their neighbors, and it was the state's responsibility to enforce the contract. Hobbes called his ideal form of government the Leviathan, a ruler or assembly that imposes its will on the people. Provoking fear of punishment, the Leviathan places security as the paramount value, above any individual liberties.

Thomas Jefferson took the opposite path. In drafting the Declaration of Independence, Jefferson wrote that God endowed every human with "unalienable" rights, which included that of liberty. Echoing Mencius, Jefferson wrote that the state's role is to secure those rights, and when it fails to do that—as had the autocratic King George III of England—"it is the right of the people to alter or abolish it, and to institute new government." In his Gettysburg Address, Abraham Lincoln argued that the Civil War tested Jefferson's thesis, and through "a new birth of freedom" provided by a Union victory (and without mentioning, an end to slavery), the United States could fully realize Jefferson's dream.

Around Lincoln's time, the British philosopher John Stuart Mill also addressed Jefferson's vision. Mill recognized the natural conflict between liberty and authority, and expressed concern about tyranny of the majority in a democracy. He argued that it was essential for individuals to have full exercise of their rights to speak, assemble, dissent, and publish. Mill suggested that the only time that limits could be placed on these freedoms was when their exercise posed a risk of harm to others. Mill recognized what Moses and the Israelites learned: that with freedom comes responsibility. Government, therefore, must always carefully balance liberty and security.

While Mill's viewpoint continues to resonate in our democracy, the debate over maintaining the appropriate balance between liberty and security remains contentious. For example, we can see these arguments resonating in today's gun-control debate. Advocates of gun control suggest that security is the paramount value; even if we save only a few lives by restricting gun sales, it is worth the cost to individual liberty. Gun-control opponents counter that the freedom to bear arms, codified in the Second Amendment of the Bill of Rights, is the most consequential value. Indeed, they argue that gun ownership provides *additional* security, particularly in rural areas where law enforcement cannot respond quickly enough in emergency situations to threats of violence.

Common ground can be found by using the "Moses-Mill" balance between freedom and responsibility. Policymakers should only restrict the rights of gun owners when to do so would save lives. This balance would permit strong restrictions and stiff criminal penalties for gun use by criminals and small children. The balance would allow sportsmen and women and rural homeowners who fear for their safety to continue to enjoy the freedom to bear arms.

The production and promotion of personalized guns, or "smart guns," is one area where compromise can be found. Through combination locks or fingerprint recognition devices, smart guns prevent anyone but the gun's rightful owner from using them. As Stephen Teret of the Johns Hopkins Center for Gun Policy and Research argues, "Personalized handguns would be inoperable by the curious young child, the depressed teenager and the criminal who steals the gun from a home or disarms a law enforcement officer."[3] Further, smart guns do nothing to restrict a gun owner's freedom.

A different battleground over the liberty/security balance involves the issue of public smoking. With science demonstrating clear links between secondhand smoke and cancer, a growing debate has emerged between smokers and non-smokers concerning the right to light up in public places. To smokers, it is a personal liberty issue; to non-smokers is it about health security—the right to live and breathe clean air, protected from the carcinogens in secondhand smoke.

Here the Moses-Mill balance weighs clearly on the side of security. With the harm of secondhand smoke unambiguous, an individual's liberty to smoke must be made secondary to his neighbor's demand for health security when they are in public. That's why cities should take active steps to promote non-smoking initiatives in public areas—including restaurants and office buildings. In order to ensure some personal liberty, smoking can never be fully prohibited—and cities should consider reasonable allowances, such as permitting smoking in designated bars and clubs restricted to adults who choose to be around smokers. The fact that my hometown of Lexington, Kentucky—in the heart of the tobacco belt—boasts a strong public-smoking ban, indicates that the nation is moving in the proper direction, balancing security over liberty in this instance.

But the debate between liberty and security in the United States has never been as fully joined as it was beginning on September 11, 2001. The terrorist-initiated murders of more than 3,000 American citizens on our own soil redefined the average American's opinion of the meaning of security. The intensification of international terrorism, particularly the variety sponsored by radical Islamic fundamentalists, compelled all of us to reassess the freedom/security balance.

Clearly, in the weeks that followed 9–11, most Americans were willing to surrender some liberties to ensure a safer and more secure homeland. But finding a balance was very difficult. During times of crisis like this, even some of our greatest presidents had overreached—such as Lincoln, by suspending the writ of habeus corpus (a judicial mandate ordering a prisoner to court) during the Civil War; and Franklin D. Roosevelt, by despicably interning tens of thousands of Japanese Americans in concentration camps during World War II.

The solution offered by the Bush administration, with near-unanimous Congressional approval, was called the PATRIOT Act. In many ways, Congress made an appropriate balance between liberty and security. Improving communication among government intelligence agencies (which failed miserably on 9–11) and relaxing restrictions on the prosecution of terrorist front groups and foreign nationals who were suspected of terrorism did not violate Mill's suggestion to only restrict liberties when there was a likelihood of harm to others.

But where the PATRIOT Act failed was in its excessive delegation of authority to intelligence agencies, allowing them to engage in surveillance activities without appropriate supervision. The drafters of the Constitution and the Bill of Rights held the freedoms of speech and assembly to be sacrosanct. Within the system of balanced government they created, these freedoms should only be subjugated when an impartial third-party—the judiciary—determines that a particular exercise of government authority is necessary. And yet, in some cases, the PATRIOT Act authorized surveillance of American citizens and businesses with the approval of only a secret military court, and sometimes with no judicial review at all. The PATRIOT Act only required the FBI to seek approval of a secret foreign intelligence court to search *any* kind of business record and seize *any* "tangible thing"— an extraordinarily broad delegation of power. And another provision of the law permitted the use of administrative subpoenas or "national security letters" to demand certain records *without any court oversight at all*.[4]

The issue exploded onto the front pages in late 2005 when it was revealed that President Bush had authorized intelligence agencies to wiretap international phone calls made by American citizens without obtaining any court approval, allegedly in violation of federal law. When, at the same time, it was revealed that the FBI was separately investigating and monitoring liberal activist groups such as Greenpeace and People for the Ethical Treatment of Animals (PETA) for suspected terrorist activities, comparisons to Richard Nixon's Administration spying on its perceived political enemies in the Watergate scandal were common.[5]

Quite simply, weighing the balance between liberty and security is always very difficult in a democratic system. It is essential to retain the careful system of checks and balances that our Framers conceived in the Constitution. The executive should not be in a position to judge the limits of its authority; it is the judiciary's role to determine when that authority inappropriately encroaches on the fundamental freedoms guaranteed by the Bill of Rights. While no solution can find the "perfect" balance, requiring judicial intervention, oversight, and supervision provide the necessary objectivity to guarantee an optimal evaluation of the factors in the Moses-Mill test.

MILITARY FAMILIES' BILL OF RIGHTS

While the PATRIOT Act, gun control, and smoking are very important to highlight in any discussion of freedom, I want to focus on a topic we often overlook, even though it is an area of public policy in which the balance between freedom and security is not difficult to assess. Indeed, when it comes to supporting the men and women of our armed forces, we are able to enhance both our liberty and our security. Our military men and women risk their lives every day to provide both the security and the freedoms that we Americans take for granted.

I grew up at a time in the country when our armed forces were not treated with the respect they deserved. Some Vietnam War opponents unfairly and shamefully blamed the young men returning from combat for the military decisions made by politicians in Washington, and many Vietnam veterans were subjected to name-calling and sometimes physical abuse.

During the Iraq War, the dynamic has changed. While the nation is divided about the wisdom and necessity of war, nearly every American honors the young men and women who volunteer to put their lives on the line. This new mindset better reflects the traditional view of our military: Throughout history, the men and women who served in battle and protected the home front earned a special level of honor and respect from those whom they protected. The compassionate community is defined by their heroic sacrifices—placing the interests of the community above even their own lives. As the Gospel of John informs us: "greater love has no one than this: that one lay down his life for his friends."

In today's politics of self-interest, however, too often these brave service men and women are not paid what they deserve. Considering the risks they take every day for their country, our citizens in the military are woefully under-compensated. With average salaries around $35,000 a year, our soldiers fall in the bottom quartile of American wage-earners. According to a 2004 report from the General Accounting Office, 16,000 active-duty service men and women filed for bankruptcy over a 12-month period.[6]

September 11 and its aftermath exacerbated this financial problem exponentially. Fighting wars on two fronts, an increasing number of individuals have been called overseas, separating families for long stretches of time, placing extraordinary burdens on their finances. The Pentagon reported what would seem obvious—that nearly one-third of all military families reported a drop in income when a spouse is deployed overseas.[7]

Further, as the traditional full-time armed forces have been stretched thin, a new issue has emerged. The U.S. military has been forced to call up National Guard soldiers and Reservists into service in a way that we have not witnessed since the Korean War. As of 2006, nearly half of all U.S. troops in Iraq and Afghanistan are members of the National Guard or Reserves. (Although the National Guard is a part of this nation's reserve forces, there are a few differences between the Army or Air Force Reserve and the Guard. Most significantly, the Guard has a unique "dual status," serving both the state and federal government.)

Unlike active troops, these men and women have civilian lives and jobs to manage, and many had not expected to ever be called into combat. The reliance on National Guard and Reserve units to serve overseas has caused many of these men and women to lose their jobs, businesses, even their homes. Others have had to put business plans on hold, sell cars, cancel home purchases or suspend their education. Up to 40 percent of Guard and Reserve personnel make less money when they are sent overseas than when they are at their civilian jobs. Many of these Guard members and Reservists are also small-business owners, and they tend to suffer tremendous setbacks as their companies lose revenue or even simply struggle to survive without active involvement.[8] As these men and women help to ensure our freedoms, they are losing many themselves.

Problems like these affect not just the service men and women themselves; their whole family unit is imperiled. The expression "military families" is not new, but it is now quite common. For many decades, there was a popular joke that "if the Army wanted you to have a wife, they would have issued you one." Today, however, the proportion of married soldiers is higher than during any previous war and a significant number are parents.[9]

Unfortunately, our troops are feeling frustrated over the lack of public support for their families. Men and women in uniform are asking why the nation they serve is so unwilling to sacrifice for their benefit. There is no draft, no tax hike, no savings bond drives, and no gas rationing as we have seen in previous wars. The *New York Times* featured a military officer arguing that "no one in America is asked to sacrifice, except us."[10] Symbolic gestures—such as flying the flag, wearing a commemorative bracelet or displaying a ribbon on a car—are simply not enough, and they rarely are witnessed by our troops overseas. As the Exodus story instructs, to guarantee our essential freedoms, we all must take responsibility, and not simply lean on the young men and women of our military.

In most every conflict, there will be a political debate as to whether a war is necessary to protect American freedom and security. The value of American efforts in Iraq toward meeting these goals is certainly debatable. As more evidence comes to light, the alleged connections between U.S. policy in Iraq and the international terrorism embodied by the 9–11 attacks appear quite tenuous indeed. But wherever our armed forces are deployed by our political leadership—rightly or wrongly— they play a vital role in ensuring the values that we all take for granted. Our American military is the symbol of our central desire for security and freedom. We must support our military men and women to guarantee freedom for all Americans.

It is essential therefore that we increase efforts to provide for our armed forces and their families back home, who, in peace and in war, guarantee our freedom and our security, but who often struggle just to make ends meet. I suggest that we develop a Military Families' Bill of Rights. Here, the compassionate community would develop an inviolable contract with the men and women of the armed forces and the families they leave behind when they go overseas to serve their country. It is only fair that we step in to provide financial security for the families of those who are ensuring our nation's security. It is only right that we guarantee a new set of liberties for these individuals who are securing our freedom. The Military Families' Bill of Rights would include the following ten provisions:

1. Every military family shall be provided a safety net to protect them from a life of poverty.

Today, thousands of military families are living in poverty. This is our modern-day "burning bush": our sacred call to rectify injustice. We cannot claim to support our troops overseas if we are abandoning them at home. Our country's great freedoms cannot be enjoyed by those who are struggling just to put food on the table.

Where the federal government is unable to provide the necessary financial support, states must step in to provide financial resources to those military families most at economic risk. One model was recently introduced by Governor Bill Richardson of New Mexico, who has proposed the creation of a voluntary fund into which residents can contribute some of their tax refunds to help military families. It would also make half of military retirement benefits exempt from state taxation. New Mexico is following the lead of several states that have proposed similar benefits. Illinois Lieutenant Governor Pat Quinn helped establish a program whereby individuals and corporations could donate all or a portion of their state and city tax refunds to a Military Family Assistance Fund. So far, Illinois has collected almost $6 million and distributed about $3 million in claims. A state commission reviews claims on a needs basis, helping families pay rent, car notes or other critical obligations. Similarly, North Carolina has proposed to use a portion of gas taxes collected on military bases to support programs that provide a safety net to military families.[11] These types of financial benefits will go a long way to ensure that military families are able to survive in today's economy, particularly when the household's bread-winner may be thousands of miles overseas.

2. A military spouse shall be able to take reasonable leave when his or her spouse has been deployed, and shall be freed from administrative red tape to earn a living.

There are many military spouses who are eager to earn a living for their families, but are struggling to meet state and local administrative burdens to secure their livelihood. Spouses are often transferred to a new base in a new state and must apply for a new set of professional licenses to work or build a business in the new location. This can be extraordinarily burdensome, and acquiring a new professional license can be quite time-consuming. Factors like this contribute to the trend in which military spouses are three times more likely to be unemployed than civilians.[12]

State policymakers should follow the lead of former Virginia Governor Mark Warner who launched an initiative that provides for expedited consideration before professional licensing boards to all spouses of active military members serving overseas. Cutting through the red tape to ensure that these military spouses can earn a sufficient living is a small but significant step states can take.

Military families who are relocated or face deployment overseas also confront another set of burdens caused by the transition. Often times a family has to scramble to make moving arrangements, deal with childcare, and pay bills. Major adjustments need to be made in a very short period of time. While single parents in the National Guard are expected to file contingency plans, with details on how to take care of their children should they be deployed, many of them have found that their plans were not easily implemented. Some spouses have been fired from their jobs because of the demands placed on them during this time of transition.

Congressman Tom Udall of New Mexico has proposed one solution to remedy these problems: He would allow spouses to use the Family and Medical Leave Act to take 12 weeks of leave from their jobs to deal with issues directly related to the deployment. On the state level, Illinois recently enacted legislation to require businesses to provide employees who are parents or spouses of deploying service members 15–30 leave days, if those employees have already exhausted all of their annual and compensatory leave time.[13] By better preparing service members and their families for deployment overseas, we can ensure that families are prepared for the psychological and financial burden they bear for the good of our nation.

3. The right of every National Guard member or Reservist called into active duty to receive supplemental income shall be encouraged through tax incentives to private employers who provide supplemental pay and state tax deductions for their service.

Federal law protects a National Guard soldier's civilian job when he or she is deployed; these servicemen and women cannot be fired from their private sector job or permanently replaced by a new employee. However, there is no such job security protection under federal law for small businesspeople and the self-employed. Further, even those who do not lose their jobs can lose significant pay and benefits from their employer, leaving their families struggling to make ends meet.[14]

Some private employers provide supplemental benefits to their employees deployed overseas. These patriots should be rewarded, and more employers should be encouraged to join in their efforts. U.S. Senator Evan Bayh has proposed federal legislation to provide tax credits to employers that provide supplemental pay for active-duty troops.[15] State legislatures should do the same. Further, when funding is available, states should explore making direct payments to Reservists and Guardsmen who are self-employed or work for companies who are not as generous. Further, states should provide tax deductions to service

members for active duty, full-time Guard duty, when calculating the
state's taxable income.

4. Adequate and appropriate death benefits shall be provided for all veterans.

We must also prepare military families for the contingency that a parent might make the ultimate sacrifice for our freedom. The federal
government currently provides limited financial benefits to the survivors of service men and women killed in the line of duty. Today, the
surviving spouse of a service man or woman receives a lump-sum
"death gratuity" of $100,000, plus life insurance of as much as
$450,000. But these amounts cannot possibly compensate a family for
the loss of a loved one, who usually is the household's principal bread-
winner. Worse, Reservists and National Guard members are not always
eligible for these full-death benefits. In prior conflicts, many of these
citizen soldiers served mainly as "rear area" support, far from the front-
line fighting. In Iraq, however, there are no front or back lines—all soldiers are vulnerable to attack. By late 2005, Reservists and National
Guard troops comprised more than half of all deaths.[16]

Accordingly, we should do more—much more. States should follow
the lead of New Mexico, which has proposed providing an additional
$400,000 life-insurance policy for every National Guard member on
active duty. Those who serve their country merit the respect of the
compassionate community. Those who are prepared to die to secure
our nation's liberties in peacetime and in war should be assured that the
community will support their families upon their death.

5. No military family shall be subjected to predatory financial practices.

The compassionate community also must protect our military families
from predatory financial practices—the ten plagues of modern times.
While predatory business scams affect Americans in all walks of life, in a
disturbing and growing trend, military personnel have emerged as a frequent target of these abusive schemes. Like college students, who have
been targeted by credit-card companies, many new service men and

women are recent high-school graduates, just released from the shelter of home. Most are financially unsophisticated; many have never used a credit card, never had a bank account, never invested money, and never managed finances. Further, as the U.S. House Judiciary Committee discovered, service men and women are easy targets for predatory companies: "They go after military members because they know that they: have a steady source of income, are young, have family obligations, are often strapped for cash, and are easy to find. Most offensive [they] target military members because they know these are people who are hard-working and honest and believe in personal responsibility and integrity."[17]

Some predatory companies hold "investment seminars," to lure service members off base—where they are otherwise protected by strong Department of Defense solicitation policies. In the guise of lucrative investment vehicles, service men and women and their families are offered savings plans with an insurance component that has a combat-exclusion clause—making it virtually worthless for an active-duty service member. As one local radio talk show host commented, these insurance scam artists "deserve a special place in Hell."[18]

Shamefully, these companies often use retired senior enlisted personnel to serve as salesmen to the active military. With troops trained to obey their superiors, military men and women do not realize that the costs of products are not readily apparent. Recent Congressional legislation purportedly designed to protect military families does little to crack down on these excesses; the insurance industry is called on to investigate this problem and share its findings with the Defense Department, but there is no federal funding provided and no corrective action mandated.[19]

Service men and women are also the victims of simple financial crimes. Senior Fort Knox officials tell me that identity theft is a growing problem on their bases, as the Social Security numbers and other pertinent information about service members are too easily available to the public, more than civilian citizens. Further, a growing crime at Fort Knox is the theft of debit cards, which leads to the loss of substantial amounts of personal savings. (Some of these financially unsophisticated young people will write their passwords on the back of their debit cards, making theft of their funds even easier.)

It is essential that policymakers act to protect these service members. On the federal level, the new bankruptcy "reform" laws (which hurt all lower-income Americans, as I highlighted in chapter three) need to be changed to prohibit payday creditors who charge exorbitant interest rates from recovering the assignment of military benefits and disability payments in bankruptcy court. Further, disabled veterans should have further protections under the bankruptcy laws if their indebtedness occurred while on active duty or after they came home with a disabling injury.[20] States also should act by forcing payday lenders to lower their interest rates, credit-card companies to comply with strict solicitation regulations (like those on college campuses that I proposed in chapter three), and banks to place video cameras in their automatic teller machines (ATMs), at least within a few miles of a military installation, to protect service members from debit card theft.

6. Every military family shall be provided free, comprehensive financial education.

Perhaps even more important than the passage of new laws and regulations is providing financial education to our troops and their families. Often times, the best weapon against unfair financial practices is an educated consumer who can distinguish between scams and good investment opportunities. Unfortunately, financial illiteracy among military families is a disturbing and growing trend.

It is essential for states and localities to work with partners in the private non-profit sector and the business community to provide free financial seminars for the military and their families. We must ensure that these military men and women are aware of the wide range of benefits and programs that are available to them specifically and to the population at large.

With this in mind, my office has launched a comprehensive program to provide financial education to military families stationed or living in Kentucky. Working with military officials at Fort Knox, Fort Campbell, the National Guard, and the Reserves, we are developing a series of programs to promote financial literacy: from financial curricula in the classroom, to seminars and handy guides to warn families about predatory financial behavior. At the heart of this initiative is a statewide partnership with chambers of commerce and civic organizations to match up financially struggling military families with volunteer money mentors from the business community. After these money mentors receive training from financial and military benefit experts, they can provide a few hours a month of invaluable advice and guidance to their "adopted" military families. I hope that this program can serve as a model for programs like it across the country and on military bases overseas.

We are also incorporating the "money and marriage" materials that I described in chapter three. With economic and emotional pressures reaching their boiling point for many military families, the divorce rate has skyrocketed.[21] Again, while financial planning is not a panacea for modern-day marriages, equipping these couples with sound financial education from the beginning of a relationship can help them avoid many of the common pitfalls.

A list of financial resources and military-specific benefits available to military families—as well as a list of common scams perpetuated against military families—can be found in appendix 3. A more comprehensive and updated listing of resources, as well as online discussion and support groups for military families, are available at my Web site.

7. All military families shall have access to counseling and emotional support when a family member is deployed, activated, killed, or disabled in action.

Of course, the overseas deployment of a parent poses more than a financial burden—there is a considerable emotional toll, particularly for children. The military has always demonstrated concern for the well-being of these children, but the unanticipated growth of military families—both from the recent Middle East conflicts and from the growing number of service men and women having families—has left many spouses and children of active troops without adequate emotional support. The military maintains a network of support groups called "family readiness groups" to help spouses and children adjust to the new circumstances. But in some cases, these groups have not been adequately prepared for the current conflict. This is particularly true with the National Guard and Reservist organizations because no one expected a mobilization of the size and duration of the Iraq war.[22]

Family problems are not solved once a soldier returns from his or her deployment overseas. Tens of thousands of soldiers who have served in Iraq or Afghanistan are expected to suffer from post-traumatic stress disorder, with more than ten percent experiencing a substantial interference with their lives, according to a recent report by the *New England Journal of Medicine*.[23] Having a parent suffer from this crippling mental disease can have a devastating impact on all members of a family.

A few national programs have been developed or expanded recently to help provide the children of service people with emotional counseling. The Tragedy Assistance Program for Survivors (TAPS) provides peer-to-peer counseling for children, while Sons and Daughters in Touch has begun inviting the children of Iraq War casualties to its Fathers' Day memorials. On the state level, some programs are going further. Through its "Operation: Military Kids," the Army is providing funding to 11 states to buy portable computer labs so that children can communicate with their parents through e-mail and video conferencing. In Ohio, a 4-H summer camp for the children of deployed Reservists has been established to provide both distractions from family stress and needed emotional counseling. In Iowa, military families have formed a speakers' bureau where children can share problems and tips for coping.[24]

It is incumbent on every state to develop programs to nurture, protect, and counsel our military children. Whether it is merely a temporary disruption in the family caused by deployment, or it is a permanent void caused by a parent's death, these emotional tolls are significant. States should partner with the private sector to ensure that every military child and spouse has adequate emotional support during these trying times.

Indeed, the mental health and social services community should take an active role in reaching and treating these military families. Since "support for our troops" is a common rallying cry for most Americans, professionals in the mental health field should find ways to volunteer their time and energies to help the spouses and children of our troops. Public leaders should help develop partnerships among local hospitals and the philanthropic community to provide private funding for such initiatives.

8. Veterans and members of the Guard and Reserves shall receive adequate and affordable health care for their entire lives.

While this chapter has focused how we should repay the families of the active military men and women who provide our freedoms, the plight of our nation's veterans must also be addressed. Anyone who has fought to guarantee our liberties should have the same opportunities to enjoy a good quality of living.

On a more practical level, it is essential that we demonstrate tangible support for our veterans in order to help recruit new men and women to join the military. As George Washington famously remarked, "the willingness with which our young people are likely to serve in any war, no matter how justified, shall be directly proportional as to how they perceive the veterans of earlier wars were treated and appreciated by their country." Currently, we do not treat or appreciate our veterans in a manner they deserve.

As the veteran population ages, the primary concern for these men and women is health care. And while combat veterans are supposed to be provided with free health care services by the Veterans' Administration, federal spending cutbacks in recent years have been devastating to the veterans' health-care system. Indeed, the recently revealed $1 billion shortfall in the Veterans' Affairs health-care budget demonstrates that renewed support is urgently needed. Lack of funding leads to insufficient medical staffing, fewer available specialists, outdated equipment, inappropriate denials of medical care, unfair rejections of benefit applications, and long waiting lines, during which some veterans actually die due to a lack of prompt attention.[25]

Substandard health care for our veterans is inexcusable—they should have the highest quality of care available at affordable prices. And while health care for veterans is largely a federal issue, states should involve themselves to ensure that health-care services are delivered in the most fair and efficient manner. For example, many states pay for field representatives to assist veterans part the Red Sea that is posed by the Veterans Administration bureaucracy. With more qualified and knowledgeable professionals out in the field advising veterans through the benefits' claims and appeals process, more of these men and women will receive the health care they need and deserve. These modern-day Moseses who have risked their lives to preserve the freedoms of their country should not be abandoned when their own health is at risk.

States should explore allowing their National Guard troops to buy into their public employee health-care systems that provide discounted coverage. As reported by *The Washington Monthly*, 20 percent of Guardsmen lack health-care coverage when their tours of duty end.[26]

These young men and women face the same dangers as full-time soldiers; they deserve this health-care coverage. Further, with military enlistment and reenlistment rates plummeting, awarding such health-care benefits to prospective National Guardsmen could encourage more recruits to sign up for duty, helping the country avoid the national security risk of inadequately staffed armed forces, as feared by George Washington.

9. Job preferences for veterans shall be provided by the state and encouraged through tax incentives to private employers, and veterans shall be protected from penalties due to time spent in service.

It is not uncommon to see a sign on a store in Kentucky, or anywhere in the South, that says "Hiring Preferences for Veterans." Indeed, many private employers proudly hire veterans whenever possible, whether as an act of patriotism, or a simple realization that men and women trained in the armed forces make good employees.

Some federal and state laws provide for veterans' preferences. For example, it is illegal to fire someone who leaves his job temporarily to serve in the armed forces—the job must be held open for his or her return from active service.[27] Further, many states build in a veterans' preference into their state's civil-service hiring systems.

Sometimes, however, these initiatives are not implemented or enforced. Too often, private employers are unaware of their legal responsibility to leave positions open, and many of these veterans are unaware of their legal rights. Many of the veterans who are allowed to return to their jobs lose the seniority they would have gained, and when layoffs occur, they lose their jobs to co-workers who did not serve in the armed forces.

On the federal level, we must ensure that the veterans' hiring and firing laws—those that guarantee that a soldier returning from war does not lose his private sector job—are strictly enforced. Education is also necessary to enable every veteran to know his or her employment rights. Further, these laws should be expanded to prohibit any discrimination in layoffs due to active military service.

States should use tax incentives to reward those employers who use veterans' preferences in their hiring decisions and encourage other employers to join their ranks. Similarly, states should provide clear procedures that give government civil-service hiring preferences to the veterans who live within their borders. Our veterans deserve an extra opportunity to pursue their happiness, simply due to their earlier willingness to risk their lives so that we all can have the freedoms to pursue our own dreams.

10. Military families shall receive access to affordable higher education and occupational training, and shall receive help in identifying and obtaining other benefits that are available to them.

A consistent theme of the compassionate community is that education is the great guarantor of opportunity, empowering millions of Americans to better their lives and the lives of their families. A critical element of the Military Families' Bill of Rights is to ensure that veterans and their families receive affordable access to higher education.

The G.I. bill, enacted in the wake of World War II, has rewarded generations of our veterans for their service by providing them with affordable higher education. The federal government and states have expanded that higher education access to the children of those disabled veterans who have a 100 percent disability.

But that still leaves millions of other spouses and children of our veterans without similar access. One obvious recommendation: to provide the same free education to the children of all disabled veterans who have been determined "unemployable"—a much larger group that the 100-percent disabled, but still deserving and needy of the hand-up provided by higher education.

Further, states should provide educational assistance scholarships and tax credits for military spouses to gain access to higher education. With their spouses away fighting for our security, these men and women should be given a better chance to afford higher education in order to support themselves and their children with good-paying jobs, which require higher education. For example, North Carolina has proposed a program to provide greater access for members of the military and their families to attend community college training programs at in-state rates.[28]

"LET OUR PEOPLE GO"

With apologies to Kris Kristofferson, freedom is *not* just another word for nothing left to lose. It is an essential value of the compassionate community. Over history, millions of men and women have died in its pursuit.

As the story of Moses teaches us, great freedoms carry tremendous responsibilities. That's why it is essential that we provide for the families of those who are protecting the freedoms we take for granted. They are the living embodiment of the central moral principle to "love your neighbor as yourself." We should reciprocate their compassion by ensuring that their families have the financial security they need and deserve.

Similarly, we must guarantee that the freedoms to all Americans provided by the Bill of Rights are treated with due respect. We may have a hard time articulating the proper balance between liberty and security. But like Moses, we must ask probing questions until we are satisfied that we are doing everything in our power to ensure that the essential, sacred liberties of our American democracy are secure.

We must always be cognizant, particularly during periods of crisis and insecurity, that our people are not entirely free unless they are provided the full protections of our Constitution and its Bill of Rights. Sometimes we need to challenge our government to "let our people go"; to provide every American citizen with the full protections of the First Amendment by placing reasonable supervision on executive authority. Whether it is the PATRIOT Act, or other laws that focus on American security, we must encourage all citizens to build a nation that values freedom and those men and women who secure it for the rest of us.

SIX

JOSHUA AND THE VALUE OF FAITH

"My servant Moses is dead. Prepare to cross the Jordan, together with all these people, into the land that I am giving to the Israelites. . . . No one shall be able to resist you as long as you live. As I was with Moses, so I will be with you; I will not fail you or forsake you. . . . I charge you: be strong and resolute; do not be terrified or dismayed, for the Lord your God is with you wherever you go."

—Joshua 1:2–9

I was born in 1967 into a Jewish family in the predominantly Christian city of Lexington, Kentucky. My family first entered the United States at the port of Philadelphia in the early nineteenth century, moving soon with a wave of German Jewish immigrants to Cincinnati, Ohio. My great-great grandfather Jacob Miller was a leader in that community, and as treasurer of the Plum Street Temple, he issued the formal invitation for the renowned Rabbi Isaac Mayer Wise to preach there, establishing the congregation as one of the premier Jewish synagogues in the country and as the foundation of Reform Judaism in America. But seeking greater opportunity for their growing family clothing business, in the early 1870s, Jacob's sons moved 90 miles south to Lexington, Kentucky, to set up shop and help establish the first Jewish congregation in their new hometown.

The slight change in geography represented an enormous cultural leap. Soon after the family store opened, it was vandalized because my family offered free toys to lower-income African American children on Christmas day. Even into my own childhood a century later, our faith presented many tangible barriers—social clubs my family could not join, classmates' parties to which I was not invited, civic organizations that excluded my parents. A subtle, but very serious anti-Semitism pervaded everyday life in Lexington in the 1970s.

In spite of the prejudice I faced as a child—or perhaps because of it—I always had a strong religious identity. With constant social reminders that we were "different," my family encouraged me to embrace my heritage. Perhaps more importantly, my parents reminded me that we faced few societal barriers in comparison to other minority groups.

My parents were Reform Jews—a denomination initially embraced by American Jews eager to assimilate in the Christian culture, but more recently redefined to emphasize spirituality and social justice over ritual practice. Even with our strong family roots in the Reform Jewish community, however, synagogue politics at the time led me to study for my Bar Mitzvah service under the training of an Orthodox rabbi.

But not just any rabbi. Bernard Schwab, a diabetic who had lost his eyesight as a result of his condition, dedicated his life to training the Jewish youth of his community. For months, we pored over the Biblical texts; I would read a Hebrew word or two to jog his near photographic memory of the Torah. Ultimately, I led a four-hour Saturday morning Sabbath service, for the most part in Hebrew, before a packed and largely Christian assembly of my family, classmates, and parents' friends. Most of all, Rabbi Schwab imbued in me a strong pride in my faith. While physical and professional challenges often lead people to question and abandon their faith, Rabbi Schwab knew that the obstacles tested his resolve and made him redouble his efforts to internalize God's teachings. This was a powerful lesson that carries with me today.

For a brief time, I considered becoming a rabbi myself. After serving as national president of the Reform Jewish youth movement, I found a role model in Rabbi David Saperstein, who led the Religious Action Center of Reform Judaism. Rabbi Saperstein helped clarify for me the links between religious principles and social action, and taught me that we could serve God by shaping public policy as much as by preaching from a pulpit. I wanted to be the next David Saperstein—succeed to his position in the Reform movement and travel the country and seek social justice. However, this young rabbi was one of a kind, and I did the math: Rabbi Saperstein was in his 30s, filled with incalculable energy, and by the time he retired and would need a successor, I would be in my 70s. So it was politics for me.

In January 2000, I was sworn in as Kentucky's first Jewish statewide elected official. While it would be ridiculous to compare myself to John Kennedy, Jackie Robinson, or even Joe Lieberman, I took small comfort in the notion that my election, in a small way, signaled a social evolution beyond the anti-Semitism I had experienced as a child.

I give partial credit to Jerry Seinfeld and Jon Stewart for my electoral success. Seriously. Twenty years earlier, it would not have been possible for a Jewish candidate to aspire to statewide office in Kentucky. Voters want public officials who share their values, and for most of the state, Jews remained very unfamiliar. However, popular shows like *Seinfeld*, *Friends*, and *The Daily Show* brought Jewish comedians, actors, and characters into the living rooms of middle America. Rural citizens who had never met a Jewish person before now understood that "they were just like us"—maybe just a little wackier.

My reelection in 2003 to a second term as state treasurer coincided with the election of our state's first Republican governor elected since the year I was born. The outgoing governor had admitted to lying about a sexual affair shortly after similar circumstances led to the impeachment of President Bill Clinton, and he left office with unprecedented public disapproval ratings.[1] Congressman Ernie Fletcher campaigned on the simple message of "cleaning up the mess in Frankfort," and a populace fed up with corrupt politics elected the optimistic doctor, fighter pilot, and lay minister by a wide margin.

The Fletcher administration set a clear tone early-on—in fact, during the prayer service that opened his inaugural celebration. The governor's brother delivered the event's main sermon, comparing the new governor with the Biblical hero Nehemiah. He argued that, like Nehemiah, Governor Fletcher would take on the forces of corruption and immorality, the ridiculing media critics, and the entrenched political powers in his noble mission to restore his people and his land to greatness.

The new governor surrounded himself with aides who shared his brother's vision and sense of moral certainty. In order to cleanse the state capital of its corruption, the governor's office handpicked a dozen personnel representatives from across state government to hasten the hiring of Republican supporters, and, like the devoted followers of Jesus chosen to spread His Word, they called themselves the "Disciples." The Biblical reference was no accident; some of the chosen ones compared their mission to their historical namesakes. "As 'change agents' and 'Missionaries' of the Governor, our tasks will not always be embraced by those around us," wrote one personnel official in an e-mail message to the hiring group that was later released publicly. It continued: "No one on earth faced more adversity than the Apostles—we should not think we are any different."[2] That their tactics may violate state civil service hiring laws did not deter the Disciples; that's why Fletcher and many of his aides were indicted by a Frankfort grand jury. Acknowledging that "mistakes were made," but declining to take responsibility for the actions of his administration (he instead blamed the indictments on "politics"), Fletcher issued a blanket pardon for all of his aides, even those not named in the indictment, sparking a political storm. With his own popularity ratings among the lowest of all chief executives in the nation, Fletcher used his State of the Commonwealth Address to propose that "intelligent design" be taught in public school classes, in an apparent effort to restore support from his conservative political base.

I know the governor, his brother, and some of his closest aides to be sincere men of faith. But too often today, Americans involved in the political sphere fall to an affliction that leads them to equate partisan battles with God's crusade against evil, or to use religious wedge issues as a way to polarize the electorate and garner political support. Far too often, this results in the self-important suggestion that the GOP is the only party amenable to serious faith and morality. Unfortunately, this lesson appears to be reinforced in many conservative congregations today. Many of my friends have expressed great frustration with the sometimes overt suggestion of fellow congregants that they cannot be both a Christian and a Democrat. A recent survey revealed that 11 percent of churchgoers were urged by their clergy to vote a particular way in the 2004 election, up from 6 percent in 2000. In one instance that drew significant media attention, a North Carolina Baptist minister went so far as to tell his congregants that anyone who voted for Democratic presidential nominee John Kerry needed to "repent or resign."[3]

This divisive message manifested itself on the national scene in April 2005, with "Justice Sunday," a gathering in Louisville, Kentucky, of some of the nation's most conservative political and religious leaders, including presidential aspirant and U.S. Senate Majority Leader Bill Frist of Tennessee. Protesting the threatened use of the filibuster by Senate Democrats to block some of President Bush's ideologically-outspoken judicial appointments, the leaders of "Justice Sunday" charged Democrats as "being against people of faith."[4]

I was honored to be asked to speak that day at a counter-event with national religious leaders, including the author and minister Jim Wallis. Because it was held during the first day of Passover, no national Jewish religious leaders could fly in. Since I was able to drive home that night to be with my family for the traditional Passover seder meal, I was enlisted.

My brief talk—like those of the other speakers—was intended to demonstrate that faith is not the monopoly of one party or one organization. Using the story of Hillel that opens this book, I reminded the audience that whatever faith we profess, we should be unified by the central moral instruction to love our neighbors. Claiming that others who disagree with your political opinion lack faith certainly does not reflect the "Golden Rule." I concluded: "Our American history and our religious traditions remind us that compassion for others is the central God-given value. All the rest is commentary, Senator Frist. Now go and learn it."

How is it possible for faith to be a positive force for social change in our diverse, multi-denominational democracy? Perhaps the Bible can offer some clues.

JOSHUA AND THE BATTLE OF JERICHO

As the book of Deuteronomy concludes, Moses died and left Joshua to lead the Hebrews into the land of Israel. Joshua's military acumen was sharp, but it was his strong faith that propelled him to leadership. Months earlier, Moses had sent 12 spies to survey the Holy Land for invasion, and only Joshua and his friend Caleb had the faith that the Israelites could prevail.

God outlined an unusual battle plan in Chapter 6 of the Book of Joshua. He chose Jericho—fortified by strong walls around the city—as the site of the initial invasion. God told Joshua to order his troops to march around the city once every day for six days. On the seventh day, the troops were to march around the walls seven times. This final time, the priests were to blow their horns, and the Israelites were to scream at the top of their lungs. Thereupon, "the walls will come tumbling down," and the troops could conquer the city.

The main ingredient in the successful battle plan was faith. In an oft-quoted passage, God told Joshua: "I charge you: Be strong and resolute;

do not be terrified or dismayed, for the Lord your God is with you wherever you go."

Joshua and the Israelites followed God's charge. They marched around the walls of Jericho for seven days, and on the seventh, the priests blew their horns, the people shouted at the top of their lungs, and the walls came tumbling down.

The Israelites entered and then conquered the city. As for Joshua, the chapter concludes: "The Lord was with Joshua, and his fame spread throughout the land." Joshua's faith was his strongest weapon. With faith in God, people unite, armies advance, and even walls fall down.

FAITH AND THE AMERICAN EXPERIENCE

It will come as no surprise that I use the story of Joshua to illustrate that the compassionate community embraces the value of faith.

It may seem redundant to say that faith is a central principle of our spiritual traditions, but, indeed, faith in God is the single most important instruction in the three great monotheistic religions. In the Old Testament, God's fury is provoked most severely when His people worshipped other gods. For example, Jewish tradition holds that the Hebrews were forced to wander in the Sinai Desert for 40 years after the Exodus because God was waiting for the death of the generation that had dared to worship a "golden calf."[5] And Abraham is claimed as the father of the three great monotheist religions because of his remarkable faith—the Bible and Koran praise Abraham's unflinching willingness to sacrifice his son at God's command, and both the Jewish and Muslim traditions tell a powerful story of Abraham smashing the false idols in his father's shop.

In fact, a fundamental tenet of all three religions is that their God is the only God; all others are false. It is telling that the first two of the Ten Commandments, the centerpiece of Mosaic law, state: "I the Lord am your God. . . . You shall have no other gods beside Me." Passages in the New Testament such as "Jesus said to him, 'I am the way, and the truth, and the life, and no one comes to the Father but through Me'"; and "There is salvation in no one else; for there is no other name under heaven that has been given among men by which we must be saved" have long been interpreted by Christians as denying salvation to all who deny Jesus's divinity. And the Muslim *Adhan* (call to prayer), chanted five times a day, repeats: "I testify that there is none worthy of worship except Allah."

In fact, it was an overabundance of religious exclusivity, applied inappropriately to public policy, that led to the formation of several of America's first colonies: Puritans escaping religious oppression by the Church of England founded Massachusetts, while Baptists fleeing Puritan rule founded Rhode Island. Pre-revolutionary America was marred by inter-religious disputes and discrimination. For example, in seventeenth-century Virginia, Baptist preachers were tarred and feathered because the Episcopal Church was decreed the only lawful church in that state.[6]

Religious freedom clearly occupied the minds of the Founding Fathers. In the Declaration of Independence, they acknowledged the central role of "Nature's God" and their "Creator" in endowing them with "unalienable rights." But they came to the Constitutional Convention recognizing that there were many different ways to worship God—indeed, some of them (including Thomas Jefferson) were reputedly Deists, who did not accept the Judeo-Christian concept of a God who is continually involved in the course of human affairs.[7]

The Founders addressed the issue in the very first sentence of the very first amendment to the Constitution. And they did so by balancing the desire for unencumbered religious expression against the fear that one denomination might impose its will on others: "Congress shall make no law respecting an establishment of religion, or prohibiting the free exercise thereof."

What seemed to be the perfect balance of two principles, however, has generated conflict for more than 200 years. Advocates of public religious expression cite the "Free Exercise Clause" for support, while those who fear religious persecution choose to emphasize the "Establishment Clause."

The late twentieth-century Supreme Court's rulings on the Establishment Clause—using it to narrow practices such as school prayer and religious displays on public property—have drawn the ire of many Americans. A common complaint is that liberals, secularists, and atheists have used the judiciary as a weapon to force religion out of the public realm. Fueling that fear are liberal politicians who are uncomfortable with the language of faith or are antagonistic to a discussion of religious values in the public sphere. As journalist Mike Gecan argues, this has played into the stereotype of a coastal elite that holds its nose to the values of people in the heartland. Americans want leaders who will communicate respect for our own personal beliefs.[8]

By contrast, those who fear the establishment of religion—be they secularist, a religious minority, or simply a civil libertarian—see an attempt by the right to impose a fundamentalist Christian theocracy on the country. A recent scandal at the Air Force Academy provides a cautionary tale. An internal investigation revealed that faculty, administrators, and senior cadets had used their positions to promote one specific form of Christianity to the rest of the school, resulting in over 100 charges of religious coercion, discrimination, and intolerance. Not surprisingly, most of these charges came from self-described *Christians*, who approached their faith in a different way. Predictably, right-wing zealots defended the Academy; Congressman John Hostettler of Indiana declared that exposure of the scandal was part of "the long war on Christianity."[9] But in fact, the environment created made it questionable to some as to whether the free expression of personal religious faith was welcome in the U.S. military.

Many Americans also strongly object when faith is used as a political weapon or a means to acquire and accumulate political power, as on Justice Sunday and by the "Disciples" in Kentucky. The Christian philosopher Reinhold Niebuhr argued, "we are never safe against the temptation of claiming God too simply as the sanctifier of whatever we most fervently desire."[10] And that temptation surely would be scorned by the Apostle Paul, who clearly recognized the importance of civil law, taught Christians to abide by legal authority, and warned Christians to be cautious in their judgment of the actions of others.

Former Republican Senator (and minister) John Danforth spoke for many Christian moderates when he recently wrote, "to assert that I am on God's side and you are not, that I know God's will and you do not, and that I will use the power of government to advance my understanding of God's kingdom is certain to produce hostility. . . . Following a Lord who cited love of God and love of neighbor as encompassing all the commandments, we reject a political agenda that displaces that love."[11] Perhaps more telling are the arguments of two former leaders of Jerry Falwell's Moral Majority, Cal Thomas and Ed Dobson, who suggest that fellow evangelical Christians should focus on spreading the Gospel, not seizing the levers of political power to impose their beliefs on others.[12]

How can we best protect the rights of Americans of all faiths in the midst of this contentious debate? The answer is not for government to extol one set of religious beliefs or even one form of Christianity over another. Instead, the compassionate community must respect all faiths and all denominations. Americans must be free to choose any religious belief—or none at all—and everyone's religious expression must be fully protected.

The American public usually is presented with a dialogue on faith with only the two extremes presented: promotion of a purely secular society versus establishment of a Christian nation. What is needed instead is a new "Faith Balance," that will allow the United States to enter a "promised land," where we can unite all Americans and, like Joshua and his army, we can break down the walls of distrust and fear.

A Faith Balance does not require individuals to abandon or even to compromise or moderate their own faith; believers of a singular Truth must be respected. Nor does it force non-believers to adopt a faith. Those want to protect their children from messages that conflict with their own personal belief systems should be honored. The Faith Balance calls for all people of good will—with or without faith—only to acknowledge and express common beliefs and values to improve the community that we all share.

The Faith Balance has a simple formulation, reflecting and expanding upon the First Amendment: (1) to welcome all kinds of religious expression, (2) to prohibit the coercive imposition of one set of religious beliefs, and (3) to promote unified interfaith armies of compassion.

This Faith Balance could be applied to many of the difficult issues that have divided many Americans. While we may disagree on its implementation (as many may disagree with the specific approaches I outline below), it is essential that we begin a dialogue to find some common ground on these highly contentious issues, five of which are discussed below.

1. School Prayer

Some on the left believe that there should be no mention of God in the public schools. Some on the right would like to see the mandatory recitation of Christian prayers such as the Lord's Prayer. The Faith Balance would prohibit government-dictated prayer readings. However, it would allow for a moment of silence to be available to all students, and would enable student-led religious groups to meet on campus and practice their beliefs freely. I have heard it said that as long as there are math tests, there will be school prayer; in reality, no student is forbidden to pray silently in school. Policymakers must ensure that that no child is forced to worship, much less in a way that conflicts with the belief system of himself and his family.

2. Creationism and Intelligent Design

For decades, some conservatives have argued that creationism should be taught in public school science classes as an alternative to Charles Darwin's evolution theory; more recently, the same groups have tried to introduce Intelligent Design into science classes. Many on the left have argued that these theories have no place in public school and should be left to our houses of worship. The Faith Balance would teach science in science class, but encourage a discussion of Biblical creation in a theology class, or in social studies, as part of a discussion on the political debate or the origin of American political philosophy. Further, our political, civic, and religious leaders should take steps to abate the debasement of dialogue on both sides of the evolution debate. We must recognize that many evolution advocates are people of sincere faith, and that they may believe that the creation story and evolution are entirely complementary and consistent. Further, all Americans should understand that many devout Christians are understandably insulted when their literal interpretation of the Bible is deemed anti-intellectual, and when their ancient, sacred fish symbol is co-opted on car bumpers as an apparent, but misguided, satirical statement concerning the primacy of science over religion.

3. Posting of the Ten Commandments

A cause célèbre on the right has been the attempted posting of versions of the Ten Commandments in courthouses and public grounds. Some on the left argue that there must be a complete separation of church and state, and therefore no religious statements should be posted on public grounds. The Faith Balance recognizes the significant role Mosaic law has played in the development of our jurisprudence, and would support the Supreme Court's ruling that if the Ten Commandments are posted, they *must* be part of a display of many of the key historical documents that influenced American law. However, Catholics, Protestants, and Jews have different versions of the Ten Commandments, and there are even theological disputes within each faith. I would suggest that a display could emphasize what we all find most important: the value of compassion for others, as I highlight in table 1.

4. Political Speech

Some conservative political activists would like to hear their leaders speak to their Christian beliefs at every possible occasion. Some liberals do not want to hear anything about religion from elected officials. (A local rabbi protested my participation in the Justice Sunday counter-event because it was held at a church, and I am a politician.) The Faith Balance understands that Americans want to know where our political leaders stand, and what they stand for; a sincere expression of faith (even from a different faith tradition) demonstrates that a candidate is driven by something greater than himself, and, in my opinion, contributes significantly to the public dialogue.[13] At the same time, politicians should avoid using religion as a weapon to vilify opponents and drive a wedge between Americans.

5. Government Funding of Faith-Based Institutions

Some Americans believe that no government dollars should ever pass through the hands of religious institutions. Others often search for every possible venue to seek state or federal funding of religious activities. The Faith Balance would prohibit any taxpayer dollars to be used for an exclusively religious purpose, such as proselytization, but would encourage public/private partnerships with faith-based institutions on issues such as strengthening marriage and organizing community volunteerism.

Indeed, it is the issue of community volunteering that occupies the third and most significant plank of The Faith Balance—unleashing a unified, multi-faith army of compassion. Like Joshua's army entering Jericho, we can marshal America's many faith traditions to reach our mutual dreams of a promised land. Indeed, when we advocate religious pluralism and interfaith activism, we not only heal some of the religious scars that divide us, but effectively tackle some of the more persistent problems in society.

A leading proponent of building multi-faith armies of compassion through cooperation among government, the private sector, and religious institutions is University of Pennsylvania political scientist John DiIulio, former head of President Bush's Office of Faith-Based and Community Initiatives. DiIulio viewed his role with the administration's faith-based initiative as enlisting churches to "rally armies of compassion" in an anti-poverty program—saving lives in the process. Unfortunately, in the words of a former DiIulio deputy, the Bush administration had a "minimal commitment" to this program.[14]

However, it is with this goal—the eradication of poverty—that we can find the greatest unity among all religious traditions. Helping the poor is a consistent and essential theme in the Hebrew Bible and the Jewish Rabbinic texts. Jesus opened up his ministry by saying, "The Spirit of the Lord is upon me, because he has anointed me to preach the gospel to the poor." As the author and minister Jim Wallis discovered, this idea dominates Christian teachings: One out of 16 verses in the New Testament refers to the poor, one of ten in the first three gospels, and one of seven in the Gospel of Luke. Indeed, one of America's greatest Christian theologians—the famous eighteenth-century Puritan preacher Jonathan Edwards—argued forcefully that Christians must tend to the poor, and was sharply critical of churchgoers who "pretend a great love to men's souls [but] are not compassionate and charitable towards their bodies." And in his very first encyclical—entitled "God is Love"—Pope Benedict XVI called for Catholics to renew their commitment to charitable giving, as an expression of the church's love: "Despite the great advances made in science and technology, each day we see how much suffering there is in the world on account of different kinds of poverty, both spiritual and material. Our times call for a new readiness to assist our neighbors in need."[15]

Unfortunately, while most Christian churches provide funding in their budgets for poverty relief, many of the rank and file are not getting this message. As journalist Bill McKibben notes in a powerful *Harper's* essay, a new Christian creed has emerged in competition with Jesus's message of compassion toward others: "It is a competing... creed, this one straight from the sprawling mega-churches of the new exurbs that frightens me most.... The pastors focus relentlessly on you and your individual needs.... Jesus, in all his teachings, made it very clear who the neighbor you were supposed to love was: the poor person, the sick person, the naked person, the hungry person." In the meantime, argues McKibben, many American Christians are neither aware of the key principles of their faith, nor are they putting God's law into practice.[16]

Former President Jimmy Carter blames many conservative ministers who focus on hot-button divisive issues, and who dismissed much more important causes such as the Civil Rights movement of the 1960s and global poverty eradication today as "social issues with which the gospel has no real concern." Carter argues that Christian religious leaders too often forget the admonition of the New Testament: "faith, if it has no works, is dead, being by itself."[17]

THE HOLY WAR ON POVERTY

By focusing on the universal mandate to rid the country of poverty, we can fulfill the third branch of The Faith Balance and, like Joshua, invigorate the spirit and unity of our people and march together toward a promised land. This is why I call for a new Holy War on Poverty. The term holy war today certainly has negative connotations—the concept of jihad has been used by radical Islamic fundamentalists as the Koranic justification for terrorist attacks on innocent civilians. However, the term originally stood both for just means and just ends; when Mohammed spoke of a jihad (which literally means "struggle"), it was intended to right the wrongs of injustice and poverty.[18]

The need for a Holy War on Poverty has never been greater. During the first three years of the twenty-first century, the number of Americans living in poverty increased by three million; as of 2003, there were 35.9 million people in poverty, including 7.6 million families and 12.9 million children. For some low-income workers, poverty has become a never-ending cycle. In his influential book *The Working Poor: Invisible in America*, Pulitzer Prize–winning journalist David Shipler describes the interwoven forces that grip the working poor: "For practically every family, then, the ingredients of poverty are part financial and part psychological, part personal and part societal, part past and part present. Every problem magnifies the impact of others, and all are so tightly interlocked that one reversal can produce a chain reaction with results far distant from the original cause."[19]

Meanwhile, the rich keep getting richer as an increasing percentage of the population falls into poverty. The top 400 taxpayers—representing 0.00014 percent of the population—take in more than 1 percent of the total income of all Americans. Their average annual income climbed to $174 million in 2000, while the average income for the bottom 90 percent of Americans declined to $27,000. And U.S. income disparity is worse than many industrial democracies. The ratio of incomes between the 20 percent richest Americans and the 20 percent poorest is 11:1. In France, the ratio is 7:1; in Japan, it is only 4:1. This disparity affects all Americans—rich and poor. It is telling that the capitalist system's most influential proponent—former Federal Reserve Chairman Alan Greenspan—has expressed strong concern about the income gap between the rich and the rest of the United States. Greenspan argues that this gap has become so wide, and is growing so fast, that it might eventually threaten the stability of democratic capitalism itself.[20]

The answer is not simply to redistribute income through a new wave of government handouts. The Holy War on Poverty recognizes that the original "War on Poverty"—declared by Lyndon Johnson in the 1960s—did not meet its ambitious goal of eradicating the crisis of poverty in the United States. Of course, public rifts over the war in Vietnam imperiled Johnson's domestic priorities, but some of Johnson's well-intentioned—but misguided—programs proved that governmental largesse cannot always be the only solution to poverty. The Holy War on Poverty must join the compassionate community in a public-private partnership, with the strong involvement of faith-based institutions. We must mobilize armies of compassion to eradicate poverty in our era.

A new state and local innovation that seems particularly adept at meeting this challenge is "governing by network." Here, government's role in providing goods and services is made secondary to its facilitation of networks of partners in private industry, nonprofit foundations, and faith-based institutions, which currently work to tackle these public problems. This strategy promotes greater specialization on complex public problems, greater speed and flexibility to explore alternative approaches, and a greater ability to build expansive alliances in order to stretch limited government resources much more broadly. Since welfare reform legislation passed Congress, many states and cities have developed networks of innovative private, nonprofit, and faith-based partners to focus on the promotion of economic self-sufficiency. In Milwaukee, for example, welfare recipients can take advantage of numerous available social services and job opportunities without ever entering a government facility.[21]

Such programs should have broad popular support. A recent survey revealed that two-thirds of Americans favored allowing churches and houses of worship to apply for government financing to provide social services.[22] This idea was supported by Democrats and Republicans when President Bill Clinton signed legislation to create "Charitable Choice"—which allowed faith-based social service providers to acquire government funds in a way that both protected the religious identity of the organizations and the religious freedom of their clients. When President Bush tried to expand funding of these groups, Democrats promptly blocked it, arguing that because it tried to remove more re-strictions on religious use of federal money than the Clinton model, it violated the separation of church and state.[23] I believe we should seek common ground: Democrats should ensure that faith-based organiza-tions who participate should not feel compelled to moderate their reli-gious teachings to their members; in exchange, Republicans should agree to significantly increase federal funding for such initiatives.

States, moreover, should adjust their tax laws to encourage more charitable behavior by individuals, as well. Currently Senators Joe Lieberman and Rick Santorum have joined in a bipartisan effort on the federal level to allow deductions for charitable contributions for tax-payers who do not itemize on their returns, which could result in an es-timated $80 billion in extra donations to private charities.[24] A similar tax advantage should be enacted on the state level to encourage and re-ward charity of all kinds. States furthermore could provide incentives to encourage farmers and food manufacturers to donate surplus food by allowing them to deduct those contributions from their state taxes.

Finally, the Holy War on Poverty should address one of poverty's greatest correlates: sickness and disease. More states should look to Georgia's example for a public/private partnership to combat cancer. The Georgia Cancer Coalition joins medical professionals, government officials, and volunteer advocates in a comprehensive and unified battle against the dreaded disease that claimed my father's life and that touches nearly every American. The private sector also has donated significant resources to assist the coalition and its programs operate economically and efficiently. Civic groups and individual volunteers contribute their time to organize events like cancer screening days, health fairs, promo-tion of breast cancer license plates, and the Tour de Georgia bicycle race that benefits the Georgia Cancer Coalition. Through accelerated pre-vention, intensive research, and early detection and treatment, Georgia is trying to reduce the number of cancer deaths, improve access to quality care, and realize the economic benefits of becoming a national leader in the fight against the disease.

By enlisting faith-based institutions in this comprehensive battle, the Holy War on Poverty can bring about a significant increase in cancer awareness. Particularly in the African American community, where churches often serve as the focal point for community involvement and interaction, faith-based groups can serve as an invaluable resource for prevention information and access to necessary health care. Hopefully, through early detection, frequent screening, and the scientific discovery of new cures and treatments, we could achieve a significant decrease in cancer fatalities.

The Holy War on Poverty would bring churches, synagogues, mosques, and temples together in one united front—linking armies of compassion in fighting poverty, the widespread existence of which is a moral outrage to all of our faiths. The compassionate community would benefit not only from poverty reduction that the march can affect, but from the march itself, with people of all backgrounds and religious beliefs finding common ground.

A few weeks before September 11, 2005, I had been reviewing the Book of James for preparation of this book. As we all remember, during early September 2005, none of us could escape the horrifying images and aftermath of the devastation caused by Hurricane Katrina, and none could deny the inadequate way that relief efforts were handled by government authorities. My phone rang with more bad news from my friend Chad Brownstein, a Tulane University alumnus who still had close ties to the Gulf Coast region. Chad was demanding that all of his friends who were in some position of power do something—anything—for the victims in the region. I looked down again at the passage: "What use is it, my brethren, if someone says he has faith but he has no works? Can that faith save him? If a brother or sister is without clothing and in need of daily food, and one of you says to them, 'Go in peace, be warmed and be filled,' and yet you do not give them what is necessary for their body, what use is that?"

The next morning, I called my friend Rev. Nancy Jo Kemper, the director of the Kentucky Council of Churches, who sat next to me during the counter-event on Justice Sunday discussed earlier in this chapter. I suggested that we use the model and logistics of Justice Sunday for the purposes of uniting people of all faiths, and to mobilize their compassion and energy to help the hurricane victims. When I shared with her that my inspiration came from "her" James, she replied that she had just been reading "my" Isaiah, which left her with the same sense of mission: "I want you to share your food with the hungry and to welcome poor wanderers into your homes. Give clothes to those who need them, and do not hide from relatives who need your help."

"Compassion Sunday" was born. Rev. Kemper and I helped to lead a service at a Kentucky Baptist congregation, and broadcast the service via the Internet to hundreds of congregations and thousands of individuals nationwide. The speakers represented a variety of faith traditions—Christian, Jewish, Muslim, and Hindu—and the message was of healing and unity. Our goal was not to blur the lines of the faith traditions presented, but to identify and express the significant value on which all of our creeds agree: compassion for others.

Instead of running the names of U.S. senators across the screen, we ran the names and contact information of the charitable organizations making a difference in saving people's lives in the affected region. (A list of these groups—which continue today to help tackle the problem of poverty in this country—is available at appendix 4.) And instead of cultivating division and anger, our message was one of hope. With public awareness heightened toward the debilitating effects of poverty here in the most prosperous nation in world history, Compassion Sunday could be a small step on the long march in what can be the Holy War on Poverty.

AND THE WALLS WILL
COME TUMBLING DOWN

The Holy War on Poverty has many similarities with the Battle of Jericho fought thousands of years ago. Like the Israelites at that time, all Americans want to reach the "promised land"—symbolized by the American Dream. But for many Americans, there are walls, metaphorically, that separate many hard-working Americans from that dream. There are also walls of misunderstanding that separate people of different faiths.

So it is our job to follow God's mandate. Through implementation of a proper Faith Balance, one that respects the right of everyone to express their faith, while prohibiting any official from imposing his beliefs on others, the compassionate community can eliminate so much of the divisiveness that serves as the mortar and brick of these walls.

And then through a Holy War on Poverty, our armies of compassion can march around those walls. As these armies of compassion march, we will blow our horns for religious harmony, and we will scream at the top of our lungs for economic opportunity for all Americans. When we do, the walls of poverty, the walls of acrimony, and the walls of distrust will finally come tumbling down.

SEVEN

DEBORAH AND THE
VALUE OF JUSTICE

Deborah summoned Barak . . . and said to him, "The Lord, the God of Israel has commanded: Go march up Mount Tabor, and take with you ten thousand men. . . . And I will draw Sisera, Jabin's army commander, with his chariots and his troops, toward you up to the Wadi Kishon, and I will deliver him into your hands." But Barak said to her, "If you will go with me, I will go; if not, I will not go." "Very well, I will go with you," she answered. "However, there will be no glory for you in the course you are taking, for then the Lord will deliver Sisera into the hands of a woman."

—Judges 4:6–9

I have been very fortunate in my life not to have someone close to me be victimized by crime. Except, of course, my close friend, Alex.

Alex and I met in 1987, shortly after Al Gore had announced he was running for President. It was the summer after my sophomore year in college, and I traveled to Washington to volunteer for the young Southern moderate who had inspired me with his creative and forward-looking approaches to issues such as arms control and science and technology development. Alex, a native of Gore's home state of Tennessee, had been working in his Senate office.

From the outside, it would have appeared that Alex and I were polar opposites. I was a brash, ambitious Harvard student; Alex was a country-boy graduate of the University of Tennessee, who prided himself on his rural roots and values. Yet with our mutual love of

American history, Kentucky basketball, and playing guitar, we became close friends. We loved to hang out at the Jefferson Memorial, the monument to our mutual political hero, particularly when the cherry trees were blossoming. We shared an apartment in Crystal City, Virginia, with several other Gore staffers, and we all became friends for a lifetime.

Throughout our 12-year friendship, I learned many valuable lessons from Alex. Alex was a fierce patriot—his signature line was, "You're a great American"—and his love of country rubbed off on everyone around him. Alex especially loved the South, our home region, and our long talks gave me a greater appreciation of the culture and the people among whom I was reared. Alex also prized the nobility of public service—there was no one who advocated my entry into electoral politics more strongly.

Most importantly, Alex cherished justice. He became involved in politics to help America live up to its ideals, and to help redress the nation's flaws, particularly in the areas of race and poverty. He had a strong and determined sense of what was right and what was wrong. He knew he was imperfect, and his choices were not always the right ones. But at his core, his strong heart continued to push him to better himself and to pursue justice for everyone, all great Americans.

In the middle of my first campaign for Treasurer, I was on the phone with Alex, who had been invaluable in helping me raise money among his contacts in Tennessee. A financial reporting deadline was approaching fast, and I was pushing Alex to collect his fundraising commitments. The last thing I told him—and I earned a hearty laugh from Alex—was that he was a great American.

A few hours later, sitting in his parked car on a busy street in Nashville, Alex was killed when an out-of-control speeding car hit his vehicle. The driver, who had been convicted previously more than 20 times for alcohol-related offenses, had a blood-alcohol level of more than two times the legal limit. Alex was 35.

It is difficult to describe the feeling of helplessness I felt. With my father's death, I had months to prepare, months in which I was able to come to closure. With Alex, there was no explanation and no understanding.

The funeral was surreal. Alex was eulogized by some of Tennessee's most powerful elected officials; including, of course, Vice President Gore, who interrupted a busy presidential campaign schedule to lend his comfort to us—something I will never forget. Alex's favorite musician, popular folk-country artist Steve Earle, performed a plaintive ballad. The highlight, however, was a speech by Alex's childhood friend, now a Nashville doctor, who reminded us of what we loved most about Alex—his imperfections, his crooked smile, and, most of all, his enormous heart.

A few months later, I returned to Nashville to attend the trial of the man who took Alex's life. I was there mostly to comfort Alex's mom, who I had come to love as family, and whose name, Joy, no longer seemed fitting. But I also wanted to get a look at the defendant. Emotionally, I was disappointed: the man I envisioned as a monster appeared small and broken. In his eyes, I saw nothing—no remorse, no anger.

In the end, we were pleased that he received the maximum sentence: twenty years in prison. Justice had been served. But we could not help but think of the injustice of the legal system that allowed this man back on the street, time and time again.

Six years later, we all gathered together back in Nashville for the wedding of one of our Crystal City crew, Amy Hayes. Another roommate, George Phillips, had the responsibility of lighting a candle for Alex, and he carried the candle with him—which he named Alex—to the dinner and reception. Alex's parents and I had the heartiest laugh when we saw George positioning the candle to make sure that "Alex" had a good view of the most attractive women on the dance floor.

In fact, Alex's light will never go out. In every campaign I run, Alex's wisdom is with me. Every time I hear a Johnny Cash song, I remember Alex's pride when the country legend had to borrow his guitar at a Gore campaign rally. But most of all, I will always continue to see that flame blazing within Alex; a light that stands for justice and hope, and a love for the country that provided those blessings.

DEBORAH:
THE JUDGE AND THE WARRIOR

Justice also burned within the heart of one of the greatest heroines in the Hebrew Bible: Deborah, the prophetess, teacher, judge, and warrior, who can be found in Chapters 4 and 5 of the Book of Judges.

Several years after Joshua's death, the Israelites were conquered by King Jabin of Canaan, who "oppressed Israel ruthlessly for twenty years." The people of Israel were led by Deborah, who sat under a palm tree and dispensed justice. One of the most inspiring images in the Bible is of Deborah holding court outside, with Israelites coming from all over the land to seek her guidance, counsel, and wisdom.

However, with her sense of injustice about the oppressive treatment of her people reaching a boiling point, Deborah summoned her army commander Barak. She told Barak that God had commanded him to conquer Jabin's army, led by the general Sisera, and secure freedom for the Israelites. Barak demurred, telling Deborah, "If you will go with me, I will go; If not, I will not go." Deborah consented, and with a jab at the male chauvinism of the time (and perhaps eternally), she declared: "However, there will be no glory for you in the course you are taking, for then the Lord will deliver Sisera into the hands of a woman."

After Sisera unleashed 900 chariots upon the Israelite army, Deborah ordered Barak to charge forward. With God's intervention, the Israelites killed all of the Canaanite troops, except for Sisera, who fled to safety. He was welcomed into a tent by Jael, the wife of a political ally. After Sisera fell asleep, Jael killed him with a pin and a mallet. Soon afterward, the Israelites destroyed the rest of King Jabin's army, and drove him from power. Because of the bravery of these two women, who took courageous actions to rid their people of injustice, the land was peaceful for forty years.

Fittingly, the Bible calls Deborah "*eshet Lapidot.*" This has usually been translated as "the wife of Lapidot." However *lapidot* is also Hebrew for "torches," so "*eshet Lapidot*" could mean "a woman of torches." Like Alex, Deborah's torches could be said to have burned brightly for justice.

THE MORAL AMERICAN VALUE OF JUSTICE

I use the story of Deborah to illustrate an essential value of the compassionate community: justice.

There is perhaps no value that so permeates the teachings of the world's religions than that of justice. The pursuit of justice is a consistent theme throughout the Judeo-Christian tradition. The Bible commands, "Justice, justice shall you pursue"; and the prophets urged us "to do justice, to love goodness and to walk modestly with your God," and instructed: "Let justice well up like water, righteousness like an unfailing stream." The Psalmists termed justice a "deliverance," rectifying the gross social inequities of the disadvantaged, and putting an end to the conditions that produce the injustice.

More specifically, the Jewish Rabbinic tradition declares that all Jews have an obligation to actively promote justice and a just legal system. For Christians, the Apostle Paul presented God's justice as a grace flowing into and through the believers to the needy. Paul wrote that the demand for justice is so central to Christianity, that other responses to God are empty or diminished if they exist without it.

The passion for justice runs through the other major world religions as well. For example, a central theme of the Koran involved Mohammed's challenging an unjust society; the Buddha made justice a sacred value and the removal of suffering a holy truth; and Hindu leaders such as Mahatma Ghandi pursued social justice for all Indians in order to honor the three basic Hindu concepts of *dharma* (duty), the *karmayoga* (the discipline of action) and *moksha* (spiritual deliverance).[1]

The value of justice has also been a subject of political debate since at least the time of the Greek philosophers. Plato argued that due to the "irrepressible appetites" of the public, wise leaders were needed to mete out justice, and distinguish among human wants and needs. Aristotle, by contrast, had a more optimistic view of human nature, and he argued that the state's "final cause" (or ultimate purpose) was to promote justice through the creation of fair and just laws, allowing individuals to pursue their own version of happiness through the exercise of reason.

Of course, as mentioned earlier, Jefferson brought the Aristotelian vision into drafting the Declaration of Independence. And most of the Declaration—which served both as a justification for revolution as well as a mission statement for the new democracy—calls for the redress of long list of abuses by an unjust king. A few years later, when the Founders drafted the first sentence of the Constitution's Preamble, they declared that to create a "more perfect union," the first step is to "establish justice."

But while the American judicial system has long been the envy of the world, there has been a huge black mark of injustice inherent in the American democracy. Even the slaveholder Jefferson understood that racial discrimination (slavery being its worst form) undermined the very core of the American promise of justice. In the words that appear above the memorial Alex and I would visit often, Jefferson's famous reflections about the institution of slavery remain: "I tremble for my country when I reflect that God is just; that His justice cannot sleep forever."

Four score and seven years after Jefferson's masterpiece, God's justice did indeed awaken from His slumber. Abraham Lincoln, in his Gettysburg Address, revealed that Jefferson's ideal that "all men are created equal" had not yet been realized, and that the Civil War tested whether the notion of justice for all was in fact viable. Only through an end to slavery could the United States consider itself a just nation.

And yet, even a century after emancipation, injustice still enveloped this country. It took America's third great messenger of justice (after Jefferson and Lincoln)—Martin Luther King, Jr.—to articulate why African Americans could no longer wait for civil rights. In his remarkable "Letter from a Birmingham Jail," King explained that "injustice anywhere is a threat to justice everywhere." With a list of examples of injustice in the Jim Crow South—that was even more persuasive than the list of regal abuses enumerated by Jefferson in 1776—King explained that the fight for civil rights was a fight for the soul of our American democracy. Citing the justice missions of Jesus, the Hebrew prophet Amos, the Apostle Paul, and Presidents Jefferson and Lincoln, King revealed that it was up to all good people to be "extremists for love"; that the fight for justice embodied the moral imperative to love your neighbor as yourself.

King's letter indeed was the culmination of his decade-long rhetorical mission to link the Civil Rights movement to the Judeo-Christian ethic. By marrying language from the Declaration of Independence with Biblical verse, King compellingly decreed that voting rights for all Americans was a manifestation of God's will to create all humans equal. As Pulitzer Prize–winning historian Taylor Branch notes, King's message was both revolutionary and a natural progression from America's last great messenger of justice, Abraham Lincoln: "It was strange or even blasphemous to put the humdrum workings of democracy on a par with a belief in God, but from the slave side of history, they were comparable wonders. In the Civil War, when both sides claimed divine blessing, Lincoln's distinctive purpose was to uphold the democratic intuition. From his cell, King did not hesitate to stress the political side of conviction to the Birmingham clergy, or to transcend race as a prophet of redemption to his own persecutors."[2] (Ironically, and amusingly from today's perspective, King's approach was met with strong criticism from the religious right: In 1965, Rev. Jerry Falwell complained: "Preachers are not called upon to be politicians, but to be soul winners.")[3]

Despite King's success in reshaping civil rights law, we still remain far removed from his dream of a colorblind society that he so eloquently described in 1963, as my father stood with tens of thousands of fellow civil rights marchers at the Mall in Washington. African Americans, other minorities, and those living in poverty continue to face injustice, even where the laws are supposed to provide equal treatment.

The most significant and socially disruptive disparities can be seen in the area of public education. While "separate but unequal" public schools were outlawed by the Supreme Court more than 50 years ago, many schools remain segregated, and many would argue that a new struggle for justice has taken King's place.

In his powerful book *Shame of the Nation*, former educator turned public-education activist Jonathan Kozol argues that the American public school system may be transforming itself into a kind of "educational apartheid." Kozol demonstrates that many of the public schools that were deeply segregated in King's time are no more integrated now. Further, he shows how many of the schools that were forcibly integrated during the 1970s have been rapidly re-segregating. Worst of all, many of the predominantly minority schools in the inner cities receive among the lowest per pupil funding in the country.[4]

Like many of the segregated institutions of the last century, these schools are both separate and *unequal*. Data from the National Assessment of Educational Progress demonstrate that African American and Latino students trail white students in most dimensions of schooling such as attendance, enrollment, completion of specific grades, and, most notably, test scores. In fact, minority students trail their white peers academically by four grade levels on average by the time they finish high school. Further, as the Urban Institute and the Harvard Civil Rights Project discovered, less than half of African American and Latino students graduate from high school nationwide. Study after study demonstrates how poverty and its manifestations, such as poor health and family disruption, directly and undeniably serve to broaden the opportunity gap between urban, minority schoolchildren and their suburban white middle-class peers.[5] This opportunity gap creates serious injustice, and it is morally unacceptable.

The point may have come, such as with the injustice of Deborah's time, where there is no other choice but to take immediate remedial action. Education efforts must target these desperately needy schools to guarantee a true equal treatment under the law. This is a moral imperative: the Biblical injunction "You shall not . . . place a stumbling block before the blind" has been applied frequently by religious scholars to the sin of keeping someone in ignorance from information that will protect them. Access to quality education must be equal, or many children will always be more predisposed to failure.[6] With no justice within our system of education, there will be no glory for any of us.

GUARANTEEING JUSTICE THROUGH QUALITY EDUCATION

One model for reform can be found in my home state. For decades, Kentucky ranked near the bottom of educational achievement in the country, and it is was no coincidence that we ranked near the top of the charts in poverty, child malnutrition and poor health care. The state, however, took an historic step in the late 1980s and provided an example for the rest of the nation. Where the politicians had failed for so long, the judicial system—like Deborah under her palm tree—intervened. In 1989, adjudicating a lawsuit against the General Assembly brought by a group of low-income county school systems, the Kentucky Supreme Court ruled that the entire state public school system was unconstitutional. In *Rose v. Council for Better Education*, the Court ordered the legislature to provide adequate funding for every school, to provide everyone with an equal opportunity to a sound education: "Equality is the key word here . . . The children who live in poor districts and the children who live in rich districts must be given the same opportunity and access for an adequate education." With very specific direction from the Court, and the guidance of the Prichard Committee for Academic Excellence—a non-profit, private group which even today is at the national vanguard of education reform—the General Assembly passed the Kentucky Education Reform Act (KERA).[7]

One significant objective of KERA was to mandate educational accountability through the establishment of quantifiable standards for achievement in subjects such as reading and math, the development of standardized tests to evaluate student performance, and the use of these test scores to measure educational progress and redress failure. Over the next decade, many other reform-minded states, such as then-Governor George Bush's Texas, followed this path. Unfortunately, however, the notion of educational accountability, and the high-stakes tests which serve as the centerpiece of the strategy, began to swallow up all of the attention—and significantly, all of the funding—of the education reform movement on the state and national level. Other critical innovations of KERA—such as student creative writing and art portfolios, financial literacy training, and community service incentives—were marginalized or even completely abandoned by policymakers.[8]

Ultimately, President Bush brought the gospel of educational accountability to the federal level in 2001, in the guise of his No Child Left Behind Act (NCLB). NCLB placed rigid mandates on every state to institute standardized testing, and to use these tests to measure pupil performance, with the goal that every American student would meet certain numerical targets, purporting to represent proficiency in reading and math by 2014.[9]

But instead of supplying a foundation for higher order learning, NCLB—and its obsession with numbers and scores—has created a ceiling, whereby the most that many students can hope for is a minimum basic education. With school systems "teaching to the test"—in other words, focused entirely on increasing standardized, multiple-choice test scores—studies show that student scores on other independent exams which measure broader knowledge (such as the SAT, ACT, and Advanced Placement tests) may actually be *declining*. Other studies demonstrate that the relentless focus on high-stakes standardized tests has resulted in a significant decline in reading for pleasure, effectively taking the joy out of learning and teaching.[10]

This tunnel-vision focus, moreover, fails to teach our children about important life-skills, such as how to write creatively (or even coherently), to apply math and science to our high-tech, information-age economy, or to understand the importance of values such as civic involvement, enjoyment of the arts, financial independence, awareness of current events, or compassion toward others. As my friend Brent McKim, a Louisville teacher, argues eloquently, "much of what we value cannot easily be measured, and much of what we measure is of little value."[11]

Worst of all, the schools that may suffer the most are the very ones that NCLB purportedly was designed to help: the poorer-resourced, mostly segregated schools of the inner city and remote rural America. Many of the inflexible mandates placed on states by NCLB discourage and sometimes even prohibit creative solutions for addressing some of the most desperate needs of at-risk schools.

Further, the dramatic under-funding of the legislation by Congress forces school systems to use all of their limited resources on achieving the sometimes arbitrary mandates, leaving no room for innovation or advancement beyond the baselines. With all funding devoted to the minimum quantifiable baselines, any grander dreams for higher learning for many of these children are stunted. And if these baselines are not met—often because the teachers and school systems do not have the resources to meet them—the law levies financial sanctions on the "failing" schools and societal scorn on students, who are deemed a "failing group of children." This perpetuates the cycle of injustice that *Brown v. Board of Education* was intended to remedy: the Supreme Court's ultimate justifications for integration were to eliminate the funding inequities and the pervasive sense of emotional inferiority experienced by African-American schoolchildren.[12] It is becoming more apparent that NCLB is leaving behind far more children than it is helping.

Accountability cannot be a one-way street. We need to be accountable *to* the students, educators, and schools, not simply exact accountability *from* them. Our public officials must provide adequate, equitable funding. And the public should hold its political leadership accountable for progress in the schools. As Deborah's example shows us, true justice can sometimes only be achieved when the status quo of the existing regime is questioned and challenged.

Moreover, accountability should be a means to an end, not an end in itself. The ultimate goal of the compassionate community must be a *quality education* for all of our children. Instead of merely improving results on quantifiable standardized tests, we should be improving the quality of our schools. Instead of focusing merely on assessment and accountability, we should be promoting student learning, growth and development. Justice demands more than our children learning how to pass multiple-choice tests. Justice demands that we empower them with the skills they need for the high-tech jobs of the twenty-first century and with the well-rounded capability to become tomorrow's civic leaders in the compassionate community.

If the United States is to compete in today's world economy, quality education should become our new mantra. Moreover, the equal opportunity provided by quality education will enable us to seek justice for all of our children, regardless of income or background. And while the educational accountability movement dominates reform efforts across the country, there are still a few innovative quality education programs that our political leaders should examine.

One very worthy American initiative is the Coalition of Essential Schools' Small Schools Project, a five-year program which seeks to enhance the quality, character, and sustainability of small schools while spurring broader change in the public education system. The initiative is dedicated to supporting new and redesigned schools that are small, instructionally powerful, sustainable, and are guided by the following principles:

- Personalized instruction to address individual needs and interests;
- Small schools and classrooms, where teachers and student know each other well and work in an atmosphere of trust and high expectations;
- Multiple assessments based on the performance of authentic tasks;
- Democratic and equitable school policies and practice; and
- Close partnerships with the school's community.

Significantly, this project is committed to meeting the needs of young people and communities that have traditionally been educationally underserved; the majority of new schools in this initiative primarily serve minority students and students from low-income families.

Another exciting quality education effort can be found in Queensland, Australia. The "New Basics Project" is organized around four clusters of practices that are essential for success and survival in the today's rapidly changing society: (1) Life pathways and social futures: *Who am I and where am I going?*; (2) Communications media: *How do I make sense of and communicate with the world?*; (3) Active citizenship: *What are my rights and responsibilities in communities, cultures and economies?*; and (4) Environment and technology: *How do I describe, analyze, and shape the world around me?* The lessons are taught through well-defined classroom strategies that teachers use to focus instruction, enhance curriculum quality and improve student outcomes. And quality accountability is provided through assessable activities that are intellectually challenging and have real-world value, two characteristics which research identifies as necessary for improved student performance.

The charter school model should also be examined as a means to promote quality education. The most attractive feature of many of these programs is that they create a broad-based partnership that requires the involvement, ownership and accountability of teachers, administrators, students and parents. Indianapolis Mayor Bart Peterson has launched a bold model charter school initiative that involves some of the city's most prominent community organizations. Families are competing to sign their children up for the schools' admissions lotteries, and parents with kids enrolled have expressed a high level of satisfaction with the schools and their academic programs. Most significantly, students in these schools are making impressive progress in reading, math, and language. Unfortunately, in other areas of the country, charter schools face significant funding problems, and access to them is often very difficult for those at-risk children whom the schools are designed to provide the greatest level of assistance.[13] Charter schools should not be manipulated as a device to divert resources from the existing public school system; as with every other school system, they must be carefully monitored.

Corporate America must act as a partner in our efforts to provide quality education for all of our children. The business community knows best the workforce challenges posed by global competition and the retirement of the baby boom generation. Instead of outsourcing the new information-age jobs to India and China, our business leaders should help provide training for American children, particularly those in underserved areas, so that they can be prepared to serve in the twenty-first century workforce. In the past, poor infrastructure and remote geography have prevented many areas of my state and others like it from sharing in the country's economic growth opportunities. In today's world, with the Internet potentially connecting rural and inner-city youth to the modern job market, the only things standing in the way of progress are the barriers to quality education. Business leaders should invest in their future workforce by ensuring that every school is hooked up to the Internet, and that by third grade, every child is provided a laptop computer. Justice requires us to remove all stumbling blocks and enable the hills of Appalachia and the projects of Los Angeles to become the new breeding grounds for tomorrow's leaders of the new economy.

A new quality education paradigm would also demand more years of affordable, mandatory education for all of our children. With our children competing for jobs not only with kids from neighboring states, but with their peers in growing economies such as India and China, the traditional K–12 model is as outdated as the software designed to run the mainframe computers of the 1970s. As discussed earlier in this book, every child needs the opportunity for higher education to have access to the high-paying jobs of the twenty-first century. At least two years of higher education—whether university, community college or technical education—must be available and affordable for every American child.

We also must look at our children's entry point into education. New research into brain development demonstrates that the first three years of a child's life are extremely critical for her emotional and intellectual growth. That's why we need to provide every American child with the opportunity to attend preschool and all-day kindergarten programs. As Delaware Senator Tom Carper argues, "children who attend high-quality preschool programs that prepare them to read and build cognitive, verbal, and social skills go on to do measurably better in school and in life than kids who don't have that opportunity. They get better scores on academic achievement tests in school, they go on to get better jobs, and they are less likely to become dependent on welfare or to commit crimes." Indeed, studies of preschool programs in Michigan and North Carolina demonstrate that public investments in such programs could deliver a sevenfold return, in the form of increased productivity and decreased social spending. Further research demonstrates that all-day kindergarten programs advance academic achievement for most children, particularly those in at-risk communities.[14]

Providing quality education to all of our children also requires us to address those who are on the front line of public education: our teachers. This is also a Biblical imperative: the practice of tithing, common to many Jews and Christians, finds its origin in the mandate to financially support the Levite priests, who served as the communities' teachers and spiritual leaders.[15] Teachers are our modern-day Levites, charged with nurturing our future leaders. We must demand quality and accountability, but we must also ensure that they are rewarded for their choice of profession and for their excellence when they nurture and train our children for the twenty-first-century workforce.

Rewarding them is not only the right thing to do for our teachers; it is the right thing to do for our students. According to a study by Education Trust, a good teacher impacts student achievement more than any other factor: socio-economic status, race or parent's education. Researcher William Sanders determined that three years of learning from good teachers can lift students' standardized test scores by 50 percentile points.[16] Similarly, attentive and caring teachers can improve writing skills, inspire students to appreciate the arts, and encourage our children to understand the importance of being involved in civic and political life and their communities.

Decades ago, teaching was one of the few professions available for smart, young women. Today, with the broad gains that women have made in the workplace, the pool of college graduates entering the profession has shrunk dramatically. Further, both women *and* men are discouraged from the profession when teacher pay decreases proportionately with private sector jobs, and as stories circulate of increased violence and disruption in the classroom.

We need to develop new incentives to draw our skilled young people into teaching, and to promote teaching in troubled school systems. An obvious start is higher pay: teacher salaries should be increased up to 25 percent across the board in order to be competitive with equivalent professional jobs in the private sector. With funding crunches affecting every state government and school district, however, policymakers and local administrators need to develop other creative approaches.

Teachers not only need more professional pay; they need a professional say—more of a voice in the educational reform process. While physicians are regularly in the center of efforts to improve the quality of the nation's health care system, too often teachers are left out or offered only a token role in developing new educational policies. Too frequently, teachers are only part of the implementation of reforms, not the planning and development, despite the fact that they are the closest observers of our children and the curricula. Giving teachers a place at the table, an ownership stake in the reform process, will not only attract more to the profession, it will ultimately improve the quality of our children's education.

Further, we should provide incentives for high school graduates to consider teaching by offering college scholarships to those who pledge to fill a vital societal or economic need in the classroom. For example, the national academies of science, engineering and medicine have suggested that the federal government establish and fund four-year merit-based college scholarships for 10,000 high school graduates, to be "paid back" by at least five years of K–12 public school teaching in science or math, where the needs are great to prepare our future workforce for the twenty-first-century economy.[17] Similarly, scholarships can be awarded to those bright young men and women who pledge to teach within an at-risk school district and help improve opportunity and achievement.

Moreover, school systems should move to provide free, quality child care for teachers with young children. Knowing that your child is down the hall in a safe environment might provide the extra assurance to draw a talented mom (or dad) away from a more lucrative, private sector occupation.

Finally, states and school districts must revisit and codify the informal compact made with all teachers upon entering the profession. In return for their hard, noble work at low pay, we are supposed to provide these modern-day Levites with good benefits: affordable health care for themselves and their own children and the promise of a safe and secure retirement.

Unfortunately, teachers are frequently being denied their end of the bargain: cuts to retirement benefits, particularly health care, are becoming more widespread across the country. This crisis has a familiar cause: dramatic increases in health care costs combined with an increasing number of baby-boom retirees makes it harder for states to financially support their teachers' pension funds.

One common method states have been utilizing to minimize their financial exposure to teachers' pension funds is moving from the traditional "defined benefit" model—in which teachers have guaranteed contractual pensions at retirement—to the new "defined contribution" model, where teachers invest their own money and the state provides a set contribution. With the latter, teachers have no guarantees—their retirement savings would depend on the success of their private earnings, and states are off the hook once the worker retires. In one promising recent development, West Virginia, which moved to a defined contribution model in 1991, voted in 2006 to return to a defined benefit approach. State policymakers responded to teachers who wanted and deserved long-term protection from economic uncertainty, and who did not want to have to deal with the vagaries of the stock market.[18]

Of course, every American has faced the squeeze of skyrocketing health insurance costs in recent years. But our retired educators deserve special consideration from lawmakers. Those of us with school-age children deeply understand the value of talented teachers who, day after day, put all of their energies into shaping young minds into powerful tools for progress. Teachers surely do not take on this incredible responsibility for the glory, and certainly not for the pay. They teach simply because they recognize that education is the building block of a progressive society and a successful economy.

There are millions of retired teachers across the country. All have contributed a portion of their salaries towards their retirement and health care benefits. All have gone into their classrooms every day, some accepting peanuts for paychecks, with the promise that future benefits would help redress many of their sacrifices. We owe it to them to uphold our side of the compact, to provide them with the secure and healthy retirement they deserve.

Every state must provide its teachers an inviolable contract. When they join the profession, teachers must have the assurance that whatever happens to the economy or to the state's finances, they must be guaranteed a secure retirement and full and affordable health care benefits. Anything less denies our moral obligation to the modern-day Levites on the front lines of our children's development. Anything less discourages tomorrow's bright young men and women from providing these essential services to our children. Like Deborah's people, they deserve justice, too.

MESSENGERS OF JUSTICE

We cannot assume that the elimination of injustice will occur organically. As Martin Luther King, Jr., wrote so eloquently in his Birmingham letter, "Justice too long delayed *is* justice denied." It is incumbent on all members of the compassionate community to answer King's call to become "extremists for love" and take immediate steps to help eliminate the injustice inherent in our public education system.

The politics of self-interest are not viable in the context of education. Only by working together to improve the quality of our education system can we see the benefits in our children. Further, all of us would profit from a higher-educated workforce that can compete more effectively in the twenty-first century with emerging competition in Europe and Asia. We must come together, as did the ancient Israelites around Deborah's palm tree, to seek justice for all American children and their teachers in order to establish economic progress for the entire country.

In the compassionate community, we must remember that from Deborah's time to the present, our strongest systems of government have been those that treat their citizens—regardless of race or socioeconomic status—with the highest sense of justice. We must urge all of our political leaders to understand that until we create a greater sense of equality and opportunity in the classroom, we are not fulfilling our nation's promise, nor are we achieving the grand dreams envisioned by our three great messengers of justice: Jefferson, Lincoln, and King.

Who will be the fourth great messenger of justice? Perhaps it will not be one person, but instead the compassionate community as a whole. It is up to every American to become messengers of justice and to remind our leaders and our neighbors that God created all of us equal. As King's contemporary, Rabbi Abraham Heschel, exclaimed, "Let there be a grain of prophet in every man."[19]

The flame of justice that burned from Deborah's torches and within my friend Alex still can illuminate our nation. We must not rest until we can see a flicker of hope within every young child, no matter their color, creed or circumstance. When we empower every child with the education and opportunity they need to become a great American, then we can proudly declare that our country does indeed provide justice for all.

EIGHT

JONATHAN AND THE
VALUE OF PEACE

Jonathan, out of his love for David, abjured him again, for he loved him as himself . . . "As for the promise we made to each other, may the Lord be witness between you and me forever."

—*First Samuel 20:17–23*

I have never been much of a fan of long plane rides. But my last international trip—helping lead a Kentucky trade mission to Israel during the summer of 2000—was nothing short of magical.

I had been to Israel on a family vacation as a child, but this mission was wholly different. We prayed at the Wailing Wall (the only remaining remnant of the Great Temple), climbed the Golan Heights overlooking Syria, and waded into the Jordan River, where Jesus had been baptized (I filled several water bottles to bring home to my Christian friends with upcoming baptisms).

We never felt any fear of violence or terrorism. We were greeted warmly by Palestinian leaders in Ramallah, rode a tank near the border of Lebanon, and walked the streets of Jerusalem as if we were in any American city, the only exception being the sight of young women dressed in military fatigues and carrying Uzi submachine guns.

The impossible dream of peace seemed at hand. While we were in Israel, President Clinton had brought Israeli Prime Minister Ehud Barak and Palestinian leader Yasser Arafat to Camp David, and reports were that a historic peace agreement would soon be signed. With Clinton's urging, Barak had agreed to significant concessions, including, for the first time, the creation of a new Palestinian state, with the capital in Jerusalem.

Our delegation was giddy. Half of the group was Christian—government officials and business leaders—who were on their first trip to the Holy Land. They arrived with a great love of and support for America's strongest ally and the only democracy in the region. A few of the Jewish participants, like me, had come of age after the severe threats to Israel of the Six Day War in 1967 and the Yom Kippur War of 1973, and had taken the existence of a strong and secure Israel for granted. The remainder were Jews who had watched the creation of the Jewish state during their childhood and had endured decades of anxiety about Israel's security.

The fact that Israel simply exists is nothing short of a miracle. After more than 2,000 years of the Jews wandering through the Diaspora, praying every day for a return to Jerusalem, suffering through the worst genocide in the history of humanity, the dreams of the Hebrew prophets were now a reality. And to think that the violence, armed conflict, and terrorism since Israel's independence in 1948 could be nearing an end! In the words of the famous Hebrew folk song that sustained Jews around the world for generations: *Am Yisrael Chai!*—Long live the people of Israel![1]

And then in an instant, the dream vanished. Arafat walked away from the deal, without offering any alternative. Within a few months, and a few failed attempts at resuscitating the negotiations, the peace process died. A new Palestinian intifada (uprising) escalated terrorist attacks and suicide bombings, killing hundreds of innocent civilians. Citizens could no longer relax when walking the streets of Jerusalem, or any Israeli city for that matter.

All Americans have a stake in the Middle East peace process. Our economy is severely influenced by oil price fluctuations during times of conflict. More significantly, Americans of all three Abrahamic faiths—Jews, Christians, and Muslims—have a deep spiritual connection to the holy sites of the troubled region. It is accordingly essential that we play a role in bringing about a just and fair resolution to the Middle East conflict.

Will there ever be peace in the Middle East? I cannot pretend to answer that question. But in helping determine the proper role for the compassionate community in the process, we can turn to some of ancient Israel's greatest leaders for guidance.

THE FRIENDSHIP OF
JONATHAN AND DAVID

Chapters 18 through 23 of the Book of First Samuel tell the story of the escalating tensions between Saul, the King of Israel, and David, whom Saul perceived as a threat to his crown. Making matters even more complex, Saul's son, Jonathan, had developed a close friendship with David. The two friends shared common values, and both were very interested in the welfare of their people. Their relationship was so deep and abiding that the Bible tells us that Jonathan loved David "as himself."

In time, Saul plotted to kill David, and asked Jonathan for his help. Jonathan not only pleaded with his father to spare David, he betrayed Saul to warn David about his father's intentions. Jonathan fundamentally believed that the people of Israel would be best served with David as their ruler.

After initial indications that Saul had backed down from his threats, it again became clear to Jonathan that Saul intended to kill his best friend. Jonathan spied for David, lied to Saul in order to protect him, and finally, after a violent confrontation with his father, joined David's troops in their battle against Saul. Ultimately, when Jonathan died at the hands of a foreign power, David's mourning was profound and intense.

What is most remarkable about Jonathan's actions is that they were entirely opposed to his self-interest. Not only was Saul his father; Jonathan also was heir to the throne. David, therefore, was Jonathan's rival—David's death likely would have ensured Jonathan's rise to power. Yet, Jonathan placed his friend's interests—as well as the long-term interests of the people of Israel—above his own selfish desires.

This marks a clear rejection in the Bible of many of the amoral values embraced by the politics of self-interest. David's death could have brought Jonathan power, achievement, and affluence beyond his wildest dreams. But Jonathan chose love of another and his community over his own self-interest, over even his own life.

THE THREE DIMENSIONS OF
THE MORAL VALUE OF PEACE

Jonathan's great love for his friend David illustrates, in a symbolic sense, a central value of the compassionate community: peace.

The moral value of peace has three distinct, albeit related, dimensions. The first, and most common, definition of peace is the absence of war among nations. The quest for this type of peace is fundamental to the Judeo-Christian tradition. Jesus, in his Sermon on the Mount, famously embraced the pursuit of peace: "Blessed are the peacemakers, for they shall be called sons of God." The Hebrew prophets condemned armed conflict and envisioned a world without war: Micah, for example, prophesized a utopian future when "They shall beat their swords into plowshares and their spears into pruning hooks. Nation shall not take up sword against nation; they shall never again know war." The Rabbis subsequently demanded that political leaders take all steps necessary to avoid war with their neighbors, arguing that rulers were obliged to promote conflict resolution, prohibit violence against the innocent, and use war only as a last resort.

By no means, however, does the Judeo-Christian tradition impose pacifism in response to aggression or injustice. The Mosaic law prohibits passivity in the face of violence to others—"Do not stand by the blood of your neighbor"—which the Rabbis interpreted to support international intervention to protect human rights abuses. Further, Jews have a fundamental obligation to do everything in their power to help release people who are enslaved or wrongly imprisoned. Under Jewish law, the highest obligation that overrides almost every other law is the saving of the life of another, ordering Jews to actively intervene to prevent the murder or injury of innocent victims. And as philosopher Reinhold Niebuhr argued, Christians also recognize that force is sometimes necessary: "Christian realism recognizes that justice can be achieved only by a certain degree of coercion on the one hand, and by resistance to coercion and tyranny on the other hand."[2]

The second component of the value of peace is the notion of civility—the desire for harmonious relations among individuals within a community. This type of peace is represented clearly by the friendship of David and Jonathan, during a time of significant conflict. Christians and Jews celebrate the affirmative value of promoting and seeking peace and prohibiting violence against the innocent. The Psalmist writes, "seek amity and pursue it." Further, the New Testament teaches, "be like-minded, live in peace; and the God of love and peace will be with you." Some of Jesus's most inspirational—and radical—teachings stemmed from God's desire to ensure that there would be peace among men: "You have heard that it was said, 'An eye for an eye, and a tooth for a tooth.' But I say to you, do not resist an evil person; but whoever slaps you on your right cheek, turn the other to him also. . . . You have heard that it was said, 'You shall love your neighbor and hate your enemies.' But I say to you, love your enemies and pray for those who persecute you." The rabbis of the Talmud similarly taught that the Torah's admonition "you . . . must raise it up with him" means that it is our duty to aid anyone in distress, even one's enemies.

But there is a third and much more spiritually significant component of the value of peace that incorporates and transcends all of our religious traditions. That is the idea of inner serenity—peace between one's self and God—which is at the heart of much of our religious instruction. Islam comes from the Arabic words for peace and surrender; the Muslim greeting, *salaam aleckem* means peace be upon you. The Jewish greeting is similar: shalom, which generally is translated as "peace," but, as Jewish scholars Eugene Borowitz and Frances Schwartz explain, the word has greater significance:

> The root of the word shalom conveys the meanings "complete," "whole," or even "perfect." So to say "shalom" is to breathe the air of Jewish hope and human aspiration, wishing the day will come soon when we are all fulfilled. No wonder, then, that loving peace, as the Psalmist puts it, or living to create peace, as the Rabbis glorify it, is a climactic Jewish ideal, the outcome of worthy living, the chief virtue of Jewish character.[3]

Christian writer Roy Herron elaborates, "For people of faith, the concepts of wholeness and integration are familiar ones. As we have seen in the Bible, these ideas are expressed in the concept of *shalom*. God calls us to have integrity and seek peace and wholeness."[4]

It is in this context that prayers for peace are so important in Christian and Jewish liturgy. Calls for peace permeate daily services, and a request for peace concludes the threefold priestly benediction: "May the Lord bestow his favor upon you and grant you peace." For Jews, the blessing after a meal concludes with the prayer: "May the Lord grant strength to His people; may the Lord bestow on His people peace." Indeed, the Rabbis made the search for inner peace a fundamental objective for religious Jews. As second-century Rabbi Simeon ben Gamaliel concluded: "The world rests on three things: justice, truth and peace. As it is said: 'Judge each other truthfully, and in your gates, render a judgment of peace.'"

The search for inner peace is at the heart of Eastern religious practice as well. Indeed, several practices of these ancient traditions have been adopted by Americans of all faith backgrounds who are searching for inner peace. For example, the teachings of Theravada Buddhism, which centers on peaceful meditation as the key to emancipation, inform many Westerners who practice transcendental meditation and other types of meditation. Further, the practice of yoga—which is now extremely popular in gyms, studios, and homes across the United States—emerges from the Hindu practice of "reaching the beyond within," escaping psychological and physical pain through meditation.[5]

THE U.S.-ISRAEL RELATIONSHIP

Nowhere is the struggle for peace—in all three of its iterations—more profound than in the Middle East. For many centuries, a highly polarizing conflict has persisted among Israel and her neighbors. Jewish statehood existed in Israel for over 1,000 years—the high watermark being the kingdom of David and his son, Solomon—until it was conquered by the Romans in 70 A.D. The land was then occupied by many other powers, including the Ottomans and the British. Despite this occupation, the land of Israel was always a focal point of the Jewish people, whose scripture, liturgy, and religious instruction consistently cried for a return to the Holy Land. At the same time, there never was a Palestinian state: A separate Palestinian movement evolved only in reaction to the emergence in the early twentieth century of Zionism, the political movement dedicated to support of a Jewish state in Israel.[6]

By 1917, the British issued the Balfour Declaration, stating that it was their goal to establish a national home for the Jewish people in Israel. However, it was not until 1947—after the world learned of the atrocities committed during the Holocaust—that the British submitted the issue to the United Nations.

In 1947, the UN decided to partition the land into a Jewish state and an Arab state. While the Jewish community was exuberant, Arab and Muslim states rejected the partition, and invaded Israel in 1948 on the day she declared independence. Israel won that war, as well as a series of other conflicts over the next several decades.

Since the first rustlings of Zionism, there has been a special relationship between Israel and the United States. Abraham Lincoln was the first president to advocate a Jewish homeland, and Harry Truman's support for and recognition of the State of Israel was vital to its creation. Since John Kennedy's administration, the United States has supplied Israel with arms critical to its defense, and in 1973, an emergency airlift ordered by Richard Nixon during the Yom Kippur War preserved its very existence. (It is a great irony that such an anti-Semite—judging by his many anti-Jewish slurs recorded on the White House tapes—may have saved the Jewish state from extinction.) In turn, Israel provides the United States invaluable strategic, military, intelligence, and economic assistance that serve to strongly bolster America's fiscal and national security.

Of course, U.S. support of Israel comes at a significant economic cost. The oil-rich Arab and Muslim states have tried to use their leverage to pressure the United States into changing its Middle East policies—most prominently during the Arab Oil Boycott in 1973, which drove up American gas prices and helped deepen our recession during the mid-1970s. More recently, rogue nations such as Iraq and terrorist leaders such as Osama bin Laden have tried to generate support for their activities and hatred toward the United States by fomenting the conflict among Israel and its neighbors.[7] Many patriotic Americans—from Noam Chomsky on the far left to Pat Buchanan on the far right—have argued that the United States should abandon its strong support for Israel in order to better preserve vital American interests.

So why does the United States stick with Israel? For the same reasons that Jonathan sided with David. Had Jonathan supported his father, Saul, he would have inherited his throne, meaning untold riches and powers. But to Jonathan, his personal power and finances were not important; he loved David, and he recognized that with David as king, their country could reach true greatness.

Like Jonathan and David, the relationship between the United States and Israel has emerged from a partnership based on shared values and interests, into a deep friendship that provides both countries with economic, strategic, and military benefits. Most Americans believe that only under Israeli control will they have access to all of the holy sites of the world's major monotheistic religions. And Americans of all political persuasions understand that it is essential that the United States protect the region's only democracy from the threat of extinction. Public opinion polls consistently have shown overwhelming support for the U.S.-Israeli relationship. Interestingly, support of Israel is one of the few issues of agreement between the American Jewish community and the so-called Christian right, who are among Israel's strongest advocates. (Some evangelical Christians believe that the Bible prophesizes a war in the Middle East against Islam, and the taking of the entire Holy Land by Jews. In this vision of the Apocalypse, ultimately, the Messiah will return and triumph, and the Holy Land will be restored to greatness.)[8]

Israel's chief critics in the United States come from two primary sources. First, hostility comes from those who oppose the very existence of the Jewish state, whether due to their support of Arab sovereignty or simple anti-Semitism. Second, resistance comes from some on the American left who support Israel's existence, but tend to blame her actions for the absence of peace in the Middle East. Some of Israel's strongest critics, in fact, have come from the progressive religious community. In his otherwise powerful and influential book, *God's Politics*, Jim Wallis states that the Israeli presence in some of the disputed lands in the region reminds him "of apartheid in South Africa," and argues that "Israeli violence is enormously disproportionate to Palestinian violence." More recently, several mainline Protestant churches in the United States—including the Presbyterian Church and the Episcopal Church—have called for an economic boycott of companies that are involved in providing military security to Israel in lands it has occupied after wars with its neighbors.[9]

Certainly, the leaders of Israel are not perfect, and should not be immune to criticism. Further, I believe that the words and actions of these progressive church leaders are well-meaning, based on love, not in antagonism to the Jewish state or the Jewish people. And as I discuss below, there is a significant role that the compassionate community can play in bringing peace to the region, and prosperity to all its residents—Jews and Arabs.

However, withdrawing American financial or political support for the Jewish state is not the answer. Indeed, the left's criticism is often inaccurate. In Israel, Palestinians and other Israeli Arabs enjoy the highest standard of living of any Arab community in the region. Israel's laws provide all of its citizens, including Arabs, the freedom of religion, full civil and political rights, and equal participation in all aspects of social, political, and civic life. Today, Israeli Arab citizens have emerged as leaders in the worlds of business, academia, and technology. Many have become popular elected officials, and even national sports heroes.[10]

Any rights that Israel must deny its residents—always after considerable debate and introspection—are the result of one desire: to promote peace in the region. Israeli policy directly targets the pursuit of peace in all three of its dimensions: (1) to prevent the outbreak of war with its neighbors; (2) to reduce the civil strife created by terrorist acts; and (3) to provide serenity for all of its citizens who live in fear of violence and terror, so that they can have peace between themselves and their God. On 9–11, Americans briefly experienced the fear of terrorism at home. Fortunately, this fear has dissipated somewhat. However, it is a continuing preoccupation of all Israelis, including most Israeli Arabs. Indeed, Israeli security forces within Israel's borders and in the occupied territories do as much to protect innocent Arab civilians as they do to protect Jewish Israelis. This became very clear when, after the Israeli pullout from the Gaza Strip in 2005, intra-Palestinian violence increased dramatically.[11]

What progressive Christian critics of Israel fail to understand is that the Biblical value of peace is more than simply a withdrawal of military forces and a prohibition on the means of war. As I have discussed, Christian and Jewish law clearly recognize that force sometimes may be necessary to save lives. And as Jonathan demonstrated, sometimes you need to fight for what is right—regardless of your immediate discomfort—in order to guarantee a longer-lasting peace. Israel's security forces, in fact, have been quite successful in promoting peace over the past several years. Since the construction of a controversial security fence across a significant swath of Israeli land—protested by many of these same American clergy—and since Israeli security forces have moved more aggressively to pursue terrorist leaders in the region, the wave of suicide bombings in Israel has declined precipitously.[12] Now, Israelis not only feel a greater sense of peace, in terms of the absence of war, but more importantly, they feel a greater sense of serenity in their cities and neighborhoods, and in their worship of God.

Consistently, Israel's critics call for the Jewish state to make concessions and trade land for peace. Israel has complied time and time again: withdrawing from the Sinai Desert, Lebanon, areas of the West Bank, and most recently Gaza. While we can continue to hope and pray for peace, Arafat's abandonment of the offer of a Palestinian state at Camp David in 2000 demonstrates that full peace simply may not be possible under the current generation of Arab leadership. Even worse, the 2006 Palestinian election, in which control of the Palestinian Authority was secured by Hamas—a terrorist organization that calls for Israel's complete destruction—sent an unambiguous signal that many Palestinians will not accept any type of peace with Israel, unless it means dissolution of the Jewish state. At the same time, some radical but powerful Middle Eastern leaders—such as Iranian President Mahmoud Ahmadinejad—were renewing calls that "Israel should be wiped off the map," blaming the existence of the Jewish state on "lies" about the European Holocaust.[13]

Arab hearts continue to be hardened by the deliberate provocations of radical Islamic fundamentalists who have seized power or accumulated influence in many Arab and Muslim lands and by the continued indoctrination of hatred of Israel and the West in Arab mosques, schools, and media. As Abdel Rahman al-Rashed of al-Arabia News told journalist Thomas Friedman,

> The mosque used to be a haven, the voice of religion that used to be that of peace and reconciliation. Religious sermons were warm behests for a moral order and an ethical life. Then came the neo-Muslims. An innocent and benevolent religion, whose verses prohibit the felling of trees in the absence of urgent necessity, that calls murder the most heinous of crimes, that says explicitly that if you killed one person you have killed humanity as a whole, has been turned into a global message of hate and a universal war cry.[14]

Indeed, Americans and Israelis might find the most commonality as targets of this global campaign of terror and hatred. Radical fundamentalist Islamic leaders have tapped a reservoir of enormous popular hostility toward the West in a cynical scheme to expand their political power. In a cautionary recent example, Iran's leaders have built public support for their nuclear program (and their transparent desire to produce a nuclear weapon) on anti-American and anti-Israeli hatred. As the author Daniel Jonah Goldhagen concludes, "Political Islam—aggressive, totalitarian—is now fully on the offensive."[15]

The global community is at a critical juncture. Unlike in the mid-1930s, when the threats posed by Hitler were underestimated by world leaders, today we must take immediate action to protect all peoples from the imminent threat posed by terrorists who distort the Koran by using it to justify the annihilation of the freedoms and culture that Americans and Israelis hold so dear.

A comprehensive military and diplomatic strategy to secure Middle East peace is beyond the province of this book. However, the compassionate community can and must intervene, by using the friendship of David and Jonathan as a model. Born rivals, they made peace with each other and joined forces for the common good. Similarly, the compassionate community should venture to build inter-faith dialogue among Jews, Christians, and Muslims in this country and in Israel. For example, for more than a decade, Seeds of Peace, a nonprofit organization with strong American financial support, has brought together Jewish and Arab teenagers and is dedicated to empowering these young men and women with the leadership skills and mutual understanding to advance reconciliation and coexistence.

However, creating an environment for long-term peace might only be possible if we can bring economic opportunity to average Arab citizens. The extraordinary poverty and lack of opportunity and hope in the Middle East serves to breed strife and violence. Through increasing investments and trade in this region, and encouraging these economies to join the information age (such as in China and India), we can provide a potential long-term solution to the crisis. American faith leaders who feel strongly about providing opportunity and justice for the Palestinian people should put their money where their mouths are; instead of *divesting* from Israel, they should *invest* in ventures that build the economies and infrastructure of the impoverished Palestinian lands. If hope is restored, the Palestinian people can focus on rebuilding their nation.

A DECLARATION OF
AMERICAN ENERGY INDEPENDENCE

One of the more powerful solutions to the Middle East conflict, however, can be developed and implemented within America itself. In 1776, some of America's brightest political minds were brought together to draft, edit, and sign the document that has served as our nation's mission statement—the Declaration of Independence. More than two centuries later, we need a gathering of the nation's brightest *scientific* minds to develop a new mission statement for the next 200 years; to both help resolve the centuries-long conflict in the Middle East, and to promote American economic and national security for the long-term future. We need a Declaration of American Energy Independence.

As discussed more extensively in chapter ten of this book, American reliance on Middle Eastern oil is creating enormous long-term ecological problems for the planet. Perhaps just as significantly, American dependence on these resources is undermining our nation's security and any short-term prospect for peace in the Middle East.

Today, the United States is funding both sides of the war on terror. As our military tries to hunt down Osama bin Laden and his conspirators, our fossil fuel–centered economy enriches the Arab and Muslim regimes that sponsor terrorist groups in the Middle East and around the world. The American predisposition to drive low fuel-economy cars and consume extraordinary amounts of energy continues to weaken our nation and make the prospects of Middle East peace more and more difficult.

The Declaration of American Energy Independence would bring together our nation's best and brightest scientists in an intense and concentrated effort to develop alternative energy technologies—using hydrogen, solar, wind, water, and other renewable resources to reduce our dependence on foreign oil. Through a greater investment in research and technology, we can drive the prices down for these renewable energy sources and make them affordable for average American families. For example, new firms recently have been formed that will finance projects to capture the energy from ocean waves in a cost-efficient manner, providing a clean, renewable, and potentially very powerful way to fuel the American economy in the future.

The declaration would also focus on the construction of cheaper, cleaner-burning power facilities that could tap America's abundant fossil fuels such as coal and natural gas to both protect the environment and build our nation's energy security. Environmentalists must understand that "clean coal" is not an oxymoron, and with an appropriate investment from the government and coal companies, we can burn coal more efficiently and cleanly as a domestic alternative to imported oil. Through new conversion technologies, coal can become a cheaper, cleaner power source for all Americans.

We should also expand the supply of natural gas because it is the cleanest fossil fuel, and because 90 percent of it is found in North

America. We must work with Canada and Mexico to develop and transport natural gas resources from all over the continent, particularly from the areas rich with natural gas, such as Alaska and the Gulf of Mexico.

The initiative would also collaborate with our nation's farmers to use the world's most abundant food supply to fuel our economy—exploring more affordable ways to tap the energy resources within corn, soybeans, and other biomass. Our farmers feed the world, and with existing technologies, they can also help us provide power for our nation's energy needs in a way that is both renewable and clean.

The plan, moreover, would enlist the country's automobile manufacturers in an effort to build cars that are far less dependent on foreign oil. Currently, public/private partnerships are developing cars that utilize hybrid and hydrogen technologies, in order to dramatically improve gas mileage and perhaps ultimately eliminate the need for fossil fuel-burning vehicles. U.S. manufacturers are falling behind Japan in the production of cleaner, more efficient cars, and their profits are suffering. The Declaration of American Energy Independence, therefore, would have the added benefit of promoting the bottom line, as well as increasing the workforces of our domestic car industry. Meanwhile, we would offer more choices of public transportation to commute to work more quickly, with less pollution, and at a significantly lower cost to average Americans.

The declaration would provide incentives for homebuilders and owners to use the most energy-efficient materials and standards. And our political leadership should follow suit. With half a million buildings and a huge fleet of cars, our government is the largest single consumer of energy in the world; by employing energy-efficient standards and conservation efforts, state and federal governmental entities could save billions of dollars. And our effort would encourage corporations, universities, and hospitals to follow suit.

The technologies enumerated here are not only possible, they are close at hand. In the late 1990s, as deputy chief of staff at the U.S. Department of Energy, I was introduced to dozens of new technological innovations to power our country in a cleaner, more affordable way. What is missing is the will, as well the moral leadership, necessary to press forward toward a Declaration of American Energy Independence.

This project would also reap enormous benefits for those men and women who suffer most at the hands of the radical Islamic fundamentalists—the world's Arab population. Arab and Muslim nations would be forced to diversify their economies, and like China and India, create a long-term progressive economic agenda and develop a middle class. Oil-rich monarchies no longer would be able to horde their profits and would have far less freedom to fund terrorism in the Middle East, allowing Arab and Muslim moderates to secure power in the region. These new leaders could press for greater political, economic, and civil rights for all Arabs. And instead of widespread destitution, which provides a breeding ground for hatred and terrorism, prosperity and opportunity could engender an environment where peace could be at hand.

Skepticism that Arab and Muslim lands can never truly be free is misguided. As Indian Nobel laureate economist Amartya Sen notes, democracy is not exclusively a Western tradition. Sen points to examples of African, Asian, and Middle Eastern cultures over the last 2,000 years in which there was a free atmosphere of open discussion and political debate. The best example may indeed be modern India. The world's largest democracy also has the second-largest Muslim population in the world. Yet India does not export terrorism, likely because the country is moving toward greater economic prosperity, and because its leaders have created a political system in which there are basic human rights and a tolerance for all faiths.[16]

SHALOM AND SALAAM ALECKEM

My best friend in Kentucky—who just happens to be named David—is a devout, evangelical Christian. While each of us is proud of and deeply committed to our separate faiths, we have learned over the course of our nearly 20-year friendship that we have far more in common then what divides us. (David likes to joke that I am his second favorite Jew, behind Jesus, of course.)

Jews and Muslims in Israel and America can learn the lesson provided by the Biblical and modern-day Davids and Jonathans. Each religion shares Abraham as a father, as well as a tradition where the first and last words of any conversation is a call for peace—shalom and *salaam aleckem*. It is the responsibility of the compassionate community here in the United States to ensure that these are not just words, but that the moral value of peace is secured throughout the world in all three of its dimensions—an absence of war, harmonious relations among people, and peace between individuals and their God. We will only progress as a society if we can match our words of shalom, with our actions of *salaam aleckem*.

The compassionate community extends across the globe, as our hearts will always be with the lands where many of our religious traditions were born or achieved greatness. Like Jonathan, we must put aside our own selfish, short-term economic demands on behalf of the value of peace for the greater global community. We must stop blaming our friends, and instead do what each of us as individuals and communities can do to reduce the terrorism promoted by radical Islamic fundamentalism and funded by our own addiction to foreign oil. Only an energy-independent America—brought to us by a Declaration of American Energy Independence—can lead the world toward a peaceful solution in the Middle East.

Promoting peace in the Middle East is the responsibility of all of us, for the inner peace of all people of faith is at stake. Shalom and *Salaam Aleckem*.

NINE

DAVID AND THE VALUE OF RESPECT

At the turn of the year, the season when kings go out to battle, David sent Joab with his officers and all Israel with him. . . . David remained in Jerusalem. Late one afternoon, David rose from his couch and strolled on the roof of the royal palace; and from the roof he saw a woman bathing. The woman was very beautiful, and the king sent someone to make inquiries about the woman. He reported, "She is Bathsheba, daughter of Eliam and wife of Uriah the Hittite." David sent messengers to fetch her; she came to him and he lay with her—she had just purified herself after her period—and she went back home. The woman conceived, and she sent word to David, "I am pregnant."

—Second Samuel 11: 1–5

When I called my parents to tell them I had decided to run for office, my mother—a respected political science professor, a woman who had raised her children to embrace public service—responded exactly as I expected. She cried. But hers were not tears of joy.

For while my mom believed that public service was a noble calling, and while she encouraged my sister and me to work on campaigns and serve as staff for elected officials, she strongly discouraged our own entry into politics.

As one of Kentucky's shrewdest political observers, commentators, and writers, my mother knew exactly what her son would be getting into. She knew that a political life would mean enduring vicious personal attacks and directly exposing my family to the worst of the political system.

By the late 1990s, the toxicity of American politics had reached absurd new levels. While the system's corruption had a thousand fathers, one man had made a science of the politics of personal destruction. And I had witnessed it firsthand.

My first government experience came in 1994, as an aide to Tennessee Congressman Jim Cooper. Jim represented everything that is right in politics—a thoughtful, introspective, policy-minded centrist who went to work every day trying to do what was best for the people of his district. All of which made him the wrong man in the wrong place at the wrong time.

In 1994, the U.S. House of Representatives was the epicenter of a political revolution, led by a brilliant radical visionary, Newt Gingrich. Gingrich had waged a decade-long battle for Republican control of Congress. Gingrich's theory was that the only way for the Republicans to seize power after more than four decades of Democratic control was to destroy public credibility for all of the institutions of government and all of its participants, particularly its Democratic leadership.

Gingrich's strategy worked. Public anger, fueled by conservative talk radio, precipitated a stunning national landslide victory for Republicans, after which they took control of both branches of Congress. Jim Cooper was a prominent victim, losing a Senate race to Fred Thompson, a movie actor whom he was heavily favored to defeat. With the electorate focused on issues such as term limits and government corruption, being a career public servant was a significant handicap for Cooper.

With a Democrat still in the White House, the Republican Congress used its political and legal authority to try to bring ill repute on the entire administration. This all culminated, of course, in the impeachment of a president for lying about a personal indiscretion. Seeing the extraordinary partisanship in Washington, and seeing many of our friends being forced to hire lawyers to defend themselves against specious, politically motivated charges, Lisa and I were even more convinced that it was time to leave Washington and return back home to Kentucky to raise our children.

The day I became state treasurer in 2000 was also the first day of divided state government in Frankfort. The state Senate had just shifted to Republican control, due to the defection of two formerly

Democratic Senators. Unfortunately, Gingrich's strategy had started spreading to the states. Grover Norquist, formerly a top Gingrich advisor, now the president of Americans for Tax Reform, vowed to shrink government "down to the size where we can drown it in a bathtub," and he took his slash-and-burn political approach to the state legislative level.[1] Norquist found a willing acolyte in Kentucky's Republican State Senate President, David Williams.

Soon after taking office, Williams started to launch a series of personal attacks against the Democratic governor—at one point, publicly calling him a "mouthy drunk"—and policy progress came to a screeching halt. In 2002, Williams copied Gingrich's obstructionist strategy on the federal level from a few years earlier, and, for the first time in the history of the Commonwealth, the General Assembly did not pass a budget.[2]

Things took another turn for the worse in 2004. When Republican U.S. Senator Jim Bunning's reelection campaign seemed endangered due to many missteps and misstatements on his part, Senator Williams publicly chastised Bunning's unmarried opponent as "limp-wristed" and a "switch-hitter," and stunningly denied he was accusing him of being gay (he said he was just using baseball analogies since Bunning was a Hall of Fame pitcher). Williams's outburst made national news, and subjected Kentucky to yet another round of unwanted national ridicule.[3]

By 2005, after three courts proclaimed that a Republican candidate for state Senate in Louisville did not meet the state constitution's definitions for residency, the state Senate defied the courts, and declared her the senator anyway. Senator Williams declared that his body had absolute power: it could even pronounce—straight out of Orwell's *Animal Farm*—that a 23-year-old was 30 years old for the purpose of the Constitution's age requirements. This led one frustrated Republican Senator, Bob Leeper, to consider resignation and then ultimately to leave the Republican Party.[4]

Today, the political atmosphere in both Washington and Frankfort is poisoned by bitter partisanship. Unfortunately, for some, the only goal is the seizure of power, solely for the sake of exercising power. And in the most unfortunate of twists, the poisoned atmosphere of today's politics drives away principled public servants such as Senator Leeper, leaving greater control to those who probably have forgotten why they entered public service in the first place.

DAVID AND BATHSHEBA

The Bible tells us a story of another public servant named David who lost his moral bearings: King David, one of the greatest leaders of the Hebrew Bible.

We first encounter David in Chapter 17 of First Samuel, as a young shepherd among a demoralized Israelite people. When the giant Goliath of Gath terrorized the Israelite troops, only the youthful shepherd was willing to stand up to him. As any Sunday School student or fan of the underdog knows, with just a slingshot and "five smooth stones," young David slayed the mighty Goliath.

David's extraordinary courage propelled him into a leadership position among the Israelites, and, some years later, he became king. Under David's strong command of the Hebrew armies, the Kingdom of Israel was finally united. David secured his place in world history, and both the Jewish and Christian traditions believe that David's lineage would produce the Messiah.

But as his power and status grew, his moral bearings collapsed. Chapter 11 of the Book of Second Samuel tells us that one day, while his troops were fighting another battle, David spotted a beautiful woman bathing in a nearby house. He inquired after her, and learned that she was Bathsheba, the wife of one of his generals, Uriah. This did not deter David, and he summoned her. The two slept together, and Bathsheba learned soon after that she was pregnant with David's child.

The cover-up began. David tried twice to trick Uriah into returning home and sleeping with his wife so as to disguise the paternity of Bathsheba's child. When that strategy failed (unlike David, Uriah was too committed to his troops to enjoy the luxuries of home), David instructed the commander of his army to send Uriah into battle, "in the front line where the fighting is fiercest, then fall back so that he may be killed." Uriah was killed in battle, leaving David free to marry the new widow.

Ultimately, God sent the prophet Nathan to David, who, through the use of parable, revealed to David the wickedness of his ways. David immediately admitted guilt, and prayed for forgiveness. God determined that the child of the illicit liaison would die, and that David's family would suffer innumerable hardships. However, because of his acknowledgement of wrongdoing and his pledge to change his behavior, David's life was spared. In fact, his next child with Bathsheba, the wise Solomon, inherited David's throne and built the great temple in Jerusalem.

THE MORAL VALUE OF RESPECT

The story of David is one of the Bible's more complex narratives. Certainly, it stands for the principle that all humans—even our greatest leaders—are fallible and vulnerable to sin. It also stands for the principle of redemption: Even those who commit the most heinous crimes can be redeemed in the eyes of God. But to me, ultimately, the story of David's fall from grace illustrates an important value of the compassionate community: respect.

By the time he met Bathsheba, David had secured absolute power over the Israelite people. He no longer joined his troops on the field of battle; he no longer had his close friend, Jonathan, to advise him because he had died several years earlier. Full of pride, arrogance, and power, he felt no restrictions against using others to satisfy his most selfish needs. David no longer showed respect—no respect for Uriah and Bathsheba's marriage, no respect for the Bible's commandments against adultery and murder, no respect for the rule of law he had been chosen to execute.

The Judeo-Christian tradition places considerable emphasis on the value of respect. The Rabbis taught that all humans must treat each other with dignity and respect; in fact, the loss of personal dignity or public humiliation at the hands of others is considered one of the greatest wrongs under God's law, akin to murder. Jesus and his disciples taught respect and mercy for all humans, even one's enemies. Indeed, a central principle of Christian theology is "Do not judge, so that you will not be judged," as all men and women have sinned and fallen short of the glory of God. (Eastern tradition is more specific; for example, the Buddha preached against the human propensity to engage in false witness, idle chatter, gossip, and slander, particularly in their covert forms—subtle belittling, accidental tactlessness, and barbed wit—which are often more vicious because their animus is veiled.)[5]

Lying about others particularly is singled out for condemnation in the Bible. Telling falsehoods is such a moral abomination that "You shall not bear false witness against your neighbor" immediately follows prohibitions against murder, adultery, and theft in the Ten Commandments. The New Testament took such offense with liars that it teaches that "the tongue is a fire, the very world of iniquity; the tongue is set among our members as that which defiles the entire body, and sets on fire the course of our life."

Only valid criticism is valued by the Judeo-Christian tradition. If you see someone acting in a way harmful to himself or his community, the Bible teaches you to denounce his action: "Reprove your kinsman, but incur no guilt because of him." But Jews and Christians are taught to be gentle in their reproach. Nathan, the prophet, did not hold a press conference to denounce King David, even though the criticism was valid; he went directly to David and, through a parable, guided the king to realize his own mistake. As the Apostle Paul instructed: "if anyone is caught in any trespass, you who are spiritual should restore such a one in a spirit of gentleness." Jesus's confrontation of a group seeking to execute an adulterous woman is worthy of imitation: He urges respect from the crowd—"He who is without sin among you, let him be the first to throw a stone at her"—but he also insists that the woman respect the law and her marriage in the future—"From now on sin no more." (In common retellings of this story, many conservatives ignore the first verse; many liberals disregard the latter.)

Since Biblical times, the greatest violators of the value of respect have been among some of the world's most powerful leaders. One example is the Egyptian Pharoah Ramses II (whose Greek name was Ozymandias), who had statues built of himself to inspire fear in his subjects. Many centuries later, the British poet Percy Bysshe Shelley discovered an abandoned and damaged statue of Ramses, and satirized the pharoah's arrogance and abuse of power:

And on the pedestal these words appear:
"My name is Ozymandias, king of kings:
Look on my works, ye Mighty, and despair!"
Nothing beside remains. Round the decay
Of that colossal wreck, boundless and bare
The lone and level sands stretch far away.[6]

For centuries, political philosophers have strongly criticized supercilious rulers such as Ramses II, and have insisted that our leaders understand and express the value of respect for their constituents. Confucius emphasized that popular trust is essential for leaders because "if the people have no confidence in their government, it cannot stand";

and he emphasized two virtues above all: *ren* (benevolence and humanity) and *li* (decorum). Greek philosopher Plato insisted that wise leaders respect their subjects and inspire the good side of human nature; by contrast, playing to the "irresistible appetites" of humans failed to instill respect for the community and its members.

America's Founders recognized the limits of human nature, and tried to build checks and balances into the Constitution to reign in unscrupulous leaders. James Madison warned of the danger of "factious leaders" who would try to divide the country, and hoped that the Constitution would be effective in placing limits on their authority. When it became clear that factions—in the American case, political parties—were already beginning to cause tumult, George Washington provided by example a voluntary restraint on power by leaving office at the height of his popularity, and by encouraging future leaders in his Farewell Address to be willing to divest themselves of power and foster the next generation of leadership.

But despite the Founders' intentions, respect is a value that has gone AWOL in today's political system. Too often, political consultants wage campaign ad wars that demonize minority groups or humiliate candidates. Today, the Democratic Party's great tradition of welcoming people of all backgrounds into its big tent—dating back to Andrew Jackson—is seen as a political liability instead of a source of great strength.

Worse, many of our national and state leaders—on both sides of the political aisle—have lost respect for the institutions of government, lost respect for their colleagues, lost respect for the governing documents of democracy, and lost respect for the people they represent. Motivated simply by the desire to secure power for the sake of power itself, they engage in rank partisanship, and worse, place their own selfish desire for reelection over any sense of what is right and good. Just because you command a majority of senators—or command the Israelite troops—does not entitle you to reinterpret the law strictly to serve your own politics of self-interest.

RE-INSTILLING RESPECT
INTO THE POLITICAL SYSTEM:
THE WEAPONS OF GATH DESTRUCTION

The long-term solution to reviving the value of respect in our political system requires us to look back at the example of the young, idealistic

David, before he became corrupted by power and wealth. As in young David's time, our society is dominated by a Goliath: the politics of self-interest, fueled by special interest dollars and the insatiable thirst for power. How can modern-day Davids quash the mighty Goliath of Gath and restore the value of respect within the political process? I suggest a contemporary version of David's weapons of Gath destruction: five smooth stones and slingshot.

Smooth Stone 1: Campaign Finance Reform

Our first smooth stone should be propelled to rid the political system of corruptive influences that encourage disrespect. And there is no influence more corrupting than money. By the late 1990s, there was growing recognition that the political system was inordinately influenced by campaign contributions, and a grassroots effort—led most visibly by Senators John McCain of Arizona and Russ Feingold of Wisconsin—forced Congress to plug some of the loopholes through which special interest money was flowing into the system.

We have learned over the years, however, that once one loophole is closed, another will emerge. President Lyndon Johnson's remarks nearly 40 years ago—that the campaign finance system is more loophole than law—still ring true in 2006. Within months of the passage of the McCain-Feingold campaign finance legislation, the political parties already were establishing new schemes and structures to pump corrupting money into the process. Further, independent advocacy groups—some of which are far from "independent" from the campaigns that they were helping—figured out ways to continue to make independent expenditures to maintain the flow of special interest money into the process, usually for negative attack ads like those of the Swift Boat Veterans for Truth, who attacked John Kerry in the 2004 presidential race. The value of respect—for opposing candidates, and particularly for the public—is sorely missing in the modern campaign.

The key obstacle to regulating such expenditures is a 1976 Supreme Court decision—*Buckley v. Valeo*. In *Buckley*, a challenge had been brought on the constitutionality of several provisions of the Federal Election Campaign Act, passed in 1974 to address some of the political abuses revealed during the Watergate scandal. While the Supreme Court allowed some of the act's provisions to stand, it struck down many of its strict expenditure limits, ruling that under the First

Amendment, money equals speech—making a political contribution is protected as free speech. Accordingly, in drafting any campaign finance reform legislation, lawmakers must recognize that any regulation of political speech has to be very limited.

A few states have been able to craft meaningful campaign finance reform laws that complied with the Supreme Court's restrictions in *Buckley*. In the late 1990s, voter referenda in Maine, Arizona, and Massachusetts, as well as the state legislature in Vermont, adopted Clean Money Campaign Reform (CMCR) laws to reduce the corruption of special interest money on their political systems. CMCR is a comprehensive campaign finance reform approach that reduces campaign spending and allows candidates to spend more time discussing the issues and meeting with voters, allowing citizens to gain greater respect for candidates and the political process. Here is how CMCR works:

- Candidates must first meet threshold requirements by obtaining a prescribed number of signatures and $5 qualifying contributions from voters in their district.
- Candidates who meet these threshold qualifications and agree not to raise or spend any private money during the primary or general election receive a set amount of money from the CMCR fund for their primary bids.
- Candidates who win their party's primaries receive more money from the CMCR fund, as well as a certain amount of free and discounted television and/or radio time for advertisements or public discussions.
- In order to comply with the *Buckley* Supreme Court decision, the CMCR program is strictly voluntary—candidates who do not wish to participate and who instead desire to express their free speech rights by raising and spending private money can do so. But in order to maintain a level playing field, CMCR candidates who are outspent by privately financed opponents, or who are targeted by independent expenditures, are entitled to a limited amount of matching funds.

Through these measures, CMCR has been able to effectively reduce campaign spending, protect the integrity of the political and lawmaking process, and instill greater respect into the democratic system.

CMCR advocates have introduced legislation to bring clean money campaigns to the federal level. Unfortunately, their prospects are bleak because many self-interested incumbents are unlikely to approve campaign finance reform measures that level the playing field and impair their ability to get reelected. More significantly, CMCR likely would not work on the federal level because too many candidates would opt out. With the easy flow of special interest money, and the limited resources of the federal government to match it, it would be make compliance the exception rather than the rule. In 2004, for example, both John Kerry and George Bush opted out of the very generous presidential federal matching fund plan established by the Federal Election Campaign Act in 1974 because they could raise significantly more money from private sources.

Accordingly, the only way to deal effectively with the campaign finance problem on the federal level is to overturn the *Buckley v. Valeo* decision. Since Supreme Court precedent makes a judicial solution unlikely, our most effective means would be through an amendment to the U.S. Constitution. With a simple instruction that Congress and the states have the authority to regulate political speech in the best interests of the public, we can have meaningful campaign finance reform, with strict campaign spending and contribution limits, and with all candidates forced to comply. With such reform, we could significantly reduce the instances of influence and jobs being bought by a load of campaign cash. With campaign contribution and expenditure limits, the need for fundraising will be reduced dramatically, allowing candidates to focus on what is truly important—contact with the voters whom they hope to represent.

It will be difficult to establish a new reform law that uses taxpayer money to fund these campaigns; such a plan is too easily subject to demagoguery by opponents as "welfare for politicians." Instead, as economist Paul Weinstein suggests, a public campaign fund could be funded by annual fees to be paid by federal lobbyists and government contractors.[7] In the end, these groups might even save money, as demands on their financial contributions would be dramatically reduced. And most significantly, the public can gain greater respect for a political system in which their voices are not drowned out by political contributions made by special interests.

Prospects for a constitutional amendment are not likely in the short term. Amending the U.S. Constitution requires a two-thirds majority in both houses of Congress, as well as the ratification of three-fourths of our state legislatures. Perhaps it will take another Watergate-type scandal to shame our elected officials into meaningful action. But now is the time for average Americans to join and develop a grassroots plan of action. Together, as a compassionate community, we can build popular consensus for returning the value of respect back into our political system.

Smooth Stone Two: Redistricting Reform

Our second smooth stone should be used to shatter the unjust process by which states draw legislative and congressional district maps after each decade's census. The strategy of gerrymandering—shaping legislative districts to protect or punish incumbents—has been around for more than a century, but never before has it been so abused. Traditionally, state legislatures and courts spend the year after the national census redrawing legislative maps, but recently, partisans in power have redrawn electoral maps mid-decade. This has led to considerable mischief, most notably in Texas, where questionable actions and expenditures relating to a mid-decade redistricting scheme have led to numerous indictments, including that of former U.S. House Majority Leader Tom DeLay.[8]

In today's system, as policy advocate Ed Kilgore argues, elected officials are choosing their voters, instead of voters choosing their elected officials. The results of the 2004 election dramatically demonstrate how political parties have used the redistricting process to protect their elected Congressmen. That year, out of 399 House incumbents running for reelection, only seven lost. Of those seven, four were Democrats targeted by the Texas mid-cycle redistricting process; so if they are excluded, there was a greater than 99 percent incumbent reelection rate for House members. Moreover, more than 85 percent of House incumbents won by landslide majorities of over 60 percent.

In analyzing the true competitiveness of House districts, the well-respected, non-partisan *Cook Political Report* determined that while there were 151 competitive U.S. House races in 1992—the first election after the 1990 census—by 2002, after another round of redistricting, only 45 seats were competitive. This means that in only 45 congressional districts are the ratio of partisans close enough to have a seriously contested, meaningfully competitive general election. (The same pattern holds true in many state legislative races; in 2004, every California state legislative incumbent seeking re-election won, and not a single seat changed party hands.)[9] As a result, some elected officials feel immune to voter recall and, like King David, show less respect for the system and their people.

Further, these incumbent-protection schemes promote much more partisan and ideologically polarized legislatures. In the vast majority of legislative districts—where there are no competitive general elections because of the imbalanced partisan makeup—in the instance when a seat becomes open due to retirement, the only truly competitive election takes place in the primary. Since candidates usually do not have to worry about appealing to a more moderate general electorate, they can gear their campaigns to the party activists, who generally are far more liberal (in the case of Democrats) or conservative (in the case of Republicans) than the average voter. Once these candidates are elected, they must focus attention on maintaining support from the more ideologically extreme elements in their parties in order to avoid potential primary challenges. This creates further partisanship and polarization in Washington and our state capitals, and less respect for the average citizen.

This phenomenon manifested itself clearly during the impeachment of Bill Clinton. While public polls showed that impeachment was opposed by a significant majority of Americans, congressional Republicans, driven by the vocal Clinton-haters who dominate their primary process, nearly unanimously voted for impeachment.

To make our elected state legislators and Congressmen more accountable to all of their constituents, we need to take the redistricting process out of the hands of partisan state legislators. We need to create legislative and congressional districts that accurately represent the population and result in truly competitive elections.

The most effective means is to transfer redistricting authority to independent, nonpartisan commissions. Six states (Arizona, Hawaii, Idaho, Montana, New Jersey, and Washington) already provide an independent commission with the final authority to draw congressional district maps, while a seventh (Indiana) uses a commission as a backup if the normal legislative process fails to develop a plan. Three more states (Maine, Connecticut, and Iowa) use commissions to draft plans, although the legislature has final approval.[10]

Today, computer software and detailed voter studies can serve as our smooth stone by enabling these independent commissions to utilize a fair, nonpartisan method to divide constituents among elected officials. As the Brookings Institution's Thomas Mann suggests, the best available model may be Arizona. Arizona's independent commission is composed of five members: two Democrats, two Republicans, and one Independent, and they approve of maps by majority vote, without review from the legislature or governor. Using detailed standards and redistricting software, they are tasked with drawing highly competitive districts without considering the residences of incumbents or other candidates. This approach provides a neutral, fair means toward developing competitive districts.[11] As other states consider redistricting reform, we must study, refine, and replicate such systems in order to have elected officials who will show proper respect to their constituents.

Smooth Stone Three: Lobbying and Ethics Reform

Our third smooth stone should be used to vanquish the extraordinary and excessive influence of special interest lobbyists on the lawmaking process. Lobbyists and the wealthy corporate clients that fund them have far too much control over the drafting and passage of legislation, which is often prepared in closed committee rooms, far from public oversight. Too often, legislators and their staff allow lobbyists to draft bills and amendments, when they should be asking average constituents for their input.

Part of the problem is that many of these same lobbyists are all too familiar to the legislative staffs: that is because they are former legislators or former staff themselves. While the "revolving door" through which elected politicians, their staffs, and senior administration officials become lobbyists has always been present, it has never spun so fast. Tom DeLay transformed the practice into an art form, developing webs of influence all over Washington with intricate ties among Congressmen, congressional staff, lobbying firms, and special-interest political action committees. As Frank Clemente, director of Public Citizen's Congress Project argues, "the revolving door is becoming more comfortably established and institutionalized."[12]

Worst of all, "pay for play" is becoming the norm in Washington and state capitals across the country. DeLay's "K Street Project" infamously encouraged Republican legislators to meet only with lobbyists and lobbying firms that contributed primarily or exclusively to Republican candidates, and even placed pressure on some firms to hire only

Republican lobbyists. (K Street is the location of many lobbying firms in Washington.) This attitude is leaking to state legislatures across the country, resulting in a more partisan and ideologically polarized political atmosphere.[13]

Some of this conduct has crossed the line into potential illegalities. For example, several prominent Congressmen, including Tom DeLay, were rocked in late 2005 by allegations of illegal dealing with super-lobbyist Jack Abramoff, who was convicted for bilking Indian casinos of millions of dollars, and has been accused of illegally bribing members of Congress with extraordinary "gifts" and funneling money through improper channels into congressional campaign coffers.[14]

Unfortunately, while much of the behavior currently seen in Washington appears unsavory, most of it is perfectly legal under current rules. That is why we need comprehensive reform of lobbying and ethics laws in Washington and in state capitals across the country. U.S. Senator Russ Feingold offered an effective model: The Lobbying and Ethics Reform Act in 2005. The Feingold bill would open up the world of lobbying to public view by requiring more frequent and much more comprehensive lobbying disclosures—to include all oral communications made with members of Congress—to be filed electronically for Internet searchable databases. His bill would also prohibit lobbyists from giving *any* gifts to members of Congress or their staffs, and provides significant penalties for violations. Feingold would also slow down the revolving door by doubling the "cooling off" period during which a former executive or legislative employee must wait before lobbying his prior employer.[15]

Former Clinton domestic policy advisor Bruce Reed would take reform even further. He suggests that there should be extensive bans on officials—as much as four years—from lobbying their former colleagues. Similarly, an industry executive who enters government would be prohibited from acting directly on policies that may benefit his former employers. Further, Reed argues that we should use the power of the Internet to require instant, real-time, substantive disclosure of lobbying activities and list the direct links between these lobbyists and their special interest funding.[16]

While lobbying reform traditionally has been advocated by progressives like Feingold and Reed (because lobbyists tend to represent the moneyed interests scorned by the left and center), true fiscal conservatives should be among reform's leading proponents. Lobbying that distorts the congressional budget process results in bloated budgets and irresponsible deficits. Cracking down on abuses in this area should contribute to more fiscally responsible federal budgets.

Finally, every state must have strong ethics rules, and establish regulatory bodies with real teeth to enforce them. Gifts to elected officials with any significant value should be prohibited, and individuals who contribute in a substantial fashion to candidates should be prohibited from doing business with the state for a significant period of time. "Pay to play" must be forever removed from the American political lexicon, even when there is only an appearance of conflict. As long as it is prevalent, many elected leaders will continue to disrespect their average constituents, and popular respect for the institutions of government will continue to decline.

Smooth Stone Four: Blogging

In today's politics, it is often very difficult for the mainstream media to report the whole truth. Too often, fearing charges of bias, or simply being too time-pressed by their cost-cutting corporate bosses, some journalists fail to delve into a political debate and determine which side is telling the truth. Articles read as "he said, she said," even when "he" or "she" is lying outright. This is particularly true in smaller communities, where news reporters are pushed in dozens of different directions, never having the time to develop the depth of understanding to provide the analysis that is needed on complex issues.

Today's new technology can serve as our fourth smooth stone. The rise of Internet reporters—some of whom are called bloggers—has the potential to become a great equalizing force. Not burdened by the pressures of ratings and corporate bosses like the mainstream media, these bloggers can report the facts to a large and growing audience. Without the limits of newspaper space or broadcast time, bloggers can pursue complex issues in great depth and can solicit instantaneous input from their readers in the blog's interactive comment section. Bloggers have the potential of emerging as the new muckrakers of the information age.

The first significant story demonstrating the power of bloggers involved a *60 Minutes II* report by former CBS anchorman Dan Rather concerning President George Bush's record of service in the National Guard during the Vietnam War. In his September 2004 report, Rather cited a document that he claimed to be a memo typed in August 1972, as proof that Bush did not fulfill his Guard duty as the president had previously claimed. Within 19 minutes after the television broadcast began, a blog commenter at the conservative FreeRepublic.com site noted that the document was not the style with which he was familiar when he came into the Air Force. Other conservative blogs such as PowerlineBlog.com and LittleGreenFootballs.com followed up with their own investigations; and, by the next morning, the Drudge Report—a conservative Web site that had broken the Bill Clinton–Monica Lewinsky sex scandal to the world—made the story known to millions of people. Within a few weeks, CBS was forced to backtrack, and many believe that the fallout ultimately led to Rather's resignation as anchor of the *CBS Evening News.*[17]

Bloggers on the left, meanwhile, have been credited with helping to encourage mainstream media reporters to cover the Iraq War in a way that is much more antagonistic to the Bush administration. In early 2005, Cindy Sheehan was an unknown mother of a soldier killed in the conflict. With the help and persistent publicity of prominent liberal bloggers such as DailyKos, MyDD, and David Sirota, Sheehan became the leading national critic of both the war and President Bush, and she soon became a staple on mainstream television news broadcasts.

Critics of blogs argue—with some merit—that this new medium is ripe for misuse; the bloggers have no filters or journalistic ethics, and they can be manipulated to spread vitriolic, libelous information. Further, since most prominent political bloggers currently are ideologically on the far left or the far right of the political spectrum, they have the tendency to further polarize an already divided nation. However, the same could have been said about newspapers early in the history of our nation. As the medium of blogging matures, the new industry too will develop standards and practices, and more objective sources of news will emerge to fill the needs of our nation's younger generations who come to the Internet to learn what is going on in their community and nation.

A comforting example can be found in Kentucky. In 2004, a number of political blogs popped up, mostly from the right, which engaged generally in gossip and unfounded attacks on politicians (usually Democrats). By the middle of 2005, Democratic political consultant Mark Nickolas founded Bluegrassreport.org, a Web site with hard-hitting analysis and originally reported news, which, within two short months, caught the attention of an average of 2,500 readers a day, including most of the state's mainstream political journalists. While Nickolas holds no pretensions that he is a nonpartisan, he has attacked corrupt Democrats and praised effective Republicans on many occasions. Most significantly, the comments sections of his posts involve a whole community of activists from all over the political spectrum, allowing for an educated debate on complex issues.

As more and more blogs move in the direction of fact-based reporting and analysis, they have several advantages over their peers in the mainstream news industry. First, the minimal costs and limited restrictions on space and time allow for in-depth coverage of complex issues that many papers cannot match. Second, the technology allows for instantaneous news; newspaper readers usually have to wait until the next morning. Third, the interactive quality of blogging allows a large and diverse community to participate in the coverage—sometimes, the most interesting and relevant information comes from commenters themselves who might have a unique perspective on the issues of the day. With blogging still in its infancy, we can expect its growth and maturity to rapidly bring new dimensions to the news-reporting business in the coming years.

But finally, and most importantly, blogging has a great potential of instilling the value of respect into the political system. Once we close the technology gap in this country—by ensuring that everyone has access to a computer and the Internet—blogging has the potential of allowing all Americans to enter into the political discussion. The Internet allows for a more robust, complex, and nuanced discussion of key issues. And when everyone can post a comment on a blog, they are empowered by having their voices heard and respected. When leaders respond, in turn, the average citizen will gain greater respect for the political system.

Smooth Stone Five: The Internet and the New Politics

The new technologies of the Internet serve as our fifth smooth stone. The Internet has the capacity of dismantling big-money politics by providing a more level playing field for political campaigns. As demonstrated by Howard Dean and John Kerry in the 2004 election, Democrats are able to use the new virtual platforms to raise significant numbers of small contributions to match the smaller numbers of large contributions that Republicans typically have been able to gather. Liberal organizations such as Moveon.org have carried this momentum forward, helping to influence elections and ballot-initiatives held across the country in 2005 and placing pressure on Democratic lawmakers on key legislative issues.

Meanwhile, Republicans have demonstrated that the Internet could be used as an effective way to organize activists under the radar screen of the mainstream media. Particularly in the key 2004 battlegrounds of Ohio and Florida, the Bush campaign, the Republican party, and conservative interest groups were able to use Internet organizing and targeted mass e-mails to mobilize conservative voters at rates much higher than expected by pollsters and political consultants. Since that election, Web-based organizations such RightOn.org and RightMarch.com—both of which style themselves as the "conservative counterpart" to MoveOn.org—have generated broad grassroots activism on political issues, such as support for the Iraq War and the Supreme Court confirmations of John Roberts and Samuel Alito.

The possibilities for future political action on the Internet seem limitless. Using e-mail and other digital modes of communication, candidates can reach much larger and much more targeted groups of voters—often at no or little cost—reducing the need to raise and spend large amounts of money on television commercials. Further, with digital video recorders such as TiVo becoming more common, allowing viewers to fast forward through television commercials, campaigns will have to look to the Internet more and more to reach voters. Just as it took a few decades for political consultants to master the art of political communication through 30-second television ads, tomorrow's challenge will be for both parties and their candidates to capture the Internet and use it to reach their constituencies and undecided voters more effectively. Potentially, this could have a dramatically positive impact on instilling respect into the process by removing the filter of media and money, and by encouraging direct communication among elected officials and their constituents.

The Internet particularly has the potential for inspiring respect for the political process in the minds of the youngest generations of voters. Many voters my age and younger have been cynical about politics over the years, are less ideological, and have lower party identification rates than our parents. Accordingly, we typically have voted in smaller numbers. At the same time, studies show that Generation X (those born between the mid-1960s and the early 1980s) and the Millennial Generation (those born since the mid-1980s) are motivated by issue-driven initiatives and are more involved in community service activities. Further, the younger the citizen, the more they use new technologies such as the Internet to gather information and news.[18] Through the Internet, campaigns and candidates can connect with these disaffected generations and offer a platform for substantive issue discussion, without the filter of the party organizations. By showing respect for younger voters, elected officials can earn the respect of a new generation of American citizens.

The Slingshot: Civic Literacy and Engagement

Unfortunately, the solutions offered by the five smooth stones listed above will never reach their intended target unless two significant barriers are addressed. As I have discussed, those who have seized power through the disrespect of others control much of the machinery that could enable needed changes. With incumbents benefiting from the status quo, it will be extraordinarily difficult to accomplish meaningful changes in the areas of campaign finance, redistricting, lobbying, and ethics reform. In addition, the principal participants in political blogs and Web-based organizations are generally political activists, usually on the left or the right. Average citizens—the very people we must involve to achieve true bipartisan reform—are still, for the most part, on the virtual sidelines.

How can we develop the value of respect for politics among ordinary Americans that will allow us all to heave the five smooth stones at the politics of self-interest, the modern-day Goliath of Gath? How can we ensure that everyday citizens will ultimately recognize that they are the true source of power and of change? We all need to train our next generation of leaders with the youthful David's weapon of choice: a slingshot, in the form of civic literacy and engagement.

Fully instilling the value of respect back into the democratic process probably will require a generational shift in leadership. The current generation that controls most of the levers of power grew up in an environment polluted by political abuses—from Watergate to Vietnam to Iran-Contra. The resulting deep cynicism for our government institutions (fueled by a media that seizes on any morsel of public discontent) has produced an electorate so disenchanted by politicians, that we often allow negative ads to dictate choices in leadership. Modern-day Machiavellis have used special-interest campaign contributions to fuel this cynical public perception. The politics of self-interest are greeted by ambivalence, as many citizens cast votes on a lesser-evil standard that often is dictated by the effectiveness of campaign ads.

I am optimistic, however. I have found that public officials of my generation are less partisan, more respectful of others, and more willing to seek the common good, instead of merely focusing on their own political prospects. In 2005, the Aspen Institute brought together 24 young Democratic and Republican elected officials from across the country to work on building a bipartisan consensus on key issues. While we will naturally disagree on a variety of subjects, we all agree that we must reinstill a sense of respect and dignity into the system. The journey has just begun, but the prospects are promising.

More significantly, as I discussed in chapter two, the emergence of the Millennial Generation—our youngest generation for whom the ethic of community service resonates—could foretell a future leadership that is dedicated to the spirit of bipartisan cooperation. The compassionate community must rear this generation with a healthy respect for others and our institutions of democracy. And we need to act now to build a slingshot for these young Davids to quash the politics of self-interest when they rise to political leadership.

Some data on the Millennial Generation is promising. Studies suggest that Millennials may be eager to assume the mantle of leadership when it is their turn. Contrary to conventional wisdom, voter turnout among 18–24 year olds has actually *risen* sharply in recent years, jumping from 36 percent participation in 2000 to 47 percent in 2004. Increases in voting rates for women and African Americans of this generation are particularly promising. Further, young people demonstrate a strong propensity to volunteer in their communities. More than 40 percent of 15 to 25 year olds participate in community activities, compared to around 30 percent of older adults. Further, volunteer rates for this generation are on the rise; for example, volunteering among college freshmen has risen every year since 1990, with over 83 percent reporting in 2003 that they had volunteered while in high school.[19]

However, while there is evidence that the younger generation believes in community service, and while they have demonstrated a willingness to mobilize during a polarizing presidential campaign, other studies demonstrate that young Americans are woefully ignorant about key concepts of our democracy. For example, recent civics assessments conducted by the National Assessment of Educational Progress and the International Education Association revealed that:

- While nearly three-quarters of all American fourth-graders knew that U.S. laws must be applied even-handedly, only 15 percent could name two government-provided services that are paid for by tax dollars;
- While four of every five eighth graders could identify Martin Luther King, Jr., as someone who was concerned about the injustice of segregation, only six percent could describe how a country can benefit from a constitution;
- While 90 percent of high school seniors knew that Social Security was a matter of considerable concern to the elderly, less than 10 percent could list two ways that a democratic society benefits from the active participation of its citizenry;
- The conceptual foundation that American students have concerning democracy and citizenship is only average when compared with students from other countries, including those in new democracies.[20]

Accordingly, there is a great disconnect. The Millennials fundamentally understand the essential moral value of compassion toward others, but, with the exception of highly publicized presidential elections, they lack a comprehension of how they can participate within the American political system to express that value. We cannot expect our next generation of leaders to have a healthy respect for the institutions of government when they are not aware of how these institutions work for everyday citizens. We cannot harness the willingness of young people to volunteer if we do not provide them a context through which they can understand how their community service plays a role in the political and civic process.

The answer—and our slingshot—is civic education and engagement. When our children learn at an early age the nobility of public and community service, the necessity of voting for a strong community, and the greatness of our democracy, they will be more likely to seek the common good when they rise to leadership positions.

This is why Kentucky Secretary of State Trey Grayson has launched a comprehensive new initiative, "Restoring Democracy." Grayson aims to empower all young Kentuckians with civic literacy—the knowledge and understanding of the basic principles of government and community processes. He will try to link that knowledge with civic engagement—active participation in the life of the community—through voting, volunteerism, and awareness of community issues. With Kentucky teens and young adults largely unaware of the basic principles and concepts that have shaped America, Grayson hopes to strengthen the civic participation of our future leadership.

After meetings across the state, Grayson developed four principles for his civic education project:

1. Civic literacy and engagement are essential to maintaining the representative form of democracy we enjoy in the United States;
2. Although schools play an important role, families, community organizations, and government agencies must also assume some responsibility;
3. Since the level of civic engagement among young adults is lower than in any other segment of the population, the private and public sectors must unite in strengthening the civic mission of our schools and in promoting civic engagement; and
4. Programs that center only on constitutional principles or political theory and foster civic literacy without encouraging active participation are not enough. Neither are service learning or internship programs that put students to work in the community but do not fully explain why their involvement is important or how it fits into the bigger picture. We must combine theory with practice in our efforts to enhance civic literacy and engagement.[21]

Early results of programs like Grayson's demonstrate that linking civic education and engagement can provide a more active and involved citizenry. One effective, mature example can be found in Maine's Fostering Youth Involvement (FYI) program. FYI sponsors mock elections and conventions, forums that bring local and state government officials and community groups into classrooms, and youth task forces that allow Maine's young people to organize voter outreach efforts and lobby legislators on laws of interest to young people. Civic programs like FYI have help ensure that Maine boasts one of the highest voter participation rates in the country.[22]

Further, studies by the National Assessment of Educational Progress and the International Education Association reveal that comprehensive civics education positively affects civic knowledge, skills, and most important, engagement. More specifically:

- Students who have studied Congress, the presidency, or political systems have greater confidence in their ability to understand political issues;
- Students who studied American government were more likely to write letters to a newspaper or a government official about political concerns as an adult or make a statement at a public meeting; and
- Students who studied the Constitution, Congress, and political parties were more likely to read newspaper articles and watch national news on television.[23]

Civic education and engagement might not provide a silver bullet to vanquish the politics of self-interest today. But with a long-term emphasis on raising the next generation of leaders with a proper understanding of our institutions of government, we have an opportunity to develop a healthy respect for our democracy, and provide us with some hope for the future of our democratic system.

LEARNING BEFORE IT IS TOO LATE

King David realized before it was too late that his loss of respect for the people of Israel would lead to great tragedy. God spared David his life, and the Kingdom of Israel prospered under the wise leadership of David and Bathsheba's son Solomon.

Before it is too late, we too must abandon the politics of self-interest which, when operating in the extreme, find some politicians acting only to get themselves reelected, doing or saying anything to fulfill those needs. By disrespecting our institutions and our rule of law, we are diverting our country from what has made it so great—a healthy respect for our people, which defines the compassionate community.

Fortunately, there is hope for change. Even today, sometimes the good guys win: By 2002, Jim Cooper was back in Congress, and Fred

Thompson's elected office was only a Hollywood mirage—he now plays the district attorney on *Law and Order.* But there will be more promise in the long run if we can reform our tainted political institutions and give average Americans a greater voice in the political process. Through civic education, literacy, and engagement, our next generation of leaders, given a louder voice in politics, will emulate noble public servants like Jim Cooper, abandon the politics of self-interest, and embrace a compassionate community. And with a healthier respect for government and its institutions, we can focus on our true shared value: respect for all Americans, regardless of status, background, or viewpoint.

TEN

ESTHER AND THE VALUE OF LIFE

Mordecai had this message delivered to Esther: "Do not imagine that you, of all the Jews, will escape with your life by being in the king's palace. On the contrary, if you are silent in this crisis, relief and deliverance will come to the Jews from another quarter, while you and your father's house will perish. And who knows, perhaps you have attained to royal position for just such a crisis." Then Esther sent back this answer to Mordecai: "Go assemble all the Jews who live in Shushan, and fast on my behalf ... Then I shall go to the king, though it is contrary to the law; and if I am to perish, I shall perish!"

—*Esther 4: 13–17*

When my daughter Abigail was six, she and my wife Lisa spotted a turtle walking out of a pond onto a busy residential street. They returned the turtle to the water. But they soon realized it would continue to leave the safety of the pond, to march in the direction of oncoming traffic. For the next several weeks, Abby and Lisa engaged in a rescue mission, transporting the wandering turtle and his friends to a safer location, far from the sprawl of suburbia, and surrounded by 30 acres of natural green space.

Rescuing and nurturing troubled animals has become Abby's natural mission. On Christmas, Abby and her sister Emily ventured to the Humane Society to volunteer. Recently, Abby and Lisa spent a week in Utah at the Best Friends Animal Sanctuary, caring for cats diagnosed with leukemia. By the time she was nine, Abigail had convinced us that adopting a dog from the pound would deeply benefit all of us. And to this day, our dog is receiving excellent care, with no complaints. Abby always puts the dog's needs ahead of her own.

Abby's love of all creatures could foretell a career as a veterinarian. But more important, Abby has developed a healthy appreciation and compassion for all of God's creation. Abby has learned about the essential fragility of life itself.

In addition, experiences like this provide children with strength and character. Indeed, animal care often provides our youngest Americans with a greater appreciation than their parents of the value of life. A respect of nature is something that too many grownups take for granted. With our hectic schedules and seemingly endless obligations, we often miss the simple pleasures and beauty of the natural world. Only when we can view the world through the eyes of our children—and look at our surroundings from their uncomplicated, unpolluted perspective— can we truly appreciate our own blessings, better understand our responsibilities to the environment around us, and place a proper emphasis on the value of life.

QUEEN ESTHER AND HER BATTLE FOR JEWISH SURVIVAL

The meaning and the very fragility of life was an issue directly confronted by one of Abby's favorite Biblical heroines. In the Book of Esther, we read the story of a young woman who saved the Jewish people. Esther was chosen by Persian King Ahasuerus to be his wife after a lengthy beauty contest. Ahasuerus did not know (nor did Esther tell him) that she was Jewish.

Soon afterward, Esther's uncle, Mordecai, learned that the king's prime minister, Haman, had hatched a plot to wipe out all of the Jews in the Persian Empire. Mordecai implored Esther to step in to protect the lives of her people. Esther initially hesitated; she felt helpless, and was concerned about revealing her own true identity. She wanted to do the right thing, but she believed that she would be risking her own life if she intervened.

Mordecai pressed further, appealing both to her sense of fear (he warned her that she might ultimately fall victim to the ethnic cleansing) and to her sense of destiny (he told Esther "perhaps you have attained royal position for just such a crisis").

Esther realized what she had to do. Even though she knew that her own life would be endangered, Esther believed that it was her moral obligation to try to save the lives of her people, announcing: "If I am to perish, I shall perish!"

After learning that her husband had no particular prejudice against the Jews, she informed the king of Haman's plot. Unfortunately, it was impossible to reverse the genocidal royal decree; so instead, Esther launched an effort to arm the Jewish people for their defense. With the help of the king's loyalists, Haman and his allies were killed. Genocide was averted, and Persian Jewry was saved and strengthened.

Because of her courage and willingness to risk her life standing up for the value of all Jewish life, Esther became one of the greatest Biblical heroines. Today, Jews celebrate the festive holiday of Purim and read aloud the story of Esther's great triumph (Haman's name is traditionally protested throughout the service with loud noisemakers). And Esther is memorialized in the "Sabbath Prayer" sung to daughters in the musical *Fiddler on the Roof:* "May you be like Ruth and like Esther."

THE ESSENTIAL MORAL VALUE OF LIFE

The story of Esther's brave, selfless efforts to save the Jewish people from extermination illustrates a crucial value of the compassionate community: life. Of course, the value of life is perhaps the most important value of all; without life, none of us can share in any of God's blessings.

Indeed, the value of life is essential within the Judeo-Christian tradition. Because every man and woman was created in God's "own image," the Bible teaches us that we should act in a loving fashion to all of our neighbors, and instructs us to "choose life if you and your offspring would live." Using the illustration of a Good Shepherd to discuss life on earth and in heaven, Jesus teaches Christians that "I came so that they may have life, and have it abundantly."[1] The traditional Jewish toast, "L'Chaim" literally means "To life!" and is announced at most public celebrations. Similarly, the spiritually significant or "lucky" number for many Jews is 18, since the numerical values of the Hebrew letters in the word *chai* (life) add up to 18. (This explains why many Jews give charitable or political contributions in factors of $18, always confusing and amusing my gentile campaign staff members.)

Because the value of life is so critical to all of us, we must take active steps, like Esther, to protect the lives of the innocent and vulnerable.

The Hebrew Bible implores Jews and Christians not to "profit by the blood of your fellow," and to actively intervene to prevent the murder of innocent people. For Jews, the highest obligation of all, overriding nearly every other law, is the saving of life. Poignantly, the Talmud teaches, God first created mankind as a single individual, rather than as a group of people, to teach us that when a person saves a single life, he saves the entire world. Jesus echoes this teaching in his parable of the Good Samaritan.

The Biblical respect for the value of life is not limited to human life. In fact, the Mosaic law prohibits cruelty to animals, and provides many rules by which humans should appropriately treat animal life. Individuals who show compassion not only for their neighbors, but also for the animal kingdom, are blessed. As St. Francis of Assisi concluded, "If you have men who will exclude any of God's creatures from the shelter of compassion and pity, you will have men who will deal likewise with their fellow men."

Furthermore, God's compassion and our stewardship responsibilities extend to all forms of life and nature—all of God's creation. In the Bible, God's love of the earth is witnessed as early as the story of creation, at the end of which "God saw all that He had made, and found it very good." By the time of man's arrival, God entrusted the earth's stewardship to human hands: "The Lord God took the man and placed him in the Garden of Eden to till it and tend it." The Jewish rabbinic tradition elaborates these notions. The Rabbis taught that God's creation of man in His image gives humans a special responsibility for the whole of creation. As the world belongs to God and not to humans, the world must be preserved for God's sake, and not be impaired because of our selfish needs.

Jews and Christians are also taught that we are not only the earth's stewards; we also receive great spiritual payback for our efforts to maintain its beauty. The author of the Psalms (traditionally attributed to King David) acknowledges that the more we observe the natural world in all of its beauty and glory, the more we come to revere the Creator. As the Psalmist declares, "the heavens declare the glory of God; the sky proclaims his handiwork."

The respect for nature is a hallmark of other belief systems as well, including the spiritual practices of our nation's original inhabitants, Native Americans, who sanctify the land as part of the greater community. A key principal of the Native American spiritual culture is the notion of a "circle of life," in which all living creatures are interrelated. Tribal spiritual leaders have taught that when a forest is felled, the entire global environment is damaged, and that the air polluted by one factory is the same air we all breathe. As the Native American teacher and civil rights advocate Wa'Na'Nee'Chee explains, "If we are to become one human family, it will be by acknowledging that we all share one Mother Earth."[2]

Indeed, reverence for nature and the environment is a significant unifying feature of all world religions. In a survey of all of the major traditions, religion professors Mary Evelyn Tucker and John Grim conclude that world religions converge to "advocate reverence for the earth and its profound cosmological processes, respect for the earth's myriad species, an extension of ethics to include all life forms, restraint in the use of natural resources combined with support for effective alternative technologies, ... and the acknowledgement of human responsibility in regard to the continuity of life and the ecosystems that support life."[3]

But while reverence for life should be a unifying force, the core American debate on the value of life has primarily concerned perhaps the most polarizing political issue of the past three decades: abortion. And it is quite unlikely that we will resolve the abortion debate any time soon. Reasonable people of sincere faith (including widely-respected religious leaders) might always disagree on complex theological and scientific issues such as when life begins; whether rape or incest victims should be treated any differently when it comes to abortion; and how we should balance the life of the unborn versus the danger to the life of a woman who may choose to seek an illegal abortion, should the procedure be criminalized. Intense focus on these contentious issues by the media, as well as by activists on the far left and right, will likely continue to exacerbate tensions among the public for decades to come.

The compassionate community, however, can help Americans find common ground. While we may disagree—even passionately disagree—on the appropriateness of access to abortion, we can all agree on a shared goal: to reduce the number of abortions performed in this country by decreasing the incidence of unwanted pregnancies, particularly among teenagers. And those of us who share this goal—whether you are strongly "pro-life" or "pro-choice," or you fall somewhere in the middle—should engage in community dialogue on how we can reduce abortion and unwanted pregnancies: Abstinence counseling, while helpful, is not sufficient on its own; we must also focus on providing medically accurate sex education, pursuing meaningful poverty reduction, promoting adoption, and ensuring stronger legal protection from sexual predators. Additionally, both sides should tone down their rhetoric—inaccurate and inflammatory mischaracterizations of policy positions (such as the all-too-common fabrication that "pro-choice" individuals are also "pro-abortion") only serve to further deepen the divide among Americans. Each of us can maintain our own strongly held positions, but we can diffuse some of the tension in the abortion debate, as we work constructively to achieve our shared goals of valuing life.

We must also remember that our responsibilities to value life do not end once a child is born. As discussed above, we have a moral obligation to ensure that every child in this country has access to affordable health care and the opportunity for a solid education. All Americans, particularly those who claim to be "pro-life," should work through their elected representatives and faith-based institutions to ensure that no American baby is born into a life of abject poverty.

GLOBAL CLIMATE CHANGE

Further, we must begin to understand that discussions about the value of life need not to begin and end with discussions of pregnancy and childbirth. In fact, where we can find the most common ground on valuing life is in the preservation of our common Earth. As discussed above, reverence for all of nature unifies all of our religious traditions. And there is one modern ecological Haman that threatens God's very creation. While it is known by several names—global warming, climate change, among others—it is a very real phenomenon that ranks among the most serious moral issues the world has ever faced.

No current debate better illustrates the conflict between the politics and the economics of self-interest and the compassionate community. Our selfish consumption of fossil fuels is solely responsible for global climate change, which will no doubt have a devastating impact on future generations. The scientific community is nearly unanimous in its conclusion that global climate change represents a real, present threat to the earth and its inhabitants. Even former vocal skeptics such as Ronald Bailey, editor of *Global Warming and Other Eco-Myths*, and Richard Cizik, lobbyist for the National Association of Evangelicals, have very recently reviewed the mounting evidence and have concluded that global warming is indeed a real and present threat.[4]

Yet lobbyists for the major manufacturing industries that cause much of the underlying pollution problems by burning fossil fuels have effectively blocked any substantial American policy action to combat global warming. The strategy of industries hostile to reform was revealed by the release of a memorandum authored by Frank Luntz, a prominent conservative pollster. The memo urged Republican politicians to persuade the public that there is no scientific consensus on the dangers of greenhouse gases:

> The scientific debate is closing [against us] but not yet closed. There is still a window of opportunity to challenge the science.... Voters believe that there is no consensus about global warming within the scientific community. Should the public come to believe that the scientific issues are settled, their views about global warming will change accordingly. Therefore, you need to continue to make the lack of scientific certainty a primary issue in the debate.[5]

Congressional leaders and White House officials, following Luntz's advice, have pooh-poohed the threat, arguing that the impact of global warming is minor, and have suggested that we can develop the technologies to deal with any problems when they emerge. Any action now to limit greenhouse gases, they argue, would cripple the economy. As recently as the July 2005 G–8 economic conference in Scotland, the Bush administration placed the primary roadblock to coordinated global measures that would have realistically addressed the growing threat of climate change.[6]

Why have Luntz and his clients been so successful in repressing public outrage toward the dangers of climate change? I would argue that because the underlying science is so complex, many Americans are confused by the debate. Just as Mordecai struggled to convince Queen Esther of Haman's threat, it is nearly impossible for the modern-day politician to articulate the scope of the global warming crisis in a 30-second sound bite. The data, however, is quite compelling.

Global warming is the result of greenhouse gases—primarily carbon dioxide (CO_2)—being released into the atmosphere and then trapping the sun's rays. The major sources of greenhouse gases are the burning of fossil fuels (which releases CO_2 into the air) and the deforestation of trees (which otherwise would absorb the CO_2). In the United States, the leading sources of CO_2 are electricity generation, transportation, and manufacturing.

The Intergovernmental Panel on Climate Change, the leading international scientific body that assesses climate change, has found that global warming is already occurring. The global average surface temperature has risen one degree since the late nineteenth century. The 1990s was, in all likelihood, the warmest decade in the last 1,000 years, and 1995 was measured as the warmest year since 1861 (when instrumented records begin); until it was surpassed by 1997, 1998, 2001, 2002, 2003, 2004, and then 2005. Scientists have determined the problem will increase in startling proportions if emissions of greenhouse gases continue to rise at expected levels. By 2100, scientists estimate that the planet will experience warming of an additional 2.5 to 10.5 degrees.[7]

Skeptical Americans have wondered why what seems like such a small change in temperature—one or two degrees is hardly noticeable to the average person—would cause such alarm. But the threat to the earth's ecological and social systems could be enormous. Consider the following:

- Within 100 years, sea levels could rise by as much as three feet, flooding coastal communities. Under some projections, the state of Florida could disappear underwater.
- Rain patterns could change, causing devastating droughts in already water-scarce areas.
- Some species of animals and plants could not adapt to the new temperatures, leading to food shortages and famine.
- Human health could suffer significantly—from increased heat stress, dirtier air and water, and the spread of infectious diseases.
- If recent trends continue, by 2050, CO_2 in the atmosphere will reach levels that have not been seen on earth for 50 million years. During that period, crocodiles roamed Colorado, and sea levels were nearly 300 feet higher than they are today.
- Weather experts predict a significant increase in Category 4 and 5 hurricanes due to warmer water temperatures, resulting—as evidenced with Hurricanes Katrina and Rita in 2005—in the potential loss of thousands of lives and trillions of dollars.[8]

The economic impact to American business could be devastating as well. Mindy Lubber, the executive director of the Coalition for Environmentally Responsible Economies (CERES), a coalition of investor and environmental groups, estimates that a small change in climate could result in multi-billion dollar losses for industries ranging from agriculture to tourism to real estate. Swiss Re, one of the world's largest reinsurance companies, predicts that within ten years, the economic impact of climate change could cost companies more than $150 billion *every year.* A recent CERES report on the affect of climate change on the insurance sector indicates that these are not simply speculative, long-term concerns: With the increasing frequency of hailstorms and hurricanes, the ineffectiveness of building codes to combat mold infestation, the growing number of people suffering from airborne diseases, and the increasing severity of droughts, global warming is having an enormous effect *now* on both the affordability and availability of a wide number of insurance lines. As a result, some major American corporations—including energy producers such as General Electric and Cinergy—are endorsing global emissions caps and taking immediate steps to develop new technologies to reduce greenhouse gas emissions from their own production and manufacturing facilities.[9]

The world's poorest people are likely to be the most profound victims of climate change. The poorest nations (and as the aftermath of Hurricane Katrina demonstrated, the poorest Americans) are most vulnerable to storms, floods, and rising sea levels. Climate models predict epidemic levels of malaria, cholera, and infectious diseases in the developing world. And food supplies for the poor are particularly at risk by the threat of global warming: As demonstrated in the aftermath of the 2004 Indian Ocean tsunami that claimed 220,000 lives, coastal areas, usually inhabited by the poor, are the most vulnerable to destruction by storms and violent weather, and the distribution chain for supplies of food and water are typically impaired significantly by severe weather.[10]

By contrast, efforts to place limits on the greenhouse gases that cause global warming would have only a small, short-term negative impact on the U.S. economy. The Energy Information Administration (EIA), an arm of President Bush's own U.S. Department of Energy, found that mandatory limits on U.S. emissions of CO_2 and other greenhouse gases would not have a significant impact on economic growth. The EIA estimated that the cost to each U.S. household of using a market-based approach to limit greenhouse gases would be less than $80 a year, and the impact on the gross domestic product would be reduced in 2025 by only one-tenth of 1 percent. Indeed, in the long run, the U.S. economy could be a major winner. As discussed below, limiting greenhouse gas production could have a simultaneous economic and national security benefit by creating new business and job opportunities in the high-tech sector, and by reducing the nation's dependence on Middle Eastern oil.[11]

Scientists agree that we must act immediately to prevent climate change from devastating all life on the planet. The longer we delay remedial action, and the more infrastructure we build without regard to its impact on the environment, the more significant problems will be. If we do not act now, the global warming crisis will be much harder for future generations to fix, and the prospects of threatening all life on the planet will be increased exponentially.[12] Just as Queen Esther led an army to save the Jewish people of ancient Persia, we all must engage in action to preserve our planet.

Addressing the dangers of climate change before they manifest themselves must be an urgent objective of modern-day Esthers in the compassionate community. As journalist Elizabeth Kolbert cogently argues, "it may seem impossible to imagine that a technologically advanced society could choose, in essence, to destroy itself, but that is what we are now in the process of doing."[13]

Fortunately, while many American politicians have remained silent, religious leaders have stepped up to fill the void and reassert the universal value of life. In June 2002, Pope John Paul II and Greek Orthodox Patriarch Bartholomew joined to issue a "Common Declaration" that stated that it is God's will "that His design and our hope for it will be realized through our cooperation in restoring its original harmony." The Archbishop of Canterbury declared at the dawn of the new millennium that a "child born in a wealthy country is likely to consume, waste and pollute more in his lifetime than 50 children born in developing nations. It may not be time to build an ark like Noah, but it is high time to take better care of God's creation." In advocating for a global effort to combat climate change, the Dalai Lama wrote that Buddhism teaches us to care about the environment: "Our practice of non-violence applies not just to human beings but to all sentient beings or any living thing."[14]

Most recently, many evangelical Christian leaders in the United States have begun to weigh in on the issue of global warming. In October 2004, more than 100 leaders adopted a platform "For the Health of the Nation: An Evangelical Call to Civic Responsibility," in which they issued a call to combat global warming, claiming that it is an urgent threat, a cause of poverty, and a Christian issue because the Bible mandates stewardship of God's creation. More recently, 86 evangelical Christian leaders—including the presidents of 39 colleges, pastors of several megachurches, and popular author Rick Warren—issued a statement calling for federal legislation that would require reductions in CO_2 emissions through "cost effective, market-based mechanisms." This same group's Evangelical Climate Initiative began running television and radio ads, stating: "As Christians, our faith in Jesus Christ compels us to love our neighbors and to be stewards of God's creation. The good news is that with God's help, we can stop global warming, for our kids, our world and for the Lord." Also, the Evangelical Environmental Network (EEN) has spearheaded a national "What Would Jesus Drive?" effort. (EEN additionally has been at the forefront of efforts to regulate mercury and other toxic substances at power plants as part of its "pro-life" agenda).[15]

Rev. Ted Haggard, president of the 30-million-member National Association of Evangelicals (NAE), explained this new activism to the *Washington Post*: "The environment is a values issue. There are significant and compelling theological reasons why it should be a banner issue for the Christian right." In addition, *Christianity Today* recently wrote: "Christians should make it clear to governments and businesses that we are willing to adapt our lifestyles and support steps toward changes that protect our environment."[16]

Without a doubt, this message is being heard by conservative Christians. In 2004, a Pew survey revealed that a majority of evangelical Protestants said they would support strict environmental restrictions. A 2005 Pew study demonstrated that fully 67 percent of social conservatives say strict environmental regulations are worth the cost. (This is compared to self-described "free enterprise" conservatives, only 16 percent of whom support strict environmental regulations.)[17]

It is now time to put our words into action; to create policies and lifestyles that truly promote the universal value of life. Just as Esther armed the Jewish people to fight Haman's army, we must arm our neighbors and our civic and political leaders with the information and public support to battle the threat of global climate change. A partnership is needed between two traditional adversaries: the environmental/scientific community and our religious leaders. Instead of debating how the earth was created, they should marshal their resources to ensure that the Creation itself is preserved. To win over skeptics in the heartland, environmentalists must not be afraid to embrace the moral language of life, stewardship, and freedom, and enlist the support of their natural allies in the clergy and in faith-based organizations.

Within this partnership, there are a wide variety of actions to be taken on the local and state levels to promote a healthier planet. These include the following:

- *Individual energy conservation:* Programs that encourage energy conservation are a dime a dozen—much easier to implement than to see actual results. However, with the scope of long-term damage so broad and the moral dimensions of preserving the earth so powerful, the country must return to a 1970s-like effort to reduce carbon emissions in our homes, cars, and offices. This means adjusting our thermostats to save energy; using more energy-efficient appliances to light our houses and to preserve our food; and teaching our children to turn off lights, computers, and electronics when they are not being used. State and local governments should advance the efforts of the U.S. Department of Energy to provide home and office conservation ideas to all Americans. (Contact information is available in appendix 1) Our religious leaders also must be involved, preaching from the pulpit about the moral outrage of global warming and its impact on humanity. Because the economic impact on developing nations would be so dramatic, a climate change action plan would fit in well with the "Holy War on Poverty" I discussed in chapter six.

- *Pension Fund Activism:* While many companies are exploring or implementing initiatives to develop new technologies to reduce greenhouse gas emissions, the lion's share of corporations are not taking any remedial action, in fear that the additional costs will negatively impact the bottom line. In so doing, they not only place their shareholders at risk of devastating regulations and lawsuits, they also face risks from the direct physical impacts of climate change. That's why a group of institutional investors have joined to place pressure on the companies in which they own stock to assess their legal, physical, and competitiveness risks and take action.[18] It is the fiduciary duty of the managers and trustees of all pension funds to examine their own portfolios and use the leverage of the purse to focus these companies on climate change risk. (See the discussion of corporate responsibility in chapter two.)

- *Investing in new technologies:* There is an economic upside to climate change. New technologies must be developed to reduce carbon emissions and make energy consumption more efficient. Those firms that are at the vanguard of producing and manufacturing these new technologies likely will make a lot of money. Entrepreneurs and existing businesses should view the growing need for environmentally friendly products as a potential economic windfall, and states should view this as an opportunity to attract these new industries and their high-paying jobs. Pension funds, similarly, should view climate change as an outstanding investment opportunity—a win-win situation—whereby a fund can promote environmental quality while enriching their pensioners. Already, California Treasurer Phil Angelides has urged the California Public Employees' Retirement System and the California State Teachers' Retirement System to place a combined $1 billion into "environmentally screened" investment funds and an additional $500 million into companies that develop "clean" technologies.[19]

- *Economic Incentives for Clean Technologies:* States must also join in promoting the development of these new technologies through incentives such as tax cuts and direct subsidies for the firms who manufacture and use environmentally friendly products. Again, this not only helps to promote the moral value of freedom through a healthier environment; the development of these new technologies also could bring states significant economic advantages through growth and new high-paying jobs. States should encourage the development of alternative energy sources—such as solar and wind—but also focus attention on the cleaner use of fossil fuels. Environmentalists must understand that "clean coal" is not an oxymoron. Instead, by using new technologies such as "carbon capture and storage" and "integrated gasification combined cycle technology," which reduce the carbon emissions of coal combustion, we can promote a cleaner environment, utilize America's most abundant natural resource, and strengthen our nation's security by reducing our dependence on foreign oil (see chapter eight for more on this subject). This will require our government to listen to modern-day Esthers such as visionary energy

CEO John Rogers of Cinergy, who has challenged his competitors in the energy industry to recognize the devastating long-term economic impact of global warming, and to support research to make these technologies more effective, and regulation to require their utilization. Coal companies are beginning to recognize that converting coal to alternative fuels will enable them both to do good and to do well: These technologies could help ensure their long-term profits deep into the twenty-first century and beyond.[20]

- *Manufacture and Purchase Cleaner Burning Cars:* The American automobile industry must immediately begin to manufacture more gas-efficient cars, using hydrogen, electric and hybrid (a mix of electric and gas) technologies. This is not simply a matter of placing emphasis on the universal value of life; it is also about the economic health of the industry. If American manufacturers continue to lose business to their more environmentally conscious Japanese rivals, share prices will tumble, and tens of thousands of American auto workers will lose their jobs.[21] States should provide economic incentives for new facilities because their presence can boost a local economy: The construction in Kentucky of a new Toyota plant that will manufacture hybrids has been viewed as a major boost to our economy, not only for the jobs at the plant, but for all of the associated industries that will be built around the area to service it. And most importantly, when *you* buy *your* next car, take a careful look at its gas-mileage efficiency: Not only will you be playing your part at reducing the threat of climate change; with rising gas prices, you could save a lot of money.

- *Implement Market-Based Emissions Trading for Carbon Dioxide:* One of the great environmental accomplishments of the late twentieth century was the development of a market-based trading system for sulfur dioxide (SO_2) emissions to curb acid rain.[22] The program sets overall limits for SO_2 in a given area, and sets targets for particular production plants. Plants that are deemed "high-polluting" (those facilities that must pollute more than the intended targets) can buy emissions "credits" from lower-polluting plants (those that pollute less than the targeted emissions), so that the overall limits are not violated. While the proposal was initially greeted by much hand-wringing from the manufacturing industry—which claimed that it would be cost-prohibitive—the program has been an extraordinary success, reducing emissions and causing no significant economic impact on the participating firms or industries. States should experiment by enacting legislation that would bring such an emissions trading system to the release of carbon dioxide. If successful, emissions trading could be brought to the federal level, and emissions of carbon dioxide could be reduced significantly. We would thereby address the climate change danger directly, and place a higher public policy emphasis on the value of life.

APPEALING TO OUR
FEAR AND OUR DESTINY

When Mordecai was trying to convince Queen Esther to save the Jewish people of Persia, he validated her personal fears and appealed to her sense of destiny: Esther's fear that her own life may be in danger, and her sense of destiny to become the great heroine of the Jewish people. This is also a time for all of us—our leaders, our neighbors, our children, and ourselves—to be afraid because, without concerted action, the lives of our children and grandchildren will certainly be impaired. But with concerted action, our destiny will be fulfilled: We can be known as the generation that saved the earth from potential devastation.

The Bible teaches us that all life is precious, because all of us are created in God's image. If even children can understand this—when they volunteer to help save animals and the environment—then American adults need to take the value of life seriously, and take meaningful steps to preserve it. While many politicians at the extremes will use the debate over life to further polarize and divide the country, it is up to the compassionate community to work to protect all life on this planet, in a way that can unite our nation and the entire world. It is up to each of us to demonstrate to our friends and neighbors that not only does the environment reflect God's majesty, but we are the greatest beneficiaries of its beauty.

Life is our most important value. Each of us must feel empowered to make the small sacrifices—conserving electricity, driving more fuel-efficient cars, exploring more energy-efficient technologies for our homes—to make the planet's future brighter. Each of us must feel responsible to convince our elected officials to take the threat of global warming seriously, and to join the rest of the industrial world in efforts to reduce carbon emissions. The compassionate community can save the planet one small step at a time. Like Esther, it is up to us; it is our destiny to guarantee the future health and welfare of Planet Earth. And in the end, our children and grandchildren will thank us for preserving God's glory.

AFTERWORD

THE FAITHFUL SERVANTS

By The Honorable Al Gore

The Parable of the Unfaithful Servant, recounted in three of the four gospels in the New Testament, offers us an instructive message. The master of the house, about to leave on a trip, places his servant in charge of his home and instructs him to be vigilant in protecting the house from vandals or thieves. The homeowner explicitly warns his servant that even if the vandals arrive while he is sleeping, he still has a responsibility to protect the house.

Today, too many of us play the role of the unfaithful servant. We sit idly by as Martin Luther King Jr.'s dreams of justice for all fall far short of fulfillment. We turn a blind eye to the ravages of poverty across the globe and even here at home—in the richest country in the history of the world.

Perhaps worst of all, we remain asleep as global vandalism wreaks unprecedented ecological destruction of planet Earth. The Earth is the Lord's creation, and we have been given the responsibility to take care of it. As in Jesus's parable, our slumber is not an acceptable excuse.

Jonathan Miller offers us a wake-up call. Miller reminds us that all of our great religious and spiritual traditions instruct us, above all else, to love our neighbors as ourselves and to value all of God's creation. His elegantly constructed, value-laden *Compassionate Community* offers us a compelling balance between respect for the past and faith in the future, between a belief in the individual and a commitment to the community, and between our love for the world and our fear of losing it.

It is up to each of us to be God's faithful servants. With such faith, we may find it possible to resanctify the earth and accept our responsibility to protect and defend it. We might even begin to make policy decisions based on long-term considerations, not

short-term calculations. But most important, each of us can take action—small steps, mutual sacrifices—to reflect our shared values and develop a united country and a healthier planet.

Some people say that we can't solve the problems Miller has identified—that they are too big or too complicated or beyond the capacity of political systems to grasp. Indeed, there are many people who move from denial to despair without pausing to think about how it might be possible to solve these problems.

To those who say that they are too big for us, I say that we have accepted and successfully met such challenges in the past. We declared our liberty, and then won it. We designed a country that respected and safeguarded the freedom of individuals. We abolished slavery. We gave women the right to vote. We took on Jim Crow and segregation. We have cured fearsome diseases, we landed on the moon, and we have won two wars in the Pacific and the Atlantic simultaneously. We brought down Communism, we vanquished apartheid, and we have even solved a global environmental crisis before—the hole in the stratospheric ozone layer. These successes were the result of leadership and vision. They were the result of people's actions—people who exercise moral authority in their local communities empowered our nation's government to take ethical actions even though they were difficult.

So there should be no doubt that we can solve today's crises, too. When it comes to climate change, for example, we can seize the opportunities presented by renewable energy, by conservation and efficiency, by some of the harder but exceedingly important challenges such as carbon capture and sequestration. The technologies to solve the global warming problem exist, and we must find the determination, wisdom, and political will to use them.

This is a moral moment. This is not ultimately about any scientific debate or political dialogue. Ultimately it is about who we are as human beings. It is about our capacity to transcend our own limitations. To rise to this new occasion.

God has left us to be the stewards of His creation. As God's faithful servants, we must wake up from our slumber. And as a compassionate community, we can and we must join together in a united effort to love all of our neighbors as ourselves, and to be good and faithful stewards of God's Earth.

EPILOGUE

PUTTING WORDS INTO
ACTION AT THE
COMPASSIONATE E-COMMUNITY

M ost Americans frankly are fed up with our political system. We see too many politicians focused exclusively on pleasing the extreme wings of the two political parties and the special interests whose financial largesse helps to keep them in power. We see government institutions that are not focused on the needs of the people that they are supposed to be addressing. We see a populace divided—polarized seemingly beyond repair.

This polarization is inflamed by extremists on the left and right who profit from our division. Shrill voices on each extreme—aided and abetted by the television and radio talk shows that thrive on ideological conflict—drive deeper wedges among Americans to win elections and raise money for their causes and campaigns. Often times, Americans are discouraged or even prevented from engaging in bipartisan dialogue or seeking common ground, particularly on the most contentious issues.

But as the preceding chapters illustrate, there is a message that can unite Americans, and there are policy ideas that, if implemented, could bring real progress to the country, helping to restore it to greatness. All it takes is a reminder of the values articulated by Hillel and Jesus, and incorporated by our Founding Fathers. All it takes is a recommitment by all Americans to show compassion for others and to demand that our elected representatives, civic activists, and religious leaders join in an effort to promote policies, programs, and partnerships that harness our new technologies and reflect our timeless values. All it takes is an understanding that we are all on this journey together, that if we look beyond our own self-interest, and make the small, shared sacrifices necessary to enhance the common good, America can reach its true potential.

Finding common ground, however, does not mean compromising our most important values. The compassionate community recognizes—indeed celebrates—the diversity of beliefs, values and opinions among Americans. But as we hold onto our core beliefs, we can work together to create a better community. We may disagree with our neighbor on certain issues, but as long as we remember the Biblical admonition to "love your neighbor as yourself," we can truly unite all Americans toward the goal of making this nation even greater.

Now it is your turn to take action. Because of the brave new world offered by the Internet, the compassionate community can live beyond these pages. Indeed, it can be a continuing work in progress.

You are invited to the Compassionate E-Community: www.TheCompassionateCommunity.com. The Web site offers you the ability to learn more about the ideas introduced in this book, and gives you the tools you need to communicate with your neighbors in order to press them on policy changes that you think will make a difference. Specifically, at our Web site, you can monitor state and federal legislative initiatives designed to implement the objectives outlined in this book, and you can follow easy links that enable you to contact your elected representatives to urge them to action. Additionally, the Web site will provide free financial and educational resources to empower your families with the tools you might need to share in the American Dream.

You can sign up for our e-mail newsletter to receive semi-regular updates on the exciting programs that are discussed above. And you can participate in blog discussions to join our virtual community in real time, and contribute to the national discussion.

If you are in a hurry to get started, contact information for many of the programs cited in the chapters above appears in appendix 1. Contact information for other organizations that are helping to provide financial education and resources for military families and average Americans is available in appendices 2–4.

So join us today. As Hillel asked: "If not now, when?"

APPENDIX 1

HOW TO FIND MORE INFORMATION ON THE PROGRAMS DISCUSSED IN THE BOOK

CHAPTER ONE:
Kentucky's Affordable Prepaid Tuition (KAPT): www.getKAPT.com
Cradle to College: www.cradletocollege. ky.gov
College Savings Plan Network (with links to all 529 plans across the country): www.collegesavings.org
SEED and its partner programs: www. gwbweb.wustl.edu/csd/asset/SEED. htm

CHAPTER TWO:
North Carolina Treasurer Richard Moore's Corporate Accountability program: www.treasurer.state.nc.us
E-Health Initiatives: www. ehealthinitiative.org

CHAPTER THREE:
"Family Friendly" Tax Reform: www.ppionlne.org
Delaware Treasurer Jack Markell's "Money School": www. delawaremoneyschool.com

Connecticut Individualized Development Accounts (IDAs): www.ctdol.state.ct. us/ida/dir/mgo.html
Kentucky Marriage and Money Curricula: www.kytreasury.com

CHAPTER FOUR:
Oklahoma Marriage Initiative: www.okmarriage.org
Girls Rock!: www.TheCompassionateCommunit y.com
Cut it Out! Domestic Violence Initiative: www.attorneygeneral. utah.gov/cutitout.html
FBI's Parents Guide to Internet Safety: www.fbi.gov/publications/pguide/ pguide.htm
Stop It Now! Vermont's Child Sex Abuse Prevention: www.stopitnow.com/vt

CHAPTER FIVE:
Kentucky's Military Families Bill of Rights and Curricula: www. kytreasury.com

Illinois Military Family Relief Fund:
www.operationhomefront.org

CHAPTER SIX:
Georgia Cancer Coalition: www.
georgiacancer.org

CHAPTER SEVEN:
Coalition for Essential Schools: www.
essentialschools.org
Queensland New Basics Projects: http://
education.qld.gov.au/corporate/
newbasics/index.html

CHAPTER EIGHT:
Seeds of Peace: www.seedsofpeace.org

CHAPTER NINE:
Clean Money Campaign Finance
Reform: www.publiccampaign.org
Kentucky Secretary of State Trey
Grayson's Restoring Democracy:
www.sos.ky.gov
Maine's Fostering Youth Initiative: www.
state.me.us/sos/kids/fyigames/
fyiinfo.htm

CHAPTER TEN:
CERES Climate Change Studies:
www.ceres.org
U.S. Department of Energy's Energy
Savings Ideas for Home and Office:
www.energysavers.org

APPENDIX 2

ORGANIZATIONS THAT PROVIDE FREE FINANCIAL EDUCATION

AMERICA SAVES

Provides adult education to encourage savings and advice to assist Americans build wealth and plan for unexpected expenses.

Contact:
Nancy Register
Consumer Federation of America
1620 Eye St. NW, Suite 200
Washington, DC 20006
(202) 387–6121
FAX: (202) 265–7989
www.americasaves.org

AMERICAN FINANCIAL SERVICES ASSOCIATION

Teaches consumers the benefits of responsible money management and middle and high school students basic money management skills.

Contact:
919 Eighteenth Street, NW
Suite 300
Washington, DC 2006–5517
(202) 296–5544
FAX: (202) 223–0321
www.americanfinsvcs.com

AMERICAN SAVINGS EDUCATION COUNCIL

This program has been developed to raise public awareness about what is needed to ensure long-term personal financial independence.

Contact:
Choose to Save or ASEC Programs
Employee Benefit Research Institute
  (EBRI)
Suite 600, 2121 K Street, NW
Washington, DC 20037–1896
(202) 659–0670
FAX: (202) 775–6312
www.asec.org

CONSUMER CREDIT COUNSELING SERVICE (CCCS)

Adult education focused on debt management, budgeting, purchasing a home, and foreclosure prevention.

Contact:
9009 West Loop South, Suite 700
Houston, TX 77096
(866) 889–9347
www.cccs.org

DEPARTMENT OF EDUCATION

Education program that provides resources and information focused on reading comprehension, math skills, and other academic subjects.

Contact:
U.S. Department of Education
400 Maryland Avenue, SW
Washington, DC 20202
(800) USA-LEARN (1–800–872–5327)
FAX: (202) 401–0689
www.ed.gov/index.jhtml

DEPARTMENT OF THE TREASURY

Developed the MoneyMath program to educate middle-school children about savings, investing, spending, and credit.

Contact:
Department of the Treasury
1500 Pennsylvania Avenue NW
Washington, DC 20220
(202) 622–2000
FAX: (202) 622–6415
www.savingsbond.gov/mar/
    marmoneymath.htm

DEPARTMENT OF THE TREASURY, OFFICE OF FINANCIAL EDUCATION

The Office of Financial Education focuses the Department of the Treasury's financial education policymaking, raises awareness about the need for financial education, and provides information about financial education resources throughout the federal government.

Contact:
Department of the Treasury
Office of Financial Education
1500 Pennsylvania Avenue, NW
Washington, DC 20220
(202) 622–9372
www.treasury.gov/financialeducation

FANNIE MAE

Adult education program that provides a comprehensive homebuyer training curriculum as well as savings and credit information.

Contact:
Fannie Mae Consumer Resource Center
3900 Wisconsin Avenue, NW
Washington, DC 20016–2892
(800) 732–6643
www.fanniemae.com/homebuyers/
    homepath/index.jhtml?p=Homepath'

FEDERAL DEPOSIT INSURANCE CORPORATION (FDIC)

Comprehensive financial education program suitable for adults and high schools students. Includes ten separate modules ranging from money skills to credit issues.

Contact:
FDIC Call Center
1776 F St., NW, Washington, DC 20006
(877) ASK-FDIC (877–275–3342)
www.fdic.gov/consumers/consumer/
    moneysmart

FREDDIE MAC

Offers two programs, one is designed to provide adults with comprehensive homebuyer education, the other is focused on savings and credit matters.

Contact:
Headquarters I (PHO I)
8200 Jones Branch Dr.
McLean, VA 22102–3110
(703) 903–2000
www.freddiemac.com/creditsmart/home.
    html

INTERNAL REVENUE SERVICE

VITA Program provides access to information and technical assistance in support of poor families and entrepreneurs.

Contact:
(800) 829–1040 (individuals)
(800) 829–4933 (businesses)
www.vita.org/about.htm

The IRS has also developed an interactive, instructional tax program to provide high schools, community colleges, and the general public with a technology-based instructional tool.

Contact:
www.irs.gov/app/understandingTaxes/
    jsp/teacher_home.jsp

JUMP $TART

Comprehensive education program teaching children Pre - K–12 life skills and money management techniques.

Contact:
The Jump$tart Coalition for Personal
    Financial Literacy
919 18th Street, NW Suite 300
Washington, DC 20006
(888) 45-EDUCATE or (202) 466–8604
FAX: (202) 223–0321
www.jumpstart.org

JUNIOR ACHIEVEMENT

Program to educate children K–12 about basic life skills, critical thinking, and solving complex problems.

Contact:
JA Worldwide
One Education Way
Colorado Springs, CO 80906
(719) 540–8000
FAX: (719) 540–6299
www.ja.org

NATIONAL COMMUNITY REINVESTMENT COALITION (NCRC)

Works directly with non-profit organizations to help promote community and economic redevelopment in low- to moderate-income areas.

Contact:
NCRC
727 15th Street, Suite 900
Washington, DC 20005
(202) 628–8866
FAX: (202) 628–9800
www.ncrc.org

NATIONAL COUNCIL ON ECONOMIC EDUCATION

Program works through a network of teachers to provide youngsters grades K–12 the principles of economics including savings, investing, uses of money, and credit.

Contact:
National Council on Economic
    Education
1140 Avenue of the Americas
New York, NY 10036
(212) 730–7007 or (800) 338–1192
FAX: 212–730–1793
www.ncee.net

NATIONAL ENDOWMENT FOR FINANCIAL EDUCATION

Offers a high-school financial planning program that provides practical money-management skills and an introduction to financial planning, covering the fundamentals of insurance, investments, tax, retirement, and estate planning.

Contact:
National Endowment for Financial
    Education
5299 DTC Boulevard, Suite 1300
Greenwood Village, CO 80111
(303) 741–6333
www.nefe.org/pages/educational.html

NEIGHBORHOOD REINVESTMENT CORP.

Works directly with nonprofit organizations to provide consumer financial education through collaboration with national programs. Web site provides general information and resources to other programs.

Contact:
1325 G St., NW, Suite 800
Washington, DC 20005–3100
(202) 220–2300
FAX: (202) 376–2600
www.nw.org/network/home.asp

OPERATION HOPE

Helps revitalize inner-city communities through adult education, community resource information, and economic literacy for teens and young adults.

Contact:
Operation Hope Corporate Office
707 Wilshire Boulevard, 30th Floor
Los Angeles, California 90017
(213) 891–2900 or (877) 592–4673
FAX: (213) 489–7511
www.operationhope.org

SALLIE MAE

Provides information about higher education including planning for college, financial resources available, managing loans, and finding a job.

Contact:
Sallie Mae Servicing
P.O. Box 4600
Wilkes-Barre, PA 18773–4600
(888) 2-SALLIE (272–5543)
FAX: (800) 848–1949
www.salliemae.com/about/index.html

APPENDIX 3

FINANCIAL RESOURCES
FOR MILITARY FAMILIES

FINANCIAL EDUCATION AND SERVICES

Association of Independent Consumer Credit Counseling Agencies: www.aiccca.org; (800) 450–1794

Better Business Bureau Military Line: www.bbb.org

Consumer Credit Counseling Service: www.cccservices.com; (800) 355–2227

Financial Planning Association: www.fpanet.org; (800) 322–4237

Insurance.com: www.insurance.com

Internal Revenue Service: www.irs.gov

Kentucky State Treasurer's Office: www.kytreasury.com; (502) 564–4722

National Association of Insurance and Financial Advisors: www.naifa.org

National Association of Personal Financial Advisors: www.napfa.org; (800) 366–2732

National Foundation for Credit Counseling: www.nfcc.org; (800) 388–2227

Tomorrow's Money: www.kentucky.tomorrowsmoney.org

CHILD CARE RESOURCES

Child Care Aware: www.childcareaware.org; (800) 424–2246

Nation's Network of Childcare Resource and Referral: www.naccrra.org; (202) 393–5501

MILITARY SUPPORT

America Supports You: www.americasupportsyou.mil

American Red Cross: www.redcross.org

Air Force Aid Society: www.afas.org

Air Force Reserve: www.afreserve.com

Air National Guard: www.ang.af.mil

Alliance for Children and Families: www.alliance1.org

Army Emergency Relief: www.aerhq.org

Army Family Liaison: www.hqda.army.mil/acsim/family/family.htm

Army Family Team Building: www.trol.redstone.army.mil/mwr/aftb/indes.html

Army National Guard: www.ngb5.ngb.army.mil

Army Reserve: www.armyreserve.army.mil/usar

Coast Guard Mutual Assistance: www.cgmahq.org

Coast Guard Reserve: www.uscg.mil/hq/reserve/reshmpg.html

Defense Finance and Accounting Service: www.asafm.army.mil/DFAS

214   THE COMPASSIONATE COMMUNITY

Department of Defense: www.
defenselink.mil
Employer Support of the Guard and
Reserve: www.ncesgr.osd.mil
Lifelines: www.lifelines4qol.org
Marine Corps Reserve: www.marforres.
usmc.mil
Military Assistance Program: www.dod.
mil/mapsite
Military Family Resource Center: mfrc.
calib.com
National Military Family Association:
www.nmfa.org
Naval Reserve: www.navalreserve.com
Navy-Marine Corps Relief Society: www.
nmcrs.org
Reserve Affairs: www.defenselink.mil/ra
TRICARE: www.tricare.osd.mil
U.S. Army Community and Family
Support Center Morale, Welfare and
Recreation: www.armymwr.com
U.S. Department of Veterans Affairs:
(800) 827–1000

SAMPLE OF MOST POPULAR INVESTMENT SCAMS

1. Senior Investment Fraud. Low interest rates, rising health-care costs, and an increased life expectancy have set senior veterans up as targets for con artists peddling investment fraud, including promissory notes, charitable gift annuities, and viatical settlements. Seniors are particularly targeted because they often have access to a large amount of assets as a result of a lifetime of savings and buildup of home equity.

2. Variable Annuities Sales. As sales of variable annuities have risen, so have complaints from investors—most notably, the omission of disclosure about costly surrender charges and steep sales commissions. These surrender charges and high fees combine with other factors to make variable annuities inappropriate for many investors, particularly for purchases in retirement accounts.

3. Charity/Natural Disaster Scam. Con artists often try to make money out of tragedy. There may be con artists attempting to collect money under the guise of being involved in the Hurricane Katrina relief effort or by offering phony bonds to finance the reconstruction of areas affected by war. Donors need to check out the charity carefully, demand details, beware of excessive pressure, and make sure any donations are tax deductible. E-mail scammers are sending out pleas for help from phony survivors, invading recipients' computers, and stealing financial and other information from those who click on links in the documents.

4. Ponzi/Pyramid Schemes. Typically an unknown company is offering eye-popping returns from some plausible sounding, but vaguely described business activity. Such schemes are often spread by word of mouth through groups such as military organizations, churches, ethnic groups, or professional affiliations, frequently in an atmosphere of secrecy. The formula is simple: Promise high returns to investors and use their money to pay previous investors.

5. Military Fraud. Predatory salespeople target military recruits and active military service personnel who are misled into purchasing unsuitable investment products. The NASD, together with the SEC, recently settled a major mutual fund practice case against a firm that specialized in selling expensive systematic investment plans to military personnel. The firm agreed to pay $12 million following findings that the plans were sold in a misleading fashion. The fines will be used for restitution to affected investors with the balance used for investor education for the U.S. military and their families.

6. Viatical Settlements. One of the riskiest investment products, viatical contracts are interests in the death-benefits of life-insurance policies.

Investors get a share of the death benefit when the insured later dies, after a fee is paid to the viatical investment broker. These investments are extremely risky for numerous reasons, including difficulty predicting life expectancy, the promoter not paying policy premiums as promised, or the promoter simply stealing the investor's money.

7. *Living Trust Mills and Other Pretext Solicitations to Seniors.* The initial approach to clients may be to solicit senior veterans at "seminars" purportedly designed to educate participants about the benefits of living trusts or other estate planning subjects or general financial planning. These seminars misrepresent the actual business of the sales representative and the true purpose of the solicitation. The real goal of the sales agent is to obtain detailed personal financial information, which will then be used to sell the senior an unsuitable or unlawful financial or investment product.

8. *Bait and Switch Schemes.* Investors should be very wary about advertising in which a particular investment promises spectacular profits, but investors have to be lured into the office to get it. This is the bait. Once in the office to purchase the investment, the sales agent discourages the investor from investing in the advertised product. The sales agent then switches an investor into a different investment.

9. *Wrong Numbers and Stock Tips Scam.* Some people are finding that they have received a "misdialed" call from a stranger, leaving a "hot" investment tip for a friend. The message is designed to sound as if the caller did not realize that he or she was leaving a hot stock tip on the wrong message machine. Con artists have also sent these fraudulent messages through e-mails and faxes.

10. *Online Escrow Fraud.* Purchases through online auction sites such as eBay have become a popular arena for fraud. Online escrow services are often used for expensive online purchases such as computers, electronics, jewelry, and cars. Legitimate online escrow companies act as a neutral third party that holds payment for merchandise until the buyer receives the merchandise. However, a fraudulent escrow company will lure unsuspecting buyers or sellers to transact business through their Web site and then keep the funds and/or goods.

Source: California Department of Corporations; www.corp.ca.gov

FAITH-BASED ORGANIZATIONS DEDICATED TO THE ERADICATION OF POVERTY

American Baptist Churches USA
(800) ABC3-USA
www.abc-usa.org

American Red Cross
(800) HELP-NOW
www.redcross.org

Adventist Community Services
(800) 381-7171
www.adventist.communityservices.org

African Methodist Episcopal Church
(843) 852-2645
http://www.ame-church.com/news-and-
    events/hurricane-katrina-
    victims.php

Baptist World Aid
(703) 790-8980
www.bwanet.org

B'nai B'rith Disaster Relief Fund
(202) 857-6600
www.bnaibrith.org

Catholic Charities USA
(800) 919-9338
www.catholiccharitiesusa.org

Christian Appalachian Project
www.chrisapp.org

Christian Church, Disciples of Christ
(317) 713-2450
www.weekofcompassion.org

Christian Contractors Association
(800) 278-7703
www.ccaministry.org

Christian Disaster Response
(941) 956-5183
www.cdresponse.org

Christian Reformed World Relief
(800) 848-5818
www.crwrc.org

Church of the Brethren
(800) 323-8039, x234
www.brethren.org

Churches of Christ Disaster Relief
    Effort, Inc.
www.disasterreliefeffort.org

Church World Service
(800) 297-1516
www.churchworldservice.org

CMF International
www.cmfi.org/

Convoy of Hope
(417) 823–8998
www.convoyofhope.org

Cooperative Baptist Fellowship
(800) 352.8741
www.thefellowship.info/Landing/relief.
   icm

Episcopal Relief and Development
(800) 352–8741
www.er-d.org

Greek Orthodox Church in America
(212) 570–3500
www.goarch.org

Habitat for Humanity International
(229) 924–6935
www.habitat.org

International Disaster and Emergency
   Service of Christian
   and Church of Christ Churches
www.ides.org

Islamic Circle of North America
(718) 658–7028
www.icnarelief.org

Islamic Relief
(888) 479–4968
www.irw.org

Islamic Society of North America
(317) 839–8157
http://www.isna.net/

LDS Philanthropies
http://www.lds.org/ldsfoundation/

Lutheran Disaster Response
(800) 638–3522
www.lwr.org

Mennonite Disaster Service
(717) 859–2210
www.mds.mennonite.net

Mercy Corps
(888) 256–1900
www.mercycorps.org

Nazarene Disaster Response
(888) 256–5886
www.nazarenedisasterresponse.org

PRC Compassion
(888) 966–6600
www.prccompassion.org

Presbyterian Disaster Assistance
(800) 872–3283
www.pcusa.org/pda/

Salvation Army
(800) SAL-ARMY
www.salvationarmy.org

Southern Baptist Convention—Disaster
   Relief
(800) 462–8657, ext. 6440
www.namb.net/dr/

Union for Reform Judaism
(212) 650–4140
www.urj.org/give/index.cfm

United Church of Christ
(866) 822–8224
www.ucc.org

United Jewish Communities
(877) 277–2477
www.ujc.org

United Methodist Committee on Relief
(800) 554–8583
www.gbgm-umc.org

World Vision
www.worldvision.org

NOTES

INTRODUCTION

1. For translations of the Hebrew Bible (known to Christians as the Old Testament), I rely on the *Jewish Study Bible*, featuring the Jewish Publication Society Tanakh Translation (Oxford: Oxford University Press, 1999). For the New Testament, I use the *Zonderman New American Standard Bible (NASB) Study Bible* (La Haba, CA: Zonderman, 1995). For other Jewish texts (such as the Talmud), I rely on the translations and sourcing of Rabbis Mark Gopin, Mark Levine and Sid Schwartz, *Jewish Civics: A Tikkun Olam/World Repair Manual* (Rockville, MD: Washington Institute for Jewish Values, 1996). The Hillel story is found in the Talmud, Shabbat 31a. Later in this chapter, the Talmud, Bez. 32b, and Yev. 79a are the source of the description of the Jewish people as "congenitally compassionate." The quotes from Jesus in this chapter come from Matthew 22:36–40 (the two great commandments); Matthew 7:12 (the "Golden Rule"); Matthew 5:3–10 (the "Sermon on the Mount"); Matthew 25:31–46 (telling the righteous from the damned); and Matthew 25:40 (returning God's love). The quote from the apostle Paul is in Philippians 2:3–4 ("do nothing from selfishness . . ."). The Hebrew Bible quotes can be found at Leviticus 19:18 ("love your neighbor . . ."); Zechariah 7:9) (compassion for disadvantaged); Isaiah 42:6–7 ("light unto the nations . . .") and Micah 6:6–8 ("to do justice . . .").
2. C. S. Lewis, *The Abolition of Man*, (San Francisco: Harper's, 1944).
3. Quoted in Roy Herron, *How Can a Christian Be in Politics?* (Wheaton, IL: Tyndale House, 2005), p. 35.
4. Remarks at the dedication of the Hubert H. Humphrey Building, November 1, 1977. *The Congressional Record*, November 4, 1977, Vol. 123, p. 37287.
5. Among people who attend church more than once a week, 64 percent voted for Bush, while only 35 percent voted for Democrat John Kerry. Among those who seldom or never attend church, 62 percent voted for Kerry, while 36 percent voted for Bush. www.cnn.com/elections/2004.
6. William Galston and Elaine Kamarck, *The Politics of Persuasion* (Washington, DC: Third Way, 2005).
7. Quoted in Michelle Cottle, "Prayer Center," *The New Republic*, May 23, 2005, Volume 232, Issue 4,714, p. 21.
8. See, for example, Huston Smith, *The World's Religions* (New York: HarperCollins, 1991), pp. 103, 228 (Mohammed's teachings demanded an end to the licentiousness that humans clung to, while Buddha believed that if the cause of life's dislocation is selfish craving, its cure lies in the overcoming of such craving. If we could be released from the narrow limits of self-interest into the vast expanse of universal life, we would be relieved of our torment.) See also, Marcus

Borg, *Meeting Jesus Again for the First Time* (New York: HarperCollins, 1993) ("The dominant values of American life—affluence, achievement, appearance, power, competition, consumption, individualism—are vastly different from anything recognizably Christian. As individuals and as a culture . . . our existence has become massively idolatrous.")

9. U.S. Census Bureau, *Income, Poverty and Health Insurance Coverage in the United States: 2003* (2004).
10. See Karl Agne and Stan Greenberg, "The Cultural Divide," *Democracy Corps*, August 9, 2005.
11. Galston and Kamarck, p. 24, citing "An Open Letter to the Democratic Party," November 5, 2004.
12. Jim Wallis, *God's Politics: Why the Right Gets it Wrong and the Left Doesn't Get It*, (San Francisco: HarperCollins, 2005); Jimmy Carter, *Our Endangered Values: America's Moral Crisis* (New York: Simon & Schuster, 2005).
13. Lawrence Kohlberg, *The Stages of Moral Development* (Philadelphia: Clark University Press, 1971).
14. See David Brooks, "A Return to National Greatness: A Manifesto for a Lost Creed," *Weekly Standard*, June 15, 1997, Volume 002, Issue 24, p. 21; Lawrence Kaplan, "American Idle," *The New Republic*, September 12, 2005, Volume 233, Issue 4,730, p. 19; Sharon Bernstein, "Donations at $500 Million, And Counting," *Los Angeles Times*, September 6, 2005, p. A–1.
15. Quoted in Thomas Friedman, *The World is Flat: A Brief History of the 21st Century*, (New York: Farrar, Straus and Giroux, 2005), p. 227.
16. Quoted in Walter Isaacson, *Benjamin Franklin: An American Life* (New York: Simon & Schuster, 2003), p. 313.
17. Vaclav Havel, "In Our Postmodern World, a Search for Self-Transcendence," Speech at Independence Hall, July 4, 1994.

CHAPTER ONE
1. See Laura Hillenbrand, *Seabiscuit: An American Legend* (New York: Ballantine Books, 2002).
2. Robert Dreyfuss, "Grover Norquist: Field Marshall of the Bush Plan," *The Nation*, May 14, 2001, p. 23; Al Franken, *Rush Limbaugh Is a Big Fat Idiot* (New York: Delacourte Press, 1996).
3. Jesus's instructions can be found at Matthew 5:42. James 2:15–16 has a similar teaching. Jewish Rabbinic law cited in this section can be found at the Talmud, M. Avot 2:7; T.B. Baba Batra 8bft. The Maimonides lesson is from Mishneh Torah, Laws of Presents to the Poor, 10:1, 7–14. Lessons from the Eastern religions can be found at Huston Smith, pp. 178, 249–250; William B. Eerdmans's *Handbook to the World Religions*, (Oxford: Lion Publishing, 1982), pp. 177, 232, 323.
4. Sean Wilentz, *The Rise of American Democracy: Jefferson to Lincoln* (New York: W.W. Norton & Company, 2005).
5. Wilentz, p. 24; Timothy Egan, "No Degree and No Way Back to the Middle," *New York Times*, May 24, 2005, p. A–15.
6. Egan at A–15.
7. Workforce Kentucky Industry Employment Projections (July 2005); "The Economic Value of Higher Education," *Special Report*, Washington Research Council (July 2001).
8. "The Economic Value of Higher Education."

9. National Academy of Sciences, National Academy of Engineering, and Institute of Medicine, *Rising Above the Gathering Storm: Energizing and Employing America for a Brighter Economic Future* (2005).
10. National Center for Public Policy and Higher Education, "Educational Pipeline Success Rate: Big Investment, Big Returns," *Policy Alert*, April 2004.
11. See David Leonhardt, "The College Dropout Boom," *New York Times*, May 24, 2005, p. A–1.
12. Neil Pierce, "Faltering U.S. Competitiveness: Blame to Go All Around," *The Washington Post*, February 12, 2006, p. A–1.
13. "Baby Trust Fund Wins Go-Ahead," *BBC News*, November 26, 2003, available at http://news.bbc.co.uk/1/hi/business/3236626.stm.
14. See New America Foundation's summary of Kerrey's proposals at http://www.assetbuilding.org/AssetBuilding/index.cfm?pg=docs&SecID=6&more=yes&DocID=317. See Kerrey's legislation at http://thomas.loc.gov/cgi-bin/bdquery/D?d105:2184:./list/bss/d105SN.lst::|TOM:/bss/d105query.html.
15. The ASPIRE Act of 2004 (KIDS Accounts), S 2751/HR 4939 (July 22, 2004, available at http://thomas.loc.gov/cgi-bin/bdquery/z?d108:s.02751; Jackie Calmes, "Building Blocks," *Wall Street Journal*, January 11, 2006, p. A–1.
16. See www.experiencecorps.org; Tom Carper, "Reinventing Retirement," *Blueprint*, May 7, 2004, Volume 2004, Issue 2, p. 28.

CHAPTER TWO

1. See Koran, sura xxxvii. 100 *et seq.*
2. Hillel's lesson comes from the Pirke Avot 1:14. Other Jewish teachings in this chapter come from the Talmud, M. Avot 3:15 (rights must be reciprocally supplemented) and Avot de Rabba Nathan 6 (community such a powerful value). The Christian teachings cited below can be found at Matthew 7:1–2 ("do not judge . . ."); Luke 6:38 ("give and it will be given . . ."); Acts 4:32 ("all things were common property . . ."); Hebrews 13:16 ("do not neglect . . ."); and 1 John 3:18 ("let us not love . . .").
    The Eastern teachings on karma can be found in Huston Smith, p. 64. See also, E. A. Burtt, *The Teachings of Compassionate Buddha* (Oxford: Signet, 1955), pp. 49–50 ("Those who, relying upon themselves only, shall not look for assistance to any one besides themselves, it is they who shall reach the topmost height"). Similarly, Confucius taught that every action an individual takes affects his future; while the Koran places great emphasis on the self's individuality: its uniqueness and the responsibility that is entrusted to it alone (Huston Smith, pp. 176 and 240). Further, the first "signpost" on the Hindu Path of Renunciation is the community, which has an importance that no single life can command (Smith, p. 19); the Muslim holiday of Ramadan is seen as a period "when social relationships are reaffirmed, reconciliations encouraged and the solidarity of the community is expressed"; while the Muslim practice of hajj (pilgrimage) also emphasizes the spirituality of community (Eerdmans, pp. 190, 322; Karen Armstrong, *A History of God* [New York: Ballantine Books, 1993], pp. 156–157, citing Ali Shariati, *Hajj*, pp. 54–56); and Confucius strongly emphasized social activism—modern-day adherents have engaged in massive projects to combat famine, floods, and epidemic disease (Smith, p. 189).
3. Tony Campolo, *Let Me Tell You a Story* (Nashville: Word Publishing, 2000), pp. 133–134, citing Ruth 1:16.

4. Neil Howe and William Strauss, *Millennials Rising: The Next Great Generation* (New York: Vintage Books, 2001).

5. See e.g., Leviticus 19:13; Jeremiah 21:12; Talmud, M. Avot 4:4, 6.

6. Martin Peretz, "Not Much Left," *The New Republic*, February 28, 2005, Volume 232, Issue 4,702, p. 17.

7. Ibid.

8. Adi Ignatius, "Crusader of the Year: Wall Street's Top Cop," *Time*, December 30, 2002, Volume 160, No. 27, p. 38.

9. The Editors, "Statehouse to White House," *Washington Monthly*, May 2005, p. 27.

10. The Editors, "Statehouse to White House"; Deborah Yetter, "Bill to Create Electronic Health Network Passes," *Louisville Courier-Journal*, March 4, 2005, p. B–1.

11. Jeffrey Rosen, "The Unregulated Offensive," *New York Times Magazine*, April 17, 2005, Section 6, p. 42.

12. Leo Hindery, *It Takes a CEO* (New York: Penguin, 2005).

13. Thomas Friedman, *The World is Flat: A Brief History of the 21st Century* (New York: Farrar, Straus and Giroux, 2005), p. 238.

14. See David Osborne, *Reinventing Government: How the Entrepreneurial Spirit is Transforming the Public Sector* (New York: Plume, 1993).

15. Shailagh Murray, "Stevens Holds Senate in Session: Fight for Oil Drilling Keeps Colleagues From Holiday Break," *Washington Post*, December 20, 2005, p. A–13.

16. Paul Weinstein, "Fiscal Salvation," *Blueprint*, December 13, 2004, Volume 2004, No. 5, p. 23.

17. Ken Silverstein, "The Great American Pork Barrel," *Harper's*, July 2005, p. 38; Joe Biesk, "Kentucky Congressman Calls for Moratorium on Special Projects," *Associated Press*, October 2, 2005, p. B–1.

18. "Budget Reform, Rocky Mountain Style," *New Dem Daily*, January 18, 2005, available at http://www.dlc.org/ndol_ci.cfm?contentid=253122&kaid=131&subid=192.

CHAPTER THREE

1. Dave Krusenklaus—"Kruser"—now hosts a popular AM drive-time talk show, on which I am a semi-regular guest. With a wink to his past, the song that succeeds every break is Led Zeppelin's "Rock and Roll," which begins: "It's been a long time since I rock and rolled."

2. Harold Kushner, *Living a Life that Matters: Resolving the Conflict between Conscience and Success* (Boston: Little Brown & Co., 2001).

3. Isaiah 65:20–23. Jewish and Hebrew Bible teachings cited later in this chapter come from the *Perkei Avot*, Chapter 2, verse 15; Deuteronomy 24:15 (wage earner to be paid); and Jeremiah 22:13 and Malachi 3:5 (condemning employers). Christian teachings are found in Luke 18:18–25 ("easier for a camel . . .") and James 5:1–3 ("come now, you rich . . ."). Eastern traditions can be found at Huston Smith, p. 37 (Hindus believe that one path to God is through work; their concept of *karma yoga* suggests that you should throw everything of yourself into your work); and Christian Humphreys, *Buddhism* (Harmondsworth, England: Penguin Books, 1951), p. 120. (Buddhists consider hard work to be a significant virtue: Christian Humphreys, a noted Buddhist scholar remarked: "Buddhas only point the way. Work out your salvation with diligence.")

4. Roy Herron, p. 45, citing Exodus 21:2–6 (slaves cannot be kept for more than six years without consent); Leviticus 25:3–4 (the land should be given a rest from planting every seven years); Deuteronomy 15:1–2 (debtors were to be forgiven every seven years); and Leviticus 25:28, 19:34 (every 50 years, land was to be returned to the families who sold it).

5. Isaacson, p. 89; Wilentz, pp. 32–33.

6. Wilentz, pp. 31, 793.

7. United for a Fair Economy, "History of the Estate Tax," available at http://www.faireconomy.org/ estatetax/ETHistory.html.

8. Ibid.

9. Bill McKibben, "The Christian Paradox," *Harper's*, August 2005, p. 28.

10. See Paul Weinstein, Jr., "Family Friendly Tax Reform," *Progressive Policy Institute Policy Report*, April 12, 2005, available at http://www.ppionline.org/ppi_ci.cfm?knlgAreaID=125&subsecID=163&contentID=253276.

11. Jeffrey B. Liebman, "The EITC Compliance Problem," *Joint Center for Poverty Research News*, Summer 1998, Vol. II, No. 3, Article 3.

12. Ibid.

13. Tamara Draut, *Strapped: Why America's 20- and 30-somethings Can't Get Ahead*, (New York: Doubleday, 2006).

14. General Accounting Office, "Consumer Finance: College Students and Credit Cards," June 2001, available at http://www.gao.gov/new.items/d01773.pdf.

    This section is drawn from testimony I delivered before the U.S. Senate Committee on Banking, Housing and Urban Affairs Hearing on "The Importance of Financial Literacy Among College Students," held on September 5, 2002. The text of my testimony is available at http://banking.senate.gov/02_09hrg/090502/miller.htm.

15. Public Interest Research Group, "The Campus Credit Card Trap," September 1998, available at http://www.pirg.org/student/consumer/credit98/.

16. Nedra Pickler, "Bush Signs Strict Bankruptcy Reform," *Associated Press*, April 21, 2005; The Editors, "Morally Bankrupt," *The New Republic*, March 7, 2005, Volume 232, Issue 4,703, p. 7.

17. See Deuteronomy 23:29–30; Exodus 22:25–27; Leviticus 25:1–7; Deuteronomy 15; Nehemiah 5:6–13; and Ezekiel 18:8–17, 22:12.

18. Edmund Andrews, "Blacks Hit Hardest by Costlier Mortgages," *New York Times*, September 14, 2005, p. C–1.

19. See Center for Responsible Lending, "Letter to Chairman Oxley," found at www.responsiblelending.org.

20. Center for Responsible Lending, "Predatory Payday Lending," found at www.responsiblelending.org.

21. Ibid.

22. House Judiciary Committee, Democratic Dissent on S.256 (April 2005), available at http://www.cazelaw.com/democratsopposed.htm.

23. Jackie Calmes, "Building Blocks," *Wall Street Journal*, January 11, 2006, p. A–1.

24. William G. Gale, J. Mark Iwry and Pete Orszag, "The Automatic 401(k): A Simple Way to Strengthen Retirement Savings," Brookings Institution, March 7, 2005, available at http://www.taxpolicycenter.org/publications/template.cfm?PubID=1000751.

25. Ibid.

26. National Center for Health Statistics, "U.S. Per Capita Divorce Rates," (2005), available at http://www.divorcereform.org/rates.html.

27. U.S. Department of Justice, "Identity Theft and Identity Fraud," available at http://www.usdoj.gov/criminal/fraud/idtheft.html#What%20Are%20Identity%20Theft%20and%20Identity.

28. Federal Trade Commission, "ID Theft," available at http://www.consumer.gov/idtheft.

CHAPTER FOUR

1. Barbara Dafoe Whitehead, "Closing the Parent Gap," *Progressive Policy Institute*, Backgrounder, April 2005, available at http://www.ppionline.org.

2. Joseph Telushkin, *Biblical Literacy: The Most Important People, Events and Ideas of the Hebrew Bible* (New York: William Morrow, 1997), p. 184, quoting Genesis 4:9.

3. Genesis 1:28 ("be fertile and increase . . ."); Exodus 20:12 ("honor your mother and father . . ."); and Ephesians 5:33 ("love his own wife . . .").

4. Eerdmans, p. 340, citing Shah Waliullah of Delhi; Huston Smith, pp. 176, 190; *The Doctrine of the Mean*, chapter 13.

5. Quoted in Cole's Quoteables, found at http://www.quotationspage.com/quote/4821.html.

6. Whitehead, "Closing the Parent Gap."

7. See, for example, Center for Law and Social Policy, "Are Married Parents Really Better for Children?," May 2003, available at http://www.clasp.org/publications/Marriage_Brief3.pdf (Research largely supports the notion that, on average, children do best when raised by two married, biological parents who have a low-conflict relationship); Jim Wallis, pp. 238–240.

8. Cris Beam, "The Changing American Family," *American Baby*, May 2005, p. 48.

9. Judith Warner, "Mommy Madness," *Newsweek*, February 21, 2005, p. 23.

10. Ruth Franklin, "Missing Joy," *The New Republic*, July 4, 2005, Volume 233, Issue 4,720, p. 30; Louise Story, "Many Women at Elite Colleges Set Career Path to Motherhood," *New York Times*, September 20, 2005, p. A–1.

11. Warner, "Mommy Madness."

12. The Editors, "Statehouse to White House."

13. Elena Cherney, "Family-Leave Advocates Look To Canada For Generous Model," *Wall Street Journal*, September 19, 2003, p. A–1.

14. See http://www.metrokc.gov/exec/news/2001/041701.htm.

15. Franklin, "Missing Joy."

16. Warner, "Mommy Madness"; Franklin, "Missing Joy."

17. Evan Bayh, *Father to Son: A Private Life in the Public Eye* (Indianapolis: Emmis Books, 2003).

18. Barack Obama, Father's Day Sermon, quoted in *Chicago Tribune*, June 22, 2005, p. A–1.

19. Florida Commission on Responsible Fatherhood, policy paper at http://www.floridafathers.org/ florida-fathers-report.htm.

20. Florida Commission on Responsible Fatherhood; John Buntin, "Father Time," *Governing*, March 2005, p. 34.

21. Bayh, *Father to Son*.

22. Kaiser Family Foundation, *Generation M: Media in the Lives of 8–18 Year Olds*, March 2005, available at http://www.kff.org/entmedia/entmedia030905pkg.cfm.

23. Chrisanne L. Gayl, Progressive Policy Institute Report, *Expanding Access & Ensuring Quality in After-School Programs*, July 2004, available at www.ppionline.org.

24. Michele Stockwell, "Childhood for Sale: Consumer Culture's Bid for our Kids," *Progressive Policy Institute*, August 4, 2005, available at www.ppionline.org.

25. For more information, go to http://www.cccco.edu/divisions/ss/americorps/foster_youth_mentor.htm.

26. Florida Department of Children and Families, "Domestic Violence," available at http://www.dcf.state.fl.us/domesticviolence.

27. Family Violence Prevention Fund, "Domestic Violence," available at http://endabuse.org/programs/display.php3?DocID=9916.

28. Domestic Violence & Mental Health Policy Initiative, available at http://www.dvmhpi.org/.

29. Rhonda M. Johnson, "Rural Health Response to Domestic Violence: Policy and Practice Issues," August 30, 2000, Federal Office of Rural Health Policy, available at http://ruralhealth.hrsa.gov/pub/domviol.htm.

30. U.S. Department of Health and Human Services, Administration for Children and Families, "National Child Abuse Statistics," (May 2005), found at http://www.childhelpusa.org/abuseinfo_stats.htm.

31. Statistics compiled by Prevent Abuse Now, and can be found at http://www.prevent-abuse-now.com/stats.htm#Impact.

32. National Center for Victims of Crime, "Child Sexual Abuse," available at http://www.ncvc.org/ncvc/main.aspx?dbName=DocumentViewer&DocumentID=32315#8.

33. Associated Press, "Sexual Predators Lose an Outlet," October 13, 2005, available at http://www.wired.com/news/politics/0,1283,69188,00.html.

CHAPTER FIVE

1. See Joseph Telushkin, p. 105.

2. See Deuteronomy 6:23, 16:12, 24:17–18. Jewish and Hebrew Bible teachings cited later in this section can be found at Isaiah 58:6, 61:1 (freeing the captives); the Talmud, T.B. Baba Bathra 8a; Yerushalmi Gittin 4:4 (obligation to release people); Karen Armstrong, p. 78 (right of liberty). The New Testament quote comes from Gallatians 5:13 ("you are called to freedom . . .").

3. Democratic Leadership Council, *Smart Guns*, July 2, 2005, available at http://www.dlc.org/ndol_ci.cfm?contentid=3572&kaid=139&subid=271.

4. Chip Pitts, "Act Out: Big Business and the Patriot Act," *TNR Online*, October 19, 2005, available at http://www.tnr.com/doc.mhtml?i=w051017&s=pitts101905.

5. Daniel Politi, "Snooping Defense," *Slate*, December 20, 2005, available at http://www.slate.com/id/2132786/.

6. House Judiciary Committee, Democratic Dissent on S.256, April 2005.

7. Ibid.

8. Kirk Semple, "Deployed: Lives Left Behind; Interrupted by War, the Struggle to Care for Family and Business," *New York Times*, February 22, 2005, p. B-1; Senator Tom Carper, "Honor the Guard," *Blueprint*, March 15, 2005, Volume 2005, No. 1, .47; House Judiciary Committee, Democratic Dissent on S.256.

9. Governor Bill Richardson, "State of the State Address," January 18, 2005, available at http://www.dlc.org/ndol_ci.cfm?contentid=253124&kaid=106&subid=122; Jerry Adler, "Children of the Fallen," *Newsweek*, March 21, 2005, p. 27; Semple, "Deployed: Lives Left Behind."

10. Thom Shanker, "Military Memo; All Quiet on the Home Front, and Some Soldiers are Asking Why," *New York Times*, July 24, 2005, Section 1, p. 18.

11. Ed Anderson, "Bill Would Benefit Military Families," *The Times-Picayune*, New Orleans, May 3, 2005, p. A–1; Staff Report, "Senate Bill Makes N.C. 'Military Friendly,'" *Fayetteville Observer*, July 30, 2005, p. A–1; Governor Bill Richardson, "State of the State Address," January 18, 2005.

12. Office of Governor Mark Warner, "Governor Warner Announces Special Employment Assistance for Military Families," January 11, 2005, available at http://www.governor.virginia.gov/Press_Policy/Releases/2005/Jan05/0111.htm.

13. "Family Relief," *Clovis News Journal*, May 6, 2005, p. A–1; Illinois Military Family Leave Act (Public Act 094–0589), available at http://www.ilga.gov/legislation/publicacts/fulltext.asp?name=094–0589&GA=094.

14. Semple, "Deployed: Lives Left Behind."

15. Sheldon Shafer, "Miller Proposes Help for Military," *Louisville Courier-Journal*, August 18, 2005, p. B–1.

16. Adler, "Children of the Fallen"; Robert Burns, "A Deadly Toll on Citizen Soldiers," *Associated Press*, October 11, 2005.

17. House Judiciary Committee, Democratic Dissent on S.256.

18. David "Kruser" Krusenklaus (see chapter three notes for a profile); Rudi Williams, "DoD Warns About Insurance, Investment Rip-Offs," *American Forces Press Service*, May 4, 2005; Diana Henriques, "Senators Demand Changes in Fiscal Advice to Soldiers," *New York Times*, November 18, 2005, p. C–3.

19. Robert Sparks, "Military Protection Act too weak," *Kentucky Post*, August 1, 2005, p. A–10.

20. Amendments to S.256 were offered by Senators Richard Durbin to achieve these ends, but they were rejected by the Senate Committee. House Judiciary Committee, Democratic Dissent on S.256.

21. Letitia Stein, "Securing the Home Front," *St. Petersburg Times*, October 9, 2005, p. A–1.

22. Semple, "Deployed: Lives Left Behind."

23. Michael Lindenberger, "New Battles Await Many Veterans," *Louisville Courier-Journal*, June 27, 2005, p. B–1.

24. Adler, "Children of the Fallen"; "Army Reaches Out to Kids of Reservists," *Associated Press*, May 5, 2005.

25. "Veterans' Affairs Faces $1 Billion Shortfall," *Associated Press*, June 24, 2005.

26. The Editors, "Statehouse to White House."

27. Soldiers and Sailors Civil Relief Act of 1940, see http://www.defenselink.mil/specials/Relief_Act_Revision.

28. Staff Report, "Senate Bill Makes N.C. 'Military Friendly,'" *Fayetteville Observer*, July 30, 2005, p. A–1.

CHAPTER SIX

1. See, for example, Tom Loftus, "Fletcher's Approval Rating Sinks to 38 Percent: Support Similar to Patton's in Scandal," *Louisville Courier-Journal*, September 17, 2005, p. A–1.

2. E-mail from Tim Hazlette, quoted in Ryan Alessi, "The 12 'Disciples' and Their Mission," *Lexington Herald-Leader*, August 21, 2005, p. A–1. The Fletcher hiring scandal was covered extensively by the two prominent Kentucky newspapers, the Louisville *Courier-Journal* and the *Lexington Herald-Leader*. A comprehensive outsider's view of the scandal can be found at Drew Jubera, "Kentucky Scandal in New Flavor: BlackBerry," *Atlanta Journal-Constitution*, December 21, 200, p. A–1.

3. Bill McKibben, "The Christian Paradox," *Harper's*, August 2005, p. 28; "Pastor Resigns after Bush Battle," CBS News.com, May 11, 2005, available at http://www.cbsnews.com/stories/2005/05/08/national/main693766.shtml.

4. James Bruggers, "Ministers Urge Cancellation of 'Justice Sunday,'" *Louisville Courier-Journal*, April 23, 2005, p. A–1.

5. Exodus 31: 1–10; Talmud, Sandhedrin 102a. Jewish and Hebrew Bible teachings in this section come from Genesis 22 (the story of Abraham and Isaac); Midrash Bereshit 38:13 (Abraham smashing the idols); and Exodus 20:1–3 (The First and Second Commandments). Muslim references are from the Koran, sura xxxvii. 100 *et seq* (Abraham and Isaac); and Koran 21:51–59 (Abraham smashing the idols).

    Christian teachings can be found at John 14:6 ("I am the way . . ."); and Acts 4:12 ("there is salvation in no one else . . .").

6. Cooper P. Abrams, III, "A Brief Survey of Independent Fundamental Baptist Churches: What They Are and What Is Their History," available at http://www.bible-truth.org/fundbapt.htm.

7. Isaacson, pp. 84–87, 449–452.

8. Mike Gecan, "Taking Faith Seriously," *Boston Review*, April/May 2005, p. 72.

9. Kenneth Baer, "Faith Healing," *TNR Online*, June 24, 2004, available at http://www.tnr.com/doc.mhtml?i=w050620&s=baer062405.

10. Quoted in David Price, "Faith and Politics," *Blueprint*, March 15, 2005, Volume 2005, No. 1, p. 38.

11. John C. Danforth, "Onward, Moderate Christian Soldiers," *New York Times*, June 17, 2005, p. A–27.

12. Cal Thomas and Ed Dobson, *Blinded by Might* (Grand Rapids, MI: Zondervan, 1999).

13. Steven Waldman, "How Prayers Poll *Slate*, October 10, 2003, available at http://www.slate.com/id/2089641 (Citing a Pew Religion Forum study that argues that the group with the most political baggage is not Jews or Catholics, but atheists and that "a Democratic candidate unable to discuss his own faith will place himself defiantly outside of the mainstream").

14. Franklin Foer and Ryan Lizza, "The Bushies' Faith-Based Brawl," *The New Republic*, April 2, 2001, p. 24; Democratic Leadership Council, "Faith-Based Fiasco," *New Dem Dispatch*, February 17, 2005, available at http://www.dlc.org/ndol_ci.cfm?contentid=253180&kaid=131&subid=192.

15. "Encyclical Letter Deus Caritas Est of the Supreme Pontiff Benedict XVI," December 25, 2005, available at http://www.vatican.va/holy_father/benedict_xvi/encyclicals/documents/hf_ben-xvi_enc_20051225_deus-caritas-est_en.html; Gerald McDermott, "What Jonathan Edwards Can Teach Us About Politics," *Christianity Today*, July 2, 2001, available at http://www.christianitytoday.com/ct/2001/127/25.0.html; Wallis, pp. 15 and 212; citing Matthew 5:3 ("Blessed are the poor"); Mark 14:7 ("For you always have the poor with you, and you can show kindness whenever you wish'"). The quote from Jesus cited earlier in this paragraph is found at Luke 4:18, in which Jesus is quoting from Isaiah 61:1. The Jewish and Mosaic law cited in this section comes from Leviticus 19:9; Leviticus 23:22; Deuteronomy 26:12; Deuteronomy 24:17; Maimonides, Mishneh Torah, Book of Knowledge, Laws of De'ot 6:10; and the Talmud, T. B. Baba Batra 8bff. Muslim law also strongly countenances support for the poor; see the Koran 92:18, 9:103, 63:9, and 102.1.

16. McKibben, "The Christian Paradox" (only 40 percent of Americans can name more than for of the Ten Commandments; only half can cite any of the four

authors of the Gospels. Twelve percent think Joan of Arc was Noah's wife; 75 percent believe that the Bible teaches that "God helps those who help themselves." (It was Benjamin Franklin who said this.)

17. Jimmy Carter, *Our Endangered Values: America's Moral Crisis* (New York: Simon & Schuster, 2005), p. 11, quoting James 2:17.

18. Huston Smith, pp. 255–257.

19. U.S. Census Bureau, *Income, Poverty and Health Insurance Coverage in the United States: 2003* (2004); National Low-Income Housing Coalition, *Out of Reach 2003: America's Housing Wage Climbs* (September 2003); David Shipler, *The Working Poor: Invisible in America* (New York: Vintage, 2004)

20. David Cay Johnston, "Very Richest's Share of Income Grew Even Bigger, Data Show" *New York Times*, June 26, 2003, p. A–1; Carter, p. 127; Peter Grier, "Rich-Poor Gap Gaining Attention," *The Christian Science Monitor*, June 14, 2005, p. A–1.

21. Stephen Goldsmith and William D. Eggers, *Governing by Network: The New Shape of the Public Sector* (Washington, DC: Brookings Institution Press, 2004); Marc Porter Magee, "Civic Enterprise," *Blueprint*, December 13, 2004, Volume 2004, No. 5, p. 64.

22. Pew Forum on Religion and Public Life and the Pew Research Center for the People and the Press, July 7–17, 2005, quoted in Laurie Goodstein, "Teaching of Creationism is Endorsed in New Survey," *New York Times*, August 31, 2005, p. A–9.

23. Ronald Sider, "Faith Based Service," *Blueprint*, July 23, 2005, Volume 2005, No. 3, p. 49.

24. The Editors, "Statehouse to White House."

CHAPTER SEVEN

1. The Jewish and Hebrew Bible sources quoted in this section include Deuteronomy 16:20 ("Justice, justice shall you pursue . . ."); Micah 6:8 ("to do justice . . ."); Amos 5:24 ("Let justice well up . . ."); Psalms 10:18; 76:9 (justice a "deliverance"); the Talmud, M. Avot 1:18; 3:2; Deuteronomy Rabbah 5, T.B. Sanhedrin 7a, 8a. (obligation on Jews to do justice). The apostle Paul is quoted from 2 Corinthians 9:8–10. The Eastern religious traditions can be found at Huston Smith, p. 227; William B. Eerdmans, pp. 177–179, 224, 231, 315 and 322.

2. Taylor Branch, *Pillar of Fire: America in the King Years 1963–65* (New York: Simon & Schuster, 1998), p. 48.

3. Quoted in E. J. Dionne, "Faith Full," *The New Republic*, February 28, 2005, Volume 232, Issue 4,702, p. 12.

4. Jonathan Kozol, *Shame of the Nation: The Restoration of Apartheid Schooling in America* (New York: Crown, 2005).

5. Andrew J. Rotherham, "The New Face of Inequality," *Blueprint*, May 7, 2004, Volume 2004, No. 2, p. 72; William Collins and Robert Margo, "Historical Perspectives on Racial Differences in Schooling," *Insights on Southern Poverty*, Spring 2004; David Berliner, "Our Impoverished View of Educational Reform," *TC Record*, August 2, 2005, available at http://www.tcrecord.org/Content.asp?ContentID=12106.

6. See Leviticus 19:14; Maimonides, Book of Commandments, negative 299.

7. Quoted in Penny Miller, *Kentucky Politics and Government* (Lexington: University of Kentucky Press, 1994).

8. Richard Rothstein, *Class and Schools: Using Social, Economic, and Educational Reform to Close the Black-White Achievement Gap* (Washington, DC: Economic Policy Institute, 2004).

9. For a full explanation of the NCLB, read *Using NCLB to Improve Student Achievement: An Action Guide for Community and Parent Leaders*, Public Education Network, found at www.publiceducation.org/pdf/nclb/nclbbook.pdf.

10. Debra Viadero, "Reports Find Fault with High-Stakes Testing," *Education Week*, January 8, 2003, p. 5; Sarah Cassidy, "Tests Blamed for Decline in Reading for Pleasure," *The Independent*, October 5, 2005, available at http://education.independent.co.uk/news/article317219.ece.

11. Mr. McKim and Alan Young, a Des Moines, Iowa teacher, report that this is their updated paraphrasing of a sign that hung in Albert Einstein's office: "Not everything that counts can be counted, and not everything that can be counted counts."

12. Peter Schrag, "Bush's Education Fraud," *The American Prospect*, February 1, 2004, Volume 15, Issue 2, p. 31; National Council of Churches, "Ten Moral Concerns in the Implementation of the No Child Left Behind Act," found at www.nccccusa.org/nmu/educaministr.html#anchorwgpel.

13. Bryan C. Hassel, Progressive Policy Institute Policy Report, *Fast Break in Indianapolis: A New Approach to Charter Schooling*, September 21, 2004, available at www.ppionline.org; *Charter School Funding: Inequity's Next Frontier*, Thomas B. Fordham Institute (August 2005).

14. See www.iamyourchild.org; Senator Tom Carper, "Universal Preschool," *Blueprint*, December 13, 2004, Volume 2004, No. 5; http://www.ericdigests.org/2002–1/kindergarten.html.

15. Deuteronomy 26:12.

16. Robert Gordon, "Class Struggle," *The New Republic*, June 6 and 13, 2005, Volume 232, Issue 4,716 and 4,717, p. 24.

17. National Academy of Science, National Academy of Engineering and Institute of Medicine, *Rising Above the Gathering Storm: Energizing and Employing America for a Brighter Economic Future* (2005).

18. The Editors, "A Momentous Policy Decision," *Daily Mail* (Charleston, WV), April 5, 2006, p. A–10.

19. Branch, p. 32.

CHAPTER EIGHT

1. Huston Smith, p. 315.

2. Quoted in David Price, "Faith and Politics."

3. Eugene Borowitz and Frances Schwartz, p. 237. Other Jewish and Hebrew Bible teachings cited in this section can be found at Micah 4:3 ("They shall beat their swords . . ."); Chapter on Peace, Minor Tractates of the Talmud; Talmud, T.B. Sotah 44b; Leviticus 19:16 ("do not stand . . ."); Talmud, T.B. Sanhedrin 7sa (international intervention); Isaiah 58:6, 61:1; Talmud, T.B. Baba Bathra 8a (release captives); Talmud T.B. Yoma 85b; M Sanhedrin 4:5; T.B. Baba Kammah 93a (save the life of another); Psalms 34:15 ("seek amity . . ."); Exodus 23:5 ("raise it up with him . . ."); Talmud, T.B. Baba Mezia 32a (aid anyone in distress); Numbers 6:26 ("May the Lord bestow his favor . . ."); Psalms 29:11 ("May the Lord grant strength . . ."); Talmud, Avot 1.18, quoting Zechariah 8:16 ("The world rests on three things . . ."). See also eleventh-century philosopher Solomon ibn

Gabirol: "He is the greatest of men whose mind is most tranquil and whose association with others is most happy" (Mivhar Hapeninim, 400); Rabbi Simha Bunim of Prysucha: "Our sages say, 'Seek peace in your own place.' You cannot find peace anywhere save in your own self . . . Only when we have made peace within ourselves, will we be able to make peace in the whole world. (Buber, Tales of the Hasidim, bk 2, the Later Masters); Yehiel b. Yekutiel, Sefer Maalot Hamiddot: "Seek peace with your friend and pursue it with your enemy. Seek it in your place and pursue it in other places. Seek it with your body and pursue it with your money. Seek it for yourself and pursue it for others. Seek it today and pursue it tomorrow. And do not despair, saying, 'I will never achieve peace,' but pursue it until you do."

4. Roy Herron, p. 116. Other Christian teachings quoted in this section can be found at Matthew 5:9 ("Blessed are the peacemakers . . ."); 2 Corinthians 13:11 ("be like-minded . . ."); Matthew 5:38–44, quoting Leviticus 24:20 ("You have heard that it was said . . .").

5. Huston Smith, pp. 22, 126.

6. My summary of the Middle East conflict and the U.S. - Israel relationship comes from three decades of reading and watching the news with acute interest. For those who are interested in a more in-depth review of this history, I recommend CNN's 2003 series, "MidEast: Land of Conflict," which can be found at http://www.cnn.com/SPECIALS/2003/mideast/.

7. See, for example, "Full Text: bin Laden's 'Letter to America,'" Observer Worldview, November 24, 2002, p. A–1.

8. Jimmy Carter, p. 114.

9. Jim Wallis, p. 233; "US Presbyterian Church Warns Companies to Boycott Israel or Face Divestment," Christian Today, August 9, 2005, available at http://www.christiantoday.com/news/america/us.presbyterian.church.warns.companies.to.boycott.israel.or.face.divestment/380.htm.

10. Alan Dershowitz, "Democracy, Freedom and Rights," Sunday Times (London), September 28, 2003, available at http://www.asiucsb.org/asiissues/blogfiles/oct_25_2003.html; Daniel Kennemer, "Arab Israelis Well-Placed in Technology," The Jerusalem Post, December 21, 2005, p. 17; David Rudge, "Israeli Arab Appointed Dean of University for First Time," The Jerusalem Post, October 11, 2005, p. 5; Jay Bushinsky, "Arab Pols Cleared for Election," Chicago Sun-Times, January 22, 2003, p. 34; Jack Bell, "Soccer Report; Arabs Become Israel's Heroes," New York Times, April 5, 2005, p. D–4. See also, www.virtuallibrary.org ("Israel has no written constitution in the formal sense, even though it has a constitution in the material sense—in other words, laws and basic rules that lay down the foundations of the system of government and the rights of the individual. Some of these are formulated in basic laws, some are scattered in other laws, and part—at least until the passing of basic laws dealing with human and civil rights—were interpreted and formulated in a series of decision by the Supreme Court. . . . The Supreme Court ruled that article 1 of the Basic Law: Human Dignity and Liberty and of the Basic Law: Freedom of Occupation relates to the principles mentioned in the Proclamation of Independence as a normative source." According to this article, "the basic human rights in Israel are based on recognition of the value of man, the sanctity of his life and his being free, and they will be respected in the spirit of the principles [mentioned] in the proclamation of the establishment of the State of Israel").

11. Greg Myre, "Palestinian Police and Hamas Battle in the Streets of Gaza," *New York Times*, October 3, 2005, p. A–10.

12. Steven Erlanger, "Twin Blasts Kill 16 in Israel; Hamas Claims Responsibility," *New York Times*, September 1, 2004, p. A–12.

13. Karl Vick, "Iran's President Sparks Fears of New Isolation," *Washington Post*, November 5, 2005, p. A–14.

14. Friedman, p. 381.

15. Daniel Jonah Goldhagen, "The New Threat," *The New Republic*, March 13, 2006, Volume 234, Issue 4,756, p. 15.

16. Amartya Sen, "Democracy and its Global Roots," *The New Republic*, October 6, 2003, Volume 229, Issue 4,629, p. 28.

CHAPTER NINE

1. Robert Dreyfuss, "Grover Norquist: Field Marshall of the Bush Plan," *The Nation*, May 14, 2001, p. 23.

2. Pat Crowley, "Kentucky Tax Reform Mocked," *Cincinnati Enquirer*, January 7, 2001, p. A–2.

3. Al Cross, "Anti-gay Vote Saved Bunning," *Louisville Courier-Journal*, November 7, 2004, p. E–1; www.cnn.com/2004/ALLPOLITICS/11/02/kentucky.senate/.

4. Amanda York, "Senate 'Ready to Work Together,'" *Kentucky Post*, January 8, 2005, p. A–1.

5. Huston Smith, p. 107. Jewish and Hebrew Bible teachings cited in this chapter can be found at Talmud, M. Avot 2:10; 4:1; 4:3; T.B. Moed Katan 9b; Baba Mezia 58bff (loss of personal dignity); Deuteronomy 5:17 ("you shall not bear false witness . . ."); Leviticus 19:17 ("reprove your kinsman . . .") Christian teachings are from Matthew 5:44–45; Romans, 5:8–10; 2 Corinthians 2:7 (demanding respect, even for enemies); Matthew 7:1 ("do not judge . . ."); Romans 3:23 (all have sinned); James 3:6 ("tongue is a fire . . ."); James 1:19–20 and 4:11; Galatians 6:1 ("if anyone is caught . . ."); John 8: 7–11 (story of the adulterous woman).

6. Percy Bysshe Shelley, "Ozymandias," Original Poetry (1818); *The Examiner* (London), p. 24.

7. See Bruce Reed, "Drain the Swamp," *Blueprint*, May 31, 2005, Volume 2005, No. 2, p. 12.

8. Sasha Abramsky, "The Redistricting Wars," *The Nation*, December 29, 2003, p. 14.

9. Common Cause, "Redistricting," available at www.commoncause.org/site/pp.asp?c+dkLNK1MQIwG&b=196481; Charlie Cook, "Mid-Decade Redistricting Becoming More Popular," *The Cook Political Report*, February 26, 2005, available at http://www.cookpolitical.com/column/2004/026205.php; Thomas Mann, "Redistricting Reform," *The National Voter*, June 2005, p. 4.

10. Thomas Mann, "Redistricting Reform."

11. Ed Kilgore, "Reform!" *Blueprint*, December 13, 2004, Volume 2004, No. 5, p. 28; Thomas Mann, "Redistricting Reform."

12. Gail Russell Chaddock, "Republicans Take over K Street," *The Christian Science Monitor*, August 29, 2003, p. A–1.

13. Nicholas Confessore, "Welcome to the Machine: How the GOP Disciplined K Street and Made Bush Supreme," *Washington Monthly*, July/August 2003, p. 12.

14. Susan Schmidt and James Grimaldi, "Lawmakers under Scrutiny in Probe of Lobbyist," *Washington Post*, November 26, 2005, p. A–1.

15. "Feingold Introduces Lobbying and Ethics Reform Bill," July 14, 2005, available at Feingold.senate.gov/Feingold/05/07/2005714641.html.

16. See Reed, "Drain the Swamp."

17. Screenshots, "September 8, 2004," available at http://www.jeffooi.com/archives/2004/09/september_8_cbs.php

18. Anna Greenberg, "New Generation, New Politics," *The American Prospect*, October 1, 2003, p. 9.

19. Circle: The Center for Information & Research on Civic Learning and Engagement, "Volunteering Among Young People" and "The Youth Vote 2004," available at www.civicyouth.org.

20. Quoted by Circle: The Center for Information and Research on Civic Learning and Engagement, "Civic Knowledge," available at www.civicyouth.org/research.

21. *Rediscovering Democracy*, A Report on the Kentucky Summit on Civic Literacy, 2005, available at http://sos.ky.gov/secdesk/initiatives/civics/clik/.

22. See www.state.me.us/sos/kids/fyigames/fyiinfo.htm.

23. Quoted by Circle: The Center for Information and Research on Civic Learning and Engagement, "Civic Knowledge," available at www.civicyouth.org/research.

CHAPTER TEN

1. Jewish and Hebrew Bible instruction cited in this section can be found at Genesis 1:27 (God's "own image"); Leviticus 19:18 (love your neighbor); Deuteronomy 30:19 ("choose life . . ."); Leviticus 19:16 (do not profit by blood of neighbor); Ecclesiastes 3:15, interpreted by Talmud, T.B. Baba Kammah 93a (prevent murder of innocents); Talmud, T.B. Yoma 85b (highest obligation); Talmud, Sanhedrin 4:5 (when a person saves a single life); Leviticus 22:28; Deuteronomy 22:6–7; 25:4 (on treatment of animals); Genesis 1:31 ("God saw all that He had made . . ."); Genesis 2:15 (man placed in Garden of Eden); Deuteronomy 20:19 (strict prohibitions against destroying nature); Talmud, Midrash Ecclesiastes Rabba 7:13 (special responsibility for man); Talmud, Avot 6:12; Yoma 38a ("Whatever God created . . ."); Psalms 104, 148 (natural world's beauty); Psalm 19:1 ("heavens declare the glory . . ."). Christian teachings are from John 10:10 ("I came so that they may have life . . ."); Luke 10:25–37 (parable of the Good Samaritan).

2. Wa'Na'Nee'Chee (Dennis Renault) and Timothy Freke, *Principals of Native American Spirituality* (San Francisco: Thorsons, 1996), p. 107.

3. Mary Evelyn Tucker and John Grim, "Introduction: The Emerging Alliance of World Religions and Ecology," *Daedalus*, Fall 2001, p. 19.

4. "Academies Call for Greenhouse Gas Reductions," cnn.com, June 7, 2005, available at http://www.itpcas.ac.cn/System/printpage.asp?ArticleID=1005; Bailey wrote: "Anyone still holding onto the idea that there is no global warming ought to hang it up." Jeff Goodell, "Was It Global Warming?" *Rolling* Stone, October 6, 2005. Cizik equated his changing viewpoint on this issue with a "conversion" that was so profound that he likened it to an "alter call" when nonbelievers accept Jesus as savior. Laurie Goodstein, "Evangelical Leaders Swing Influence behind Effort to Combat Global Warming," *The New York Times*, March 10, 2005, p. A–16.

5. This memo was obtained by the Environmental Working Group, and it can be found at http://www.ewg.org/briefings/luntzmemo/

6. Goodell, "Was it Global Warming?"; John Carey, "Global Warming," *Business Week*, August 16, 2004, p. 23; Juliet Eilperin, "US Pressure Weakens G–8 Climate Plan," *Washington Post*, June 17, 2005, p. A–1.

7. J. T. Houghton, et al., *Climate Change 2001: The Scientific Basis*, Contribution of the Working Group I to the Third Assessment Report of the Intergovernmental Panel on Climate Change, 2001; Elizabeth Kolbert, "The Climate of Man—III," *The New Yorker*, May 9, 2005 (citing a February 2002 report of the Environmental Protection Agency); Sandi Doughton, "The Truth About Global Warming," *Seattle Times*, October 11, 2005, p. A–1; MSNBC, "2005 Warmest Year on Record," January 24, 2006, available at http://www.msnbc.msn.com/id/11009001/.

8. Coalition for Environmentally Responsible Economies (CERES), *Institutional Investor Summit on Climate Risk*, "Background," May 10, 2005; Kolbert, "The Climate of Man—III"; Goodell, "Was It Global Warming?"

9. "Toting Up the Potential Toll of Global Warming," *Barron's*, April 19, 2004, p. 23; Coalition for Environmentally Responsible Economies (CERES), *Availability and Affordability of Insurance Under Climate Change*, September 2005, available at www.ceres.org.; Jeffrey Ball, "Cinergy Backs U.S. Emissions Cap," *The Wall Street Journal*, December 2, 2004, p. A–6.

10. Donald A. Brown, "Ethical Dimensions of Global Environmental Issues," *Daedalus*, Fall 2001, p. 59.

11. "Energy Study Finds Greenhouse Gas Limits Affordable," *Associated Press*, April 15, 2005.

12. Kolbert, "The Climate of Man—III."

13. Ibid.

14. Jim Motavalli, "Stewards of the Earth," *E/The Environmental Magazine*, November/December 2002, p. 3; *Archbishop of Canterbury's New Year Message*, December 31, 1999, which can be found at http://www.archbishopofcanterbury.org/carey/releases/001231.htm.

15. Laurie Goodstein, "Evangelical Leaders Join Global Warming Initiative," *New York Times*, February 8, 2006, p. A–12; *www.creationcare.org.*

16. Mike Lee, "Faith Spurs Odd Union to Battle House Bill," *San Diego Union-Tribune*, September 24, 2005, p. A–1; Jan Mazurek, "Green Gospel," *Blueprint*, July 23, 2005, Volume 2005, No. 3, p. 36; Editorial, "Heat Stroke," *Christianity Today*, October 2004.

17. Pew Center on Global Climate Change, "The U.S. Electric Power Sector and Climate Change Mitigation," June 16, 2005, at www.pewclimate.org.

18. Andrew Revkin, "New York City and 8 States Plan to Sue Power Plants," *The New York Times*, July 21, 2004, p. A–15; Sarah Murray, *Financial Times*, "Investors demand action on climate change," January 16, 2004, p. 10.

19. Jeffrey Ball, "State Aides Mull Pension Funds and Environment," *The Wall Street Journal*, November 21, 2003, p. A–12.

20. Kenneth Stier, "Inside the News: Dirty Secret: Coal Plants Could be Much Cleaner," *New York Times*, May 22, 2005, Section 3, p. 3; Edward Peeks, "Conversion Looks Like Coal's Best Alternative," *Charleston Gazette*, January 10, 2006, p. A–1.

21. See Ford Motor Company, "Ford Report on the Business Impact of Climate Change," December 2005, available at http://www.ford.com/NR/rdonlyres/e6vzmdwyz2ycyehpwvuj5sdkrmfknipsreoyznmwwfqtzlwqfbfbcq44ckquxgn5xfir532knjvkq3ovbyhuscz7sfh/fordReptBusImpClimChg.pdf.

22. One of the key architects of the emissions-trading legislation was my former boss, Tennessee Congressman Jim Cooper, whom I profiled in chapter nine.

INDEX

Aaron, 91
Abdel Rahman al-Rasheed, 154
Abel, 73
abortion, 3, 4, 5, 189–90
Abraham, 7, 31–46, 47, 49, 116, 146, 158
Abramoff, Jack, 174
adhan, 116
adoption, 84, 190
Afghanistan, 97
Ahasuerus (King), 185–7
Ahmadinejad, Iranian President
    Mahmoud, 154
Air Force Academy scandal, 118
akedah, 32–4
Akiva, Rabbi, 14
Ali, Ameer, 14
Alito, Supreme Court Justice Samuel,
    178
"America Saves," 55
America Saving for Personal Investment,
    Retirement and Education
    (ASPIRE) Act, 27–8
American Dream, 7, 10, 21, 64, 127, 206
    American Revolution, 36, 117,
    133
Americans for Tax Reform, 163
Amos, 134
Am Yisrael Chai, 146
Angelides, California Treasurer Phil,
    197
anti-Semitism, 112–13, 151–2
apocalypse, 152
Arab Oil Boycott, 151
Arafat, Palestinian Authority President
    Yasser, 146, 154
Archbishop of Canterbury, 194
Aristotle, 20, 74, 133
    influence on Thomas Jefferson, 20,
    133

Armed Forces Loans, 63
Armstrong, Karen, 92
Aspen Institute, ix, 180
Auschwitz death camp, 35

baby boom generation, 30, 143
Bailey, Ronald, 191
Bank of the United States, 52
bankruptcy reform, 59, 103–4
    effect on military families, 103–4
Barak, 129, 132
Barak, Israeli Prime Minister Ehud, 146
bar mitzvah, 32, 112
Bartholomew, Patriarch, 194
Bathsheba, 161, 164–5, 183
Battle of Jericho, 111, 115, 116, 119,
    127–8
Bayh, U.S. Senator Evan (Indiana), 80,
    101
Benedict XVI, Pope, 122
Best Friends animal sanctuary, 185
Bhagavad Gita, 74
bin Laden, Osama, 151, 156
Blagojevich, Illinois Governor Rod, 83
Blair, British Prime Minister Tony, 26
Bloomfield, Michael, x
body image, 82–3
Borowitz, Eugene, 149
Boston Red Sox, 17
Boston University, 89
Boys and Girls Clubs of Delaware, 28
brain drain, 26, 79
Branch, Taylor, 134
Brandeis, U.S. Supreme Court Justice
    Louis, 8
    "laboratories of reform," 8, 29, 81
Brookings Institution, 65, 173
Brooks, David, 11
Brown v. Board of Education, 135, 138

Declaration of Independence, ix, 2, 12–3, 20, 93, 117, 133–4, 155
deism, 117
DeLay, U.S. Congressman Tom (Texas), 171, 173–4
K Street Project, 173–4
Democracy Corps, 5
Democratic Leadership Council (DLC), ix
de Tocqueville, Alexis, 2
DiIulio, John, 122
Dixon, David, x
Dobson, Ed, 118
Dobson, James, 75
domestic violence, 85–6
Cut it Out! (Utah), 85–6
Domestic Violence and Mental Health Policy Initiative (Chicago), 86
drunk-driving, 38, 130–1

Earle, Steve, 131
earmark (legislative), 44
Earned Income Tax Credit (EITC), 53–4
economics of self-interest, 8, 41, 46, 54, 72, 75, 82, 190
contribution to a coarsened culture, 8, 72, 75
Edwards, Rev. Jonathan, 122
e-health technology, 41
energy independence, 155–9, 194, 196–200
alternative and renewable energy, 156, 197–9
clean coal, 156, 197–8
conservation, 196, 199
energy efficiency, 157, 196, 199
hybrid and hydrogen cars, 157, 198–9
Enron, 38, 59
Environmental Protection Agency (EPA), 41
Esau, 49, 73
estate tax, 52–3
Esther (Queen), 7, 185–200
Evangelical Climate Initiative, 195
Evangelical Environmental Network (EEN), 195
Experience Corps, 30

Falwell, Rev. Jerry, 118, 134
family leave, 78, 100–1
Family and Medical Leave Act, 101
Family Research Council, 75
farmers/agriculture policy, 53, 125, 157, 193
fatherhood, 70–1, 80–1
"Father to Father" (South Carolina), 81
Federal Bureau of Investigation (FBI), 88, 96
Federal Reserve, 62, 124
Federal Trade Commission (FTC), 41, 69, 84
Feingold, U.S. Senator Russ (Wisconsin), 168, 174
Fiddler on the Roof, 187
financial literacy education, 54–70, 104–5, 136–7, 206, 209–15
Delaware's Money School, 55–6
for military families, 104–5, 206, 213–5
Flake, U.S. Congressman Jeff (Arizona), 44
Fletcher, Kentucky Governor Ernie, 113–14
"Disciples," 113–14, 118
hiring scandal, 114
Force One Lending, 63
Ford, President Gerald, 53
Fort Campbell, 63, 104
Fort Knox, 63, 103, 104
foster care, 28, 84
Foster Youth Mentoring Program (California), 84
Fostering Youth Involvement (Maine), 182
Franklin, Benjamin, 12, 51
Friedman, Thomas, 12, 42, 154
Frist, U.S. Senator Bill (Tennessee), 114–15
Fundación Chana Goldstein y Samuel Lewis (Puerto Rico), 28

G–8 Conference, 191
Garden of Eden, 188
gay marriage, 3, 4, 5, 65
Gecan, Mike, 117
General Accounting Office (GAO), 56–8
General Electric, 42, 193